The New American Cultural Sociology presents a serious challenge to British Cultural Studies and European grand theory alike. This exciting new volume brings together sixteen seminal papers by leading figures in what is emerging as a new and important intellectual tradition. It places them in the context of related work in sociology and other disciplines, exploring the connections between cultural sociology and different approaches, such as comparative and historical research, postmodernism, and symbolic interactionism. The book is divided into three parts: Culture as Text and Code, The Production and Reception of Culture, and Culture in Action. Each part contains edited contributions, both theoretical and empirical, to address the key debates in cultural sociology, including the autonomy of culture, power and culture, structure and agency, and how to conceptualize meaning.

PHILIP SMITH is Senior Lecturer in Sociology in the Department of Anthropology and Sociology at the University of Queensland. He has researched and taught widely in cultural sociology, social theory, crime and deviance, and comparative and historical research, in North America, Britain and continental Europe, as well as in Australia. He is co-author of *Sociology: Themes and Perspectives* and of *Analyzing Visual Data*, and author of *Cultural Theory*.

The New American Cultural Sociology

Cambridge Cultural Social Studies

Series editors: JEFFREY C. ALEXANDER, *Department of Sociology, University of California, Los Angeles, and* STEVEN SEIDMAN, *Department of Sociology, University at Albany, State University of New York.*

Series list continues at end of book

The New American
Cultural Sociology

EDITED BY
Philip Smith

CAMBRIDGE
UNIVERSITY PRESS

PUBLISHED BY THE PRESS SYNDICATE OF THE UNIVERSITY OF CAMBRIDGE
The Pitt Building, Trumpington Street, Cambridge CB2 1RP, United Kingdom

CAMBRIDGE UNIVERSITY PRESS
The Edinburgh Building, Cambridge, CB2 2RU, United Kingdom
  http://www.cup.cam.ac.uk
40 West 20th Street, New York, NY 10011–4211, USA   http://www.cup.org
10 Stamford Road, Oakleigh, Melbourne 3166, Australia

First published 1998

Printed in the United Kingdom at the University Press, Cambridge

Typeset in Monotype Times New Roman in QuarkXPress™   [SE]

A catalogue record for this book is available from the British Library

ISBN 0 521 58415 9 hardback
ISBN 0 521 58634 8 paperback

Contents

Contributors

JEFFREY C. ALEXANDER is Professor of Sociology at the University of California, Los Angeles. He is the author of numerous works in the area of social and cultural theory. As well as being a founder of the neofunctionalist paradigm, he is noted as an advocate of Durkheimian approaches to culture. Representative publications include *Fin de Siècle Social Theory* (Verso) and the edited collection *Durkheimian Sociology: Cultural Studies* (Cambridge).

NICOLA BEISEL is Associate Professor of Sociology at Northwestern University. Her work is concerned with the role that morals and ethics play in mediating public responses not only to the arts, but also to public policy issues like contraception and abortion. Her study of censorship was published as *Imperilled Innocents* (Princeton).

RICHARD HARVEY BROWN is Professor of Sociology at the University of Maryland. Much of his early work concerned the role of language and rhetoric in social life and social theory. His more recent work has continued these concerns, but with an increasing postmodernist emphasis. He is author of *Social Science as Civic Discourse* (Chicago) and *Society as Text* (Chicago).

PAUL DIMAGGIO is Professor of Sociology at Princeton University. His research embraces diverse areas including organizational theory, cultural capital, the arts, and the distribution of attitudes and values in American society. Publications reflecting these interests include *Nonprofit Enterprise in the Arts* (Oxford) and *The New Institutionalism in Organizational Analysis* (Chicago).

GARY ALAN FINE is Professor of Sociology at the University of Georgia. He is best known as an authority on, and advocate for, symbolic interactionism.

His empirical work has covered areas as diverse as play, childhood, and food and can be found in books such as *With the Boys* (Chicago) and *Shared Fantasy* (Chicago).

NINA FORTIN is with the Graduate Center of the City University, New York. She has researched extensively in the area of gender and society. Together with Gaye Tuchman she is responsible for the book *Edging Women Out* (Yale).

WILLIAM A. GAMSON is Professor of Sociology at Boston College. Much of his present research covers the interface between social movements, public discourses, and the media. Some of this is presented in *Talking Politics* (Cambridge).

WENDY GRISWOLD is Professor of Sociology at the University of Chicago. She is particularly interested in the interplay between literature and society. One of her more recent works, *Culture and Societies in a Changing World* (Pine Forge) provides a global view of the role of culture in contemporary society. Her work on the early theatre was published as *Renaissance Revivals* (Chicago).

ANNE KANE is Assistant Professor of Sociology at the University of Texas, Austin. Her research interests lie in the area of comparative and historical sociology with a particular emphasis on agrarian politics in the nineteenth and early twentieth centuries. She is currently working on a book entitled *Culture and Social Change*, which looks at the Irish Land War of 1879–82.

MICHÈLE LAMONT is Professor of Sociology at Princeton University. In her research she is particularly concerned with exploring the role of cultural capital in society. Some of this work is contained in *Money, Manners and Morals* (Chicago). She is also co-editor of *Cultivating Differences* (Chicago), an influential collection of essays on the ways that culture sets up moral and political boundaries.

CALVIN MORRILL is Associate Professor of Sociology at the University of Arizona. His research is in the area of corporate life and corporate culture. He also has an interest in qualitative methods. His research on corporate culture can be read about in more detail in *The Executive Way* (Chicago).

BARRY SCHWARTZ is Professor of Sociology at the University of Georgia. His recent research has explored the question of collective memory and has resulted in a number of pathbreaking analyses of the ways that various American presidents have been remembered.

STEVEN SEIDMAN is Professor of Sociology at the State University of New York, Albany. His more recent work is markedly influenced by postmodernism and queer theory as well as mainstream sociological traditions. These interests are reflected in books such as *Contested Knowledge* (Oxford), *Queer Theory Sociology* (Blackwell), and *Difference Troubles* (Cambridge).

WILLIAM H. SEWELL, JR. is Professor of Sociology at the University of Chicago. He is well known among historians as well as sociologists for his studies in the area of class and political culture such as *Work and Revolution in France* (Cambridge) and *Structure and Mobility* (Cambridge).

PHILIP SMITH is Senior Lecturer in Sociology at the University of Queensland. Although now based in Australia, he describes himself as an American cultural sociologist in exile. His research explores themes such as civil discourse, ritual and violence. Publications include *Sociology: Themes and Perspectives* (Longmans), *Analyzing Visual Data* (Sage), and *Cultural Theory* (Blackwell).

ANN SWIDLER is Professor of Sociology at the University of California, Berkeley. Whilst her contribution to this volume is mostly theoretical, other aspects of her work are more strongly empirical and consider areas such as education, organizations, and civic values. She is author of *Organization Without Authority* (Harvard) and co-author of the seminal *Habits of the Heart* (Harper and Row).

GAYE TUCHMAN is Professor of Sociology at the University of Connecticut. She has research interests in gender and the media as well as in culture more broadly. Her books include *Making News* (Free Press) and *Edging Women Out* (Yale). The latter expands upon her chapter in this volume.

ROBIN WAGNER-PACIFICI is Associate Professor of Sociology at Swarthmore College. Much of her research has concerned the links between rhetoric, narrative, and political crisis. Important publications in this area include *The Moro Morality Play* (Chicago) and *Discourse and Destruction* (Chicago).

ROBERT WUTHNOW is Professor of Sociology at Princeton University. His work is influenced by structural and poststructural theory and has been concerned with issues such as cultural innovation, public discourses, and religious belief. Representative books include *Vocabularies of Public Life* (Routledge) and *The Restructuring of American Religion* (Princeton).

Preface

This book owes much to the intellectual and moral generosity of colleagues on three continents. Cambridge Cultural Social Studies series editors Jeffrey Alexander and Steven Seidman supported the project from its inception. Thanks also to Catherine Max, Chris Doubleday, and Jo Barker at Cambridge University Press. Given the sheer volume of candidate work and the need to produce an affordable and helpful volume, difficult decisions had to be made about what should be included and what excluded. Comments from a number of people helped ease this burden. Advice-givers included: Jeffrey Alexander, Mike Emmison, Ronald Jacobs, Michèle Lamont, Tim Phillips, Steven Seidman, Lyn Spillman, Eleanor Townsley, Mark Western, and the three referees of the book proposal who remain anonymous. The introductory essay has had the generous benefit of ideas, discussion, and/or feedback from Jeffrey Alexander, Mike Emmison, Stuart Hall, Steve Sherwood, Laurent Thevenot, Ken Thompson, and Loic Wacquant. My thanks to the University of Queensland, the Pavis Centre at the Open University, and the EHESS, Paris for providing supportive environments for preparing the book.

With the exception of the introductory essay, this book contains previously published research. In an effort to include a greater variety of work and to provide thematic continuity, the material has been edited for length, with proposed cuts vetted by the authors. Titles have been slightly amended to flag the fact that the contributions here differ from the originals. Readers are asked to remember that the process of editing has inevitably entailed a loss of information. In my opinion this has been most notably the case for the contributions by Wagner-Pacifici and Schwartz, Morrill, and Sewell. In the case of the first two, rather substantial sections of ethnographic detail have had to be excised. In Sewell's essay an important and sophisticated theoretical critique of Giddens and Bourdieu was removed on the grounds

that it dealt with complex issues and literatures that were outside the immediate scope of this book. In these and all other cases I am very grateful to
the authors for their forbearance and helpful suggestions on where cuts
could be sensibly made. On account of these considerations, readers are
urged to consult the full text of any contribution (see details below) before
judging it in a negative way. Another set of changes that it is important to
note here is to be found in Anne Kane's article. In her original paper Kane
drew upon and quoted from an unpublished manuscript by Michael Mann.
Because this work has now been published, quotations and references have
been adjusted accordingly.

Aside from the kind permission of the authors, this book would not have
been possible without the gracious cooperation of diverse publishers in
providing reproduction permissions. Details of copyright holders and original publication are:

"Textuality and the postmodern turn in sociological theory" by Richard
Harvey Brown was first published in 1991 as "Rhetoric, textuality, and the
postmodern turn in sociological theory" in *Sociological Theory* 8(2):
188–197. It is reproduced here by kind permission of the American
Sociological Association.

"The computer as sacred and profane" by Jeffrey C. Alexander was first
published in 1992 as "The promise of a cultural sociology: technological
discourse and the sacred and profane information machine" in N. Smelser
and R. Munch (eds.), *Theory of Culture* (Berkeley: University of California
Press), pp. 293–323. It is reproduced here by kind permission of the
University of California Press.

"AIDS and the discursive construction of homosexuality" by Steven
Seidman was first published in 1988 as "Transfiguring sexual identity: AIDS
and the contemporary construction of homosexuality" in *Social Text* 9(20):
187–206. It is reproduced here by kind permission of Duke University Press.

"Fundamentalism and liberalism in public religious discourse" by Robert
Wuthnow was first published in 1988 as "Religious discourse as public
rhetoric" in *Communication Research* 15(3): 318–338. It is reproduced here
by kind permission of Sage Publications Inc.

"Analytic and concrete forms of the autonomy of culture" by Anne Kane
was first published in 1991 as "Cultural analysis in historical sociology: the
analytic and concrete forms of the autonomy of culture" in *Sociological
Theory* 9(1): 53–69. It is reproduced here by kind permission of the
American Sociological Association.

"The reception of Derrida's work in France and America" by Michèle Lamont was first published in 1987 as "How to become a dominant French philosopher: the case of Jacques Derrida" in the *American Journal of Sociology* 93(3): 584–622. It is reproduced here by kind permission of the University of Chicago Press.

"Censorship, audiences and the Victorian nude" by Nicola Beisel was first published in 1993 as "Morals versus art: censorship, the politics of inter-pretation, and the Victorian nude" in the *American Sociological Review* 58(1): 145–162. It is reproduced here by kind permission of the American Sociological Association.

"The Devil, social change, and Jacobean theatre" by Wendy Griswold was first published in 1983 as "The Devil's techniques: cultural legitimation and social change" in the *American Sociological Review* 48(2): 668–680. It is reproduced here by kind permission of the American Sociological Association.

"Victorian women writers and the prestige of the novel" by Gaye Tuchman and Nina Fortin was first published in 1980 as "Edging women out: some suggestions about the structure of opportunities and the Victorian novel" in *Signs* 6(2): 308–325. It is reproduced here by kind permission of the University of Chicago Press.

"The ambiguous and contested meanings of the Vietnam Veterans Memorial" by Robin Wagner-Pacifici and Barry Schwartz was first pub-lished in 1991 as "The Vietnam Veterans Memorial: commemorating a difficult past" in the *American Journal of Sociology* 97(2): 376–420. It is reproduced here by kind permission of the University of Chicago Press.

"Culture and social action" by Ann Swidler was first published in 1986 as "Culture in action: symbols and strategies" in the *American Sociological Review* 51(3): 273–286. It is reproduced here by kind permission of the American Sociological Association.

"Culture, structure, agency, and transformation" by William H. Sewell, Jr. was first published in 1992 as "A theory of structure: duality, agency, and transformation" in the *American Journal of Sociology* 98(1): 1–29. It is reproduced here by kind permission of the University of Chicago Press.

"Discourse, nuclear power, and collective action" by William A. Gamson was first published in 1988 as "Political discourse and collective action" in *International Social Movement Research* 1(2): 219–244. It is reproduced here by kind permission of JAI Press Inc.

"Moral boundaries, leisure activities, and justifying fun" by Gary Alan Fine was first published in 1991 as "Justifying fun: why we do not teach exotic dance in high school" in *Play and Culture* 4(1): 87–99. It is reproduced here by kind permission of Human Kinetics Publishers Inc.

"Honor and conflict management in corporate life" by Calvin Morrill was first published in 1991 as "Conflict management, honor and organizational change" in the *American Journal of Sociology* 97(3): 585–621. It is reproduced here by kind permission of the University of Chicago Press.

"The role of cultural capital and school success" by Paul DiMaggio was first published in 1982 as "Cultural capital and school success: the impact of status culture participation on the grades of U.S. high school students" in the *American Sociological Review* 47(1): 189–201. It is reproduced here by kind permission of the American Sociological Association.

The new American cultural sociology: an introduction

Philip Smith

Over the past ten to fifteen years "culture" has developed to become one of the most popular and important areas within sociology in the United States. This increasing awareness attests to both the scope and the quality of contemporary cultural work. As this new wave of discourse matures, and as its practitioners and ideas become more central to the discipline, the need grows for an overview of the area. This collection of papers is intended to provide such a guide. The contributions to this book illustrate the variety of work that is now being done by American cultural sociologists. But they also do more than this. Sometimes the whole can be greater than the sum of its disparate parts, and in combination the work presented here suggests and documents a distinctive, new, American tradition in cultural sociology. The aim of this introductory essay is to indicate the genesis and form of this tradition. The first section positions contemporary American cultural sociology in an historical context, via an exploration of the shifting theoretical tides of the discipline. The second part documents the cluster of family resemblances which constitute the discursive field, drawing contrasts with other modes of socio-cultural inquiry. I turn first to the issue of genesis.

The new-found appreciation of culture in American sociology can be explained in terms of a pendulum effect linking intellectual cohorts with theoretical positions. This has seen culture swing back into the analytic spotlight from a dark exile at the margins of the profession. During the late 1960s and the 1970s there was a massive reaction against cultural explanation in American sociology. Culture was tainted by its association with Parsonian normative functionalism. During this period it was argued, with sometimes more, sometimes less justice, that the elaborate model of society developed by Talcott Parsons contained a number of theoretical and empirical errors. It was held to emphasize harmony over conflict, structure over agency and integration over fragmentation. Uniting all these themes was the central role given by Parsons to an overarching system of values and norms. This cultural system directed and coordinated both personality and social systems so as to produce a stable, "functioning" society. It is not surprising, then, that the various reactions against Parsons all refused normative explanation.[1] The need to confront the obvious inadequacies of Parsons's structural theory was fatefully conflated with a need to abandon, rather than refine, the project of elaborating the role of culture in society.

Resulting from this rebellion against norms was the rapid ascent of a series of profoundly anti-cultural social theories. In the "macro" field there was a vogue for "conflict sociology" which drew upon Marx, Simmel and a Max Weber who was now interpreted as a kind of neo-Marxist historian rather than as a forefather of hermeneutic sociological inquiry.[2] As conflict sociology hit a theoretical dead-end it gave birth to the fruitful, if clumsily named, field of "comparative and historical sociology" which highlighted the omnipresence of struggle and oppression to social process. Studies in this field placed a relentless emphasis on power and social structural resources as the ultimate determinants of historical outcomes in processes like state formation and imperialism and in forms of collective action such as revolutions and social movements. Such work respecified its objects of study in radically anti-cultural terms. In the work of Skocpol and Tilly, for example, the state was no longer seen through the lenses of contract theory as the legitimate guardian of a collective order invested with normative authority. Rather it was depicted as the arena of class struggle or as the locus of class rule, or as a selfish, predatory bureaucracy, intent on consolidating its own power. Under this rubric, culture could be variously understood either as a system of more or less cynical ideological frameworks for establishing claims to legitimacy, the unconscious product of social structural (usually class) locations, or as completely irrelevant to sociological explanation. Whichever scenario one chose, it was hardly worth investing any time in the study of a weak, almost irrelevant, dependent variable.

Those not attracted to quasi-materialist thinking could find other, equally anti-cultural, theoretical traditions to work in. It is true that the new "micro" perspectives that emerged during the 1960s were initially somewhat cultural. Garfinkel's work on trust, Sacks's work on membership categorization devices, and early conversation-analytic analyses of adjacency pairs, for example, held out the promise of linking a collective moral order to the exigencies of individual practical action. Yet during the 1970s micro theories became increasingly antithetical to normative explanation and quasi-cultural theorizing. The muscular new fields of conversation analysis and ethnomethodology gained support most rapidly when they offered ways of relating action to meaning without recourse to collective norms or common symbolic structures. This theoretical coup was achieved by demoting "norms" as a valid topic of inquiry and by insisting on the purely "local" production of social order. The theoretical resources for accomplishing this came from a synthesis of an American pragmatist tradition that emphasized individual experience and local contexts and a German phenomenological tradition which understood meaningfulness primarily in cognitive, not evaluative terms. The rational choice theories which also gained in popularity, especially towards the end of the 1970s, went even further in rejecting culture. By positing a society made up of rational, selfish actors they abandoned all pretence of studying meaning in favor of refining the mathematical equations and game scenarios that, in their view, best explained profit-maximizing social actions.[3]

Many of the intellectual generation that rose to prominence during the 1980s embraced culture, swinging with the pendulum into an almost empty field. Career opportunities began to open up as the previous generation of Parsonian cultural theorists moved towards retirement and attractive new theories of culture became available for empirical deployment. Moreover, culture offered a way for promising scholars to differentiate themselves from their mentors and peers in the academic marketplace. This embrace of culture was neither unreflexive nor nostalgic, for the new wave of cultural theory has been anxious to avoid the perceived theoretical mistakes of Parsonian "normative consensus" theorizing. At the same time it has been positively influenced by the research agendas and models of the social put into play by Parsons's immediate critics. And so the assumption of consensus has been replaced by an examination of the role culture plays in struggle and inequality. Studies of sub-cultures and organizational cultures replaced the examination of a purportedly overarching, unified "cultural system." In the same spirit explorations have been made of the highly fractured, contested, multilayered, sometimes even self-contradictory nature of symbolic and cultural systems. Studies of the dynamics of the production and reception of culture have confronted the idealism of the more or less free-floating Parsonian value system. The critiques of the micro theorists have also been taken seriously with scholars stressing the contingent, negotiated, multifaceted qualities of action with respect to culture and the ways in which agents use culture in concrete interactional settings.

In a sense, then, we can say that America now displays a genuinely post-Parsonian cultural sociology. Surprisingly few contemporary practitioners of cultural sociology in America make reference to Parsons in either a positive or negative context. This fact reflects not only the pervasive influence of European cultural theory (discussed below), but also the fact that today (notwithstanding the recent work of neofunctionalists) Parsonian theory sets neither the terms of debate, nor the questions to be explored, nor even the tenor of argument. Yet we should use the term "post-Parsonian" with some caution – a caution flagged by the "in a sense" at the start of this paragraph. There are two reasons for this. Firstly, an earlier generation of scholars like Geertz, Shils, and Bellah had confronted Parsons's cultural theory from within his camp. They argued that Parsons's approach was insufficiently hermeneutic and that in tying culture too closely to structure and function, it prescinded consideration of the autonomous textuality of social life. Because these scholars remain important figures for almost all contemporary American cultural sociologists, Parsons can be seen as still exerting a force on current scholarship via his students. Secondly, the voices and agendas of Parsons's critics during the 1960s and 1970s still inflect the work of contemporary cultural sociologists.[4] Here, then, we can discern a dialectical process at work in which Parsons plays the part of the now almost invisible "other" through which knowledge-producing discourses have asserted their identity and purpose. In so far as the contemporary sociological field in America has been decisively shaped by these anti-Parsonian positions, one can see his influence persisting at two steps' remove.

The fall of Parsons and the turn away from and then back towards culture provide only a partial explanation of the current form of American cultural sociology. Such an analysis can go quite a long way towards explaining why culture has come back in, but it cannot tell us much about how meaning *itself* is conceptualized. To understand this we have to turn towards Europe, and then, like Henry James or Alexis de Tocqueville, explore tensions between European ideas and their translation into an American idiom.

During the 1960s and 1970s, just as Parsonian normative analysis in America was on the ebb, Europe produced a massive intellectual tide of structuralist and poststructuralist thought. Major scholars within the social sciences like Lévi-Strauss, Foucault, Lacan, Dumont, Douglas, Baudrillard, Lyotard, and Bourdieu emphasized the role of discourses and myths, symbols and signs, codes, rituals and beliefs in shaping social life. Contemporary American cultural sociology can be understood as a product of the intersection of these European movements with its own disciplinary history and theoretical traditions (Lamont and Wuthnow 1990).[5]

The attraction of the European theorists for American sociologists has been not so much their methodological rigor (often perceived to be lacking) or their contribution to understanding ongoing sociological debates about substantive empirical issues (often understood as marginal due to a European preference for philosophical abstraction), but rather their creative thinking and the tools that they have provided for a dynamic new style of cultural analysis, most particularly in decoding culture itself. During the heyday of functionalism in the 1950s and 1960s cultural analysis was stunted by a rudimentary tool-kit consisting of concepts like "norms," "values," and "beliefs." Although capable of operationalization by survey researchers and social psychologists, these concepts could only produce a wooden and lifeless form of cultural sociology that was profoundly unsatisfying from a hermeneutic point of view. That is to say concepts such as "values" failed to capture the structures and meanings of the cultural system in a rich, textured, and analytically powerful way. The functionalist cultural model was also difficult to link up to action and process convincingly. In consequence, studies produced using this tool-kit (for example, those of national cultures, peasant attitudes, democratic beliefs, and so on) now strike us as often absurdly general, at times somewhat dull, and usually profoundly ahistorical.

As American sociologists embraced culture once again, they found that European structuralist and poststructuralist thought provided the models of culture they needed. These were new, exciting, exotic. Aside from these positive virtues European thought was attractive because it was untainted by the vice of association with functionalism. In a Durkheimian sense this new knowledge was "pure" rather than "polluted" and allowed theorists to conduct cultural research without fear of stigma. Yet although foreign ideas about culture were taken up with the greatest enthusiasm, they were reworked in a distinctive, American style. This style arose from the organization and culture of the American sociological field. Its characteristics can best be identified through contrast with two other modes of cultural inquiry. The first of these is the continental European tradition of "high theory" associated with names like Habermas, Foucault, and Lévi-Strauss. The other is the approach of British cultural studies. This school of thought, which is at present growing in influence in the American tertiary sector, is linked to scholars like Stuart Hall, John Fiske, and Lawrence Grossberg.

Sweeping comparisons between forms of discourse can, of course, be dangerous in that they obscure diversity and conflict within each field. The geographical tags through which these schools have been identified must also be treated with caution as they tend to mask the existence of "outliers" – researchers in particular geographical locations who conduct research according to the norms most associated with another tradition. Finally, we have to be aware of the perils of comparing phenomena of different orders. European cultural theory, British cultural studies, and American cultural sociology are different animals almost by definition. It is therefore hardly surprising that we can detect significant points of divergence. But, although imperfect, the contrasts developed here offer a foundation upon which we can later construct a more nuanced understanding about particular types of research enterprise. In particular, they afford the intellectual distance from which we can begin to construct a reflexive understanding of the cultures that guide research activity.

A useful starting point for this three-way comparison is the issue of disciplinarity. The research of American cultural sociologists remains very strongly tied to disciplinary themes and debates, with the primary audience a peer group of scholars within the same sub-area of the same discipline. Links with other disciplines are weakly developed, with the strongest links being perhaps with the field of social and cultural history through figures like William Sewell, Jr. (see Wacquant and Calhoun 1989). By contrast the European model demands an interdisciplinary and occasionally mass audience. Academic prestige comes from exerting the widest possible influence on intellectual life through becoming a "total intellectual" who is able to engage in multiple spheres of public debate and even, in some cases, various media of cultural production (e.g., novels and drama as well as academic texts).

The contents of scholarly texts reflect these contrasting expectations and audiences. In the works of European sociologists like Habermas or Bourdieu, for example, we find frequent references to core problems in philosophy and borrowings from fields like linguistics and aesthetics. Whilst the American cultural sociologist might draw upon these fields in developing theory, few would feel motivated or qualified to develop a sustained critique of a Noam Chomsky or a Susan Sontag or a Sigmund Freud. The American cultural sociologist is also less likely to produce work as an "intervention" in ongoing political and social movement struggles. In the American discipline of sociology, academic work is narrower in scope, more limited in its ambitions, more cautious in its claims, and more precise in its formulations, if less visionary in its diagnoses. It is concerned more with issues in the specifically sociological tradition rather than with engaging the icons of Western thought or producing a global theory of how the world works. And so most textual debate is about focusing issues within academic sub-fields rather than taking on major intellectual and political movements located in other disciplines or wider society.

Like the European mode of inquiry, the British cultural studies model (e.g., Grossberg, Nelson, and Treichler 1991) is also strongly interdisciplinary in orientation. Although early texts by sociologists centered on traditional sociological fare such as work, the state, or crime and deviance, the British model of cultural studies has always been strongly interdisciplinary. The ongoing destabilization of disciplinary boundaries in recent work marks a continuation of an existing trend rather than a break with the past. Collaboration is common between scholars in different traditional disciplines and books are often aimed at broad audiences and market segments in general areas like media, culture and society, or women's studies. This interdisciplinary edge is now being reflected in academic organization, with new departments of "cultural studies," "culture and media studies," or "cultural studies and cultural policy" being set up in many universities. These departments will typically be staffed by academics with backgrounds in a number of traditional disciplines, such as history, sociology, communications, English, and anthropology.

The British cultural studies tradition also shares with the European model a concern with social engagement, usually from a radical political perspective. A major consequence of this has been a presuppositional commitment to a power-based frame of analysis. Culture is to be analyzed in terms of the extent to which it supports or confronts existing social inequalities patterned around race, class, and gender. From an American perspective such an approach has been perceived as unduly restrictive (Sherwood, Smith, and Alexander 1993) and in particular as circumscribing the range of theories that can be drawn upon in investigating the role that culture plays in society. Consequently if the analysis of power and engagement with the problematics identified by critical theories remains central to the European and British models, in the American tradition these have far less influence (Lamont and Wuthnow 1990). Weberian and Durkheimian ideas about issues of religion, symbolism, ritual and social structure, solidarity, salvation, and charisma continue to exert a powerful influence on American cultural analysis (see Emirbayer 1996; Smith and Alexander 1996). This ongoing connection with foundational debates reflects, yet again, the strongly disciplinary character of American cultural sociology.

Differential rates of participation in disciplinary, interdisciplinary, and extra-academic fields are also embodied in the forms of self-identification that scholars display. Whilst the self-description as a "cultural sociologist" is common in the American context (imagine the exchange at an ASA convention: "What kind of work do you do?" "Oh, I'm a cultural sociologist"), this term would have little meaning or currency in continental Europe. There a researcher in the tradition of Lévi-Strauss, Foucault, Bourdieu, or Barthes is likely to see themselves as simply a "sociologist" or perhaps, in some cases, as an "intellectual" or a "philosopher." Similarly, a practitioner writing in the Birmingham tradition with a sociology Ph.D. is likely to identify themselves as doing "cultural studies," not as a "cultural sociologist," thereby pointing to the subject matter of their research, rather than their disciplinary background, as a primary source of professional identity.

In understanding the development and nature of this disciplinary collective identity among American cultural sociologists it is important to acknowledge an institutional base. Within American sociology the American Sociological Association constitutes an immensely powerful force. The division of this organization into "sections" promotes the empirical and perceptual division of its members into specialisms each with their own territory. The designation of a Culture Section in 1987 must therefore be considered a foundational moment. It provided for the identification of cultural sociology as a distinctive form of sociological enterprise (much like "stratification research," "social studies of science," or "health") that has to carve out its own niche in the marketplace of ideas if it is to survive. Associated with this institutional trend towards formal differentiation is the idea that cultural sociology is a specialism with its core of canonical texts (e.g., Geertz on the Balinese cockfight, Shils on charisma, and Bellah on civil religion) and central debates (e.g., structure and agency). Familiarity with these texts and debates is required if one is to be called a competent cultural sociologist. A final symptom and cause of solidarity among American cultural sociologists have been the relatively dense social networks that tie people together who work in the field. These are also sustained, in no small part, by the ASA Culture Section through its conference activities, newsletters, and e-mail discussion groups.

With this emerging identity and growing institutional differentiation in America there have come a series of arguments on behalf of cultural sociology within the discipline as a whole. These claims center on the issue of the "autonomy of culture." Such arguments are to some extent the atavistic legacy of European structuralist rhetorics, especially those of Lévi-Strauss and Foucault. To some extent they mimic both the "relative autonomy of the state" propositions used, with great success, by political sociologists in the early 1980s and the somewhat earlier claims of "micro" sociologists for the autonomy of the "interaction order." Such assertions undoubtedly have a strategic dimension in that they seek to legitimate a space for cultural sociological inquiry. But they also reflect the genuine theoretical concerns of the line of interpretive inquiry that runs from the hermeneutics of Dilthey to the poststructuralism of Derrida. So they can be correctly understood as the authentic manifestation of an emergent, solidaristic collective identity "for culture." What is easy to overlook in the search for origin and motivation is the fact that these claims are made within a disciplinary context. That is to say they really amount to a call for space and status recognition within the framework of mainstream sociology. They point, in other words, to the fact that American cultural sociology is conservative rather than revolutionary in its academic program, unlike the British cultural studies model which has attempted to transgress disciplinary boundaries and create a completely new academic and discursive field.

Calls for the autonomy of culture also signpost the influence of positivism on American cultural sociology. In the American context these calls often take the form of demands that culture be taken seriously as an "independent variable." Yet at the same time there is a competing dynamic against transcendental idealism. This position, arising in part from post-Parsonian anxieties about overvaluing culture, has precluded the Lévi-Straussian option of bringing culture back in as the sole significant variable, thereby treating the social world as the product of free-floating myths and texts. The result has been widespread endorsement of a middle-ground position calling for multidimensional explanations that provide space for social structure, culture, and individual actors as simultaneous "causes" of the same events and processes. Therefore debates between cultural sociologists often concern the relative weights that are given to each level of analysis. In a curious, roundabout way this concern for multidimensionality reiterates Parsons's call for the mutual interpretation of social, cultural, and personality systems. However, causality tends to be proximate and grounded rather than abstract and systemic as in Parsons's own work.

Assertions about the autonomy of culture also characterized British cultural studies during its salad days. Today this sort of discourse has all but disappeared. As cultural studies has shifted towards the arts for its institutional support and academic market, and as cultural studies has become a self-supporting intellectual field, there has been less need to engage in debates or polemics against social structural or material determinism or against instrumental views of social action. Field autonomy has brought with it the luxury of being able to assume, rather than needing to demonstrate, that culture is worth taking seriously. It is possible that American cultural sociology will also follow this path as it becomes more central to the discipline.

The European tradition differs again when it comes to thinking about culture and causality. Here, thinking in terms of variables is alien to the discourse, with greater emphasis being placed on exploring the fusion of the cultural, the social, and the material than on bringing about their analytic separation. This differing style of discourse explains the frustration American scholars and students often experience in reading Europeans like Foucault or Lévi-Strauss, where discrete "variables" and lines of cause and effect are almost impossible to identify. This kind of writing is also to be found in ancestral figures like Marx, Durkheim, and Weber, and it accounts for the range of interpretations to which they have been subjected, with each of them having been described on the gamut running from idealism to materialism. Disjunctures between European cultural theory and American modes of thinking often lead American researchers to translate European cultural theory into a workable set of propositions so they can "test" it. A telling exception here is the work of Pierre Bourdieu. Although the philosophical and Marxist elements of Bourdieu's theories have found little favor in America, much of his work is already structured in a positivistic guise with relatively clear hypotheses and elegant empirical tests. It is no accident, therefore, that Bourdieu has exerted a profound influence on American cultural sociology.

A final defining characteristic of American cultural sociology is the preference for empirically grounded, middle-range research. The European tradition of "high theory" assigns prestige to the ability to speak in global and abstract terms about how culture works. In American cultural sociology and British cultural studies far greater attention is paid to exploring how culture works in specialist topic-fields. This preference reflects, yet again, the continuing importance of the Anglo-American empiricist tradition in shaping academic life in the United States and Britain, as opposed to the more speculative, literary, and discursive style of European intellectual output. Culture tends to be conceptualized in terms of its concrete interplay with institutions, organizations, and specific historical sequences rather than in terms of the grand historical meta-narratives and philosophical abstractions which dominate the European mode of discourse. The result has been a form of discourse which usually anchors analysis in empirical materials, with even papers of a purely theoretical bent providing brief examples to illustrate their point. Evidence for this preference for empirically grounded, middle-range work can be seen, once again, in the reception of European works and scholars in Britain and America. Empirical studies have been more influential than purely theoretical tracts. Foucault is most accurately thought of as a philosopher, yet the data-rich *Discipline and Punish* has been far more widely read than abstruse texts like *The Order of Things* or *The Archaeology of Knowledge*. Similarly Habermas's slender empirical study of the public sphere now stimulates more interest than his difficult *magnum opus* on communicative action.

Perhaps inevitably this attention to concrete, middle-range, real-world detail has seen both British and American traditions introduce agency into inquiry, stressing the way that actors mediate cultural codes in particular settings. Such mediations may involve using culture for strategic ends, cultural innovation, or reading and interpreting texts in individual- or group-specific ways. In the American case, this has been anchored in a powerful pragmatist tradition (see Lamont and Wuthnow 1990) and the influence of comparative social history (Wacquant and Calhoun 1989) as well as in phenomenological resources. In the British case, agency was originally introduced via the Western Marxist tradition – in particular Gramsci. The aim of this research agenda was to displace the brand of monolithic Marxist theorizing that left little room for analyzing strategy and negotiation in the struggle for cultural hegemony (Hall 1980). Despite these differing origins, in recent years both American and British approaches have come to be strongly influenced by poststructural theories of reading. This has shifted the analysis of contingency towards the reception of cultural codes and away from the circumstances surrounding their production.[6]

Yet, although the British cultural studies tradition shares the empirical, middle-range quality of American cultural sociology, positivist norms are weakly developed. The ever-intensifying push towards wider interdisciplinary relevance has seen the orientation of the field shift from the social sciences towards the arts. Traditional issues of measurement and methodology have become displaced in favor of innovative, virtuoso interpretations of media texts, youth sub-cultures, popular music lyrics, etc. Consequently the style of much contemporary work on sociological themes has more in common with the aesthetic discourses of literary and art criticism than with sociology. This shift has undoubtedly helped British cultural studies to colonize other disciplines, enabling scholars without social scientific methodological training to participate in debates about quasi-sociological issues. By contrast, success in adapting to disciplinary norms about sociology as science has been central to the rise of cultural work within the discipline of American sociology. These adaptations have included a preference for quantitative analysis or, in the case of qualitative work, controlled comparisons which attempt to rule out the influence of other variables (typically things like rational interest, social structure, money, or power). Theoretical work conducted by American cultural sociologists has, in consequence, something of the quality of Kuhnian "normal science" when compared to work in the British and Continental traditions. It tries to accumulate small, specialism-specific gains in fact and theory rather than construct bold new paradigms or speculative interpretations. Of course, theoretical disputes persist between schools of thought within American cultural sociology. Contestation is only natural given a vibrant and dynamic research environment. Yet, in the final analysis, the greatest strengths of American cultural sociology lie in its relatively non-dogmatic, middle-rangeness, its concern with data and rules of evidence and its ability to address core disciplinary issues. The result has been a style of research where creative thinking coexists with intellectual modesty and methodological caution. These are the qualities that best define a growing, and exciting, field of cultural exploration.

Organization of the book

The claim made here, then, is that American cultural sociology is an enterprise that is both distinctive and worthwhile. Such a grand claim about substance and value must be substantiated. The best proof of the pudding, as they say, is in the eating, and therefore we turn from abstract description to the research product itself. For the most part the papers collected in this book are by a younger generation of scholars, all of them based at United States institutions. Most were published over the past fifteen or so years in American journals, the majority in the two core professional journals in the United States – the *American Journal of Sociology* and the *American Sociological Review* – where the traits of American cultural inquiry are most clearly developed. The essays were selected not with the aim of promoting any particular type of cultural sociology, in terms of theory or methodology, but rather to map out the field of American cultural sociology by presenting a range of its most exemplary work. It is hoped they will allow the reader to leave this book understanding more precisely what this general approach offers and how it adds up to a distinctive new mode of cultural inquiry.

With a view, therefore, to emphasizing strong family resemblances and avoiding the divisive separation of essays according to traditional "schools of thought," works have been grouped into three parts: "Culture as text and code," "The production and reception of culture," and "Culture in action." These represent, respectively, the exploration of meaning and meaning systems, the processes by which culture is transmitted and received, and how culture actually brings about changes in the real world. Notwithstanding each area reflecting a major concentration of study in contemporary cultural sociology, this classification should be considered as a set of ideal types. In practice we find that many essays deal with issues of concern to more than one of these approaches. Indeed, perhaps it is the case that a complete approach to culture must include some explanation at each level. Whilst bearing in mind the limitations of this provisional classification, the book turns first to the study of meaning and the cultural structures through which it is sustained.

Notes

1 The most complete account of this reaction against Parsons is provided by Jeffrey Alexander (1987). Alexander's interesting thesis is that the flight from norms (i.e., culture) was one that was doomed to failure. By abandoning reference to a collective cultural order, scholars advocating alternative perspectives found themselves inevitably led into theoretical aporias, contradictions, and dead-ends. The turn back towards culture by these various schools may well constitute a response to these theoretical conundrums, although such a thesis has yet to be demonstrated in detail.

2 Witness the rediscovery of Weber's early work *The Agrarian Sociology of Ancient Civilizations*, the changing meaning of *herrschaft*, and the popularity of interpretations of Weber by Roth and Bendix as opposed to those of, say, Eisenstadt and Parsons.

3 It is doubtful whether these attempts to go beyond culture in micro-sociology have been entirely successful. This failure can be reflected in intellectual ambivalence. In the field of conversation analysis, for example, there remain latent tensions between two broad camps. The minority position hints that we may be seeing norms and their associated roles instantiated in interactions and argues that analysts should use their competencies as members to detect these. The majority position is more cautious, formalist and empiricist, arguing that analysts should document patterns in talk without attributing motivation or causality unless there is a clear mandate for these claims in each and every utterance in the transcript. The former position offers as-yet-unrealized potential for the connection of conversation analysis with mainstream cultural sociology (and vice versa). The latter position, according to some commentators, appears to take conversation analysis towards the field of linguistics and away from the core debates and concerns of both ethnomethodology and sociology (see Lynch and Bogen 1994). In the case of rational choice theories, like their ancestral exchange and game theories, we often find culture and norms slipping in through the back door. Hence concepts like "trust," "tradition," and "belief" can find themselves specified in formal models in order to explain behaviors which deviate from the analyst's idea of the rational.

4 I have argued elsewhere (Alexander and Smith 1993) that this continuing influence has not been entirely positive in its consequences. The reaction against Parsonian idealism has produced strands of contemporary cultural theorizing which often fail to recognize the autonomy of culture, reducing it to a dependent variable of the social structure or else treating it as the product of contingent individual actions. These two perspectives can be broadly represented as the contemporary cultural legacy of the "conflict" and "micro" critiques of Parsons.

5 Lamont and Wuthnow (1990) provide an extremely useful essay contrasting American and European cultural sociologies (see also Lamont, this volume, ch. 6). Their argument is notable for its emphasis on the influence of pragmatism on American cultural sociology and its discussion of the role and positioning of

intellectuals in France and the United States. The argument presented here seeks to augment, rather than confront, their position.

6 In this chapter the backdrop of European high theory has led to the fore-grounding of certain similarities among Bourdieu, the Birmingham school, and American cultural sociology as middle-range, empirically grounded projects. When this point of reference is removed, the comparison takes on a different hue. For the most part, American cultural sociology is not only the most middle-range and causally precise, but also the least ambiguous about the autonomy of culture (see Alexander and Smith 1998).

References

Alexander, Jeffrey. 1987. *Twenty Lectures*. New York: Columbia University Press.

Alexander, Jeffrey, and Philip Smith. 1993. "The Discourse of American Civil Society: A New Agenda for Cultural Studies." *Theory and Society* 22: 151–207.

    1998. "Cultural Sociology or Sociology of Culture: Towards a Strong Program." *Sociologie et Sociétés*, special edition, International Sociological Association World Congress, Montreal.

Emirbayer, Mustafa. 1996. "Useful Durkheim." *Sociological Theory* 14(2): 109–130.

Grossberg, Lawrence, Cary Nelson, and Paula Treichler. 1991. *Cultural Studies*. New York: Routledge.

Hall, Stuart. 1980. "Cultural Studies and the Centre: Some Problematics and Problems." In Stuart Hall, Dorothy Hobson, Andrew Lowe, and Paul Willis (eds.), *Culture, Media. Language*. London: Unwin Hyman, pp. 15–47.

Lamont, Michèle, and Robert Wuthnow. 1990. "Betwixt and Between: Recent Cultural Sociology in Europe and the United States." In George Ritzer (ed.), *Frontiers of Social Theory*. New York: Columbia University Press, pp. 287–315.

Lynch, Michael, and David Bogen. 1994. "Harvey Sacks' Primitive Natural Science." *Theory, Culture and Society* 11: 65–104.

Sewell, William. 1985. "Ideologies and Social Revolutions: Reflections on the French Case." *Journal of Modern History* 57(1): 57–85.

Sherwood, Steven, Philip Smith, and Jeffrey Alexander. 1993. "The British are Coming . . . Again! The Hidden Agenda of Cultural Studies." *Contemporary Sociology* 22(2): 370–375.

Smith, Philip, and Jeffrey Alexander. 1996. "Durkheim's Religious Revival." *American Journal of Sociology* 102(2): 585–592.

Wacquant, Loic, and Craig Calhoun. 1989. "Intérêt, rationalité et culture." *Actes de la recherche en sciences sociales* 78: 41–60.

PART I

Culture as text and code

At its core the study of culture is the study of meanings. It is a process involving the distillation of essences of significance from the base material of social life. There is a broad consensus among American cultural sociologists that this alchemical task can be best accomplished using the *apparatus criticus* of structuralist and poststructuralist concepts. Signs, symbols, narratives, discourses, myths, and so forth are the alembics through which the process of refinement takes place. Yet, if there is agreement on basic tools and concepts, there is discord on broader questions of approach. Differences center around two sets of issues. The first of these is the relationship between cultural inquiry and "mainstream" sociology. What is at stake here is whether cultural analysis should be understood as a radical enterprise which fundamentally transforms the nature of sociology, or whether it can best be accommodated within existing conceptual and methodological frameworks. The second, and related, issue is the question of the autonomy of culture and its links with social structure. Some sociologists, especially those strongly influenced by postmodernisms, consider that these kinds of traditional distinctions are no longer relevant or helpful. To the contrary they assert that culture and social structure are so deeply implicated that it is both futile and misguided to attempt to define where their boundaries might lie. In the introduction to this book I argued that most American cultural sociologists can be understood as holding to a conservative, disciplinary view of their enterprise – a position which tends to sustain the concept of culture as a separate "variable." Nevertheless, it is important to recognize a tension that exists between this vision of culture and more radical and relativistic alternatives.

The first essay in this part is a theoretical treatise by Richard Harvey Brown which presents arguments representative of this minority position. Brown rejects the view that cultural sociology should be limited in its domain of inquiry, and challenges existing understandings of the boundaries between culture and social structure. Brown's position draws upon French deconstructionism and relativistic programs in the sociology of knowledge to assert that there is no reality which we can access outside of language and language conventions. Drawing on Foucault, as well as the American tradition of labeling theory and rhetorical analysis, he goes on to suggest that the aim of sociological inquiry should be to illuminate the ways in which language and social texts are routinized in everyday life and how they not only reinforce, but also constitute, relationships of power and domination. This amounts to a call for greater reflexivity in exploring the linguistic and political processes through which knowledge and its associated institutions are constructed.

The contribution following Brown's, by Jeffrey Alexander, is in agreement with it about the importance of social texts and the need to engage in discursive and cultural analysis. But whereas Brown stresses the ties between texts and power, Alexander calls for an inquiry which prioritizes uncovering the internal "cultural structures" within discourses. The argument that he gives for this approach is worth stressing here: it is only through recovering and reconstructing the internal logic of meaning structures that a really strong claim can be made for the autonomy of culture. Alternative perspectives on culture, he claims, all too often see it reduced to a dependent variable of power, social structure, networks, or contingent individual actions. Typically for an American cultural sociologist, Alexander draws heavily on the more cultural dimensions of Weber and Durkheim in building this argument. His main point is that even discourse about technology – surely the domain of the most rational of discourses – is best understood as a structure of quasi-religious symbols and mythologies rather than in terms of domination and power.

Steven Seidman's chapter takes a middle road between Brown and Alexander. Like Brown's, Seidman's essay is strongly influenced by postmodernism. This is manifest not only in its emphasis on the role of discourses in constructing and legitimating the social, but also in its focus on desire and sexuality as legitimate subjects of sociological inquiry. But whereas Brown has modified postmodernism by rooting it in the American tradition of labeling theory and rhetorical analysis, Seidman has adapted the postmodern agenda to the cultural contributions of classical sociological theory. We find in Seidman's essay, as in Alexander's, the echoes of Durkheim and Weber. Discourses on AIDS and homosexuality are interpreted by Seidman in terms of a moral drama or salvation narrative involving concepts of the polluted, pure, and apocalyptic. Yet power is not excluded from this analytic frame, with Seidman pointing to the way that these binary discourses fostered the further vilification and exclusion of marginal social groups by more dominant ones. A final, unconnected, point is also worth making here: another trace of the American sociological tradition (indeed literary tradition) is to be found in Seidman's and Brown's writing style. In contrast to much European postmodern sociology each treats analytically complex issues in a straightforward, lucid way.

In his classic work *The Savage Mind*, the French anthropologist Claude Lévi-Strauss had a chapter entitled "The Logic of Totemic Classifications." What he argued there was that it is as profitable to explore the formal structures in which discourses are arranged as it is to look at the meanings they convey. Robert Wuthnow's unusual and somewhat difficult essay can be seen as a study in this tradition. It draws upon postmodernism and structural semiotics to assert that in the study of language and discourse we can sometimes push the exploration of meaning to one side. So, whereas the primary aim of Seidman's and Alexander's analyses was to reconstruct a social text, crystallizing patterns of meaning through a deeply hermeneutic analysis, Wuthnow turns away from the exegesis of religious doctrine. What is said, Wuthnow asserts, matters less than how it is said if we wish to explain the impact of religious discourses on publics. Readers might disagree as to whether Wuthnow is able to reject meaning altogether in identifying discourse structures as centrifugal or centripetal, but it is certainly clear that his approach resembles structural linguistics more than Gadamer's hermeneutics.

The final work arguing for the need to decode meaning is by Anne Kane. Her contribution acts as a bridge between this part of the book and the next two. She is concerned with exploring both meaning structures and the ways they are deployed in concrete situations. Her point is as much methodological as theoretical: cultural sociologists should attend to both the autonomy of structures of meaning and empirical or "causal" autonomy. We have to know what culture *is* before we can fully understand what it does and how it does it. This two-step process allows cultural autonomy to be affirmed in sociological analysis without falling into the trap of a one-sided idealism.

1

Textuality and the postmodern turn in sociological theory*

Richard Harvey Brown

Over recent years the "rhetorical turn" has become an important intellectual movement in the human sciences. It has become a commonplace that social and cultural reality, and the social sciences themselves, are linguistic constructions. Not only is society viewed increasingly as a text, but scientific texts themselves are seen as rhetorical constructions. In this rhetorical view, reality and truth are formed through practices of representation and interpretation by rhetors and their publics. This view can be located in the contexts of poststructuralism, critical rhetoric of inquiry, and the social construction (and reconstruction) of science. All these tendencies of thought reject the simple bifurcation of reason and persuasion, or of thought and its expression. Instead, knowledge is viewed as poetically and politically constituted, "made" by human communicative action that develops historically and is institutionalized politically.

In this view, realistic representations become true descriptions not by correspondence to noumenal objects, but by conformity to orthodox practices of writing and reading. Thus theories can be seen as the practices through which things take on meaning and value, and not merely as representations of a reality that is wholly exterior to them. Indeed, insofar as a theoretical representation is regarded as objectively true, it is viewed in that way because its methods of construction have become so familiar that they operate transparently (Shapiro 1988, p. XI). For example, if we show a chart and call it "Income Distribution in the United States," we assume that the chart has a certain equivalence with things that people have or do. That is, we see the realism of the chart as independent of our conceptions of statistics, demographic research, and social theory that guide our way of

---

* First published in 1991 as "Rhetoric, textuality, and the postmodern turn in sociological theory," *Sociological Theory* 8(2): 188–197.

seeing and reading that image. Yet every representation is always a representation from some point of view, within some frame of vision. Absolutist conceptions of sociological truth are merely those modes of representation which have "made it" socially and thence deny their necessary partiality. The distinctions between fact and fiction are thereby softened because both are seen as the products of, and sources for, communicative action; both are viewed as representations of reality that also represent various groups, interests, ideologies, and historical impositions. By untangling the relationship between textual and political practices, we gain insight into the ways in which the true has been fashioned, and could be refashioned anew.

In the presence of such a relativization of formerly privileged discourses of truth, many people feel nostalgia for a lost foundation for lawlike knowledge, whereas others hope for the creation of a new ethical ontology and normative epistemology. That is, even after deconstructive criticism has done its work, we still are faced with the challenge of establishing cognitive authority and inventing positive values as central elements of any rational moral polity. What is needed, then, is a critical assessment of the deconstructivist, rhetorical effort to date, a clearer understanding of its dialectical relationship to intelligibility within historical communities of discourse, and an analysis of how such academic discourses both reflect and influence their larger political contexts of production. In other words, we need to extend sociological analysis to uncover the methods by which, as sociologists and as citizens, we encode what is taken as real, normal, and to be accepted without question and even without awareness.

Thus the postmodernist project has the potential to radicalize the methods, the objects, and the very conceptions of our sociological enterprise. In particular, the postmodern transvaluation of epistemology wrenches us away from our most treasured beliefs about the constitution of science, knowledge, and even reason itself. It does so by leading us to question the traditional foundations of knowledge and scientific inquiry; then it asks us to adopt a *rhetorical* posture as we are subsequently faced with redefining, metatheoretically, what theory and research are. Then the task will be to define a more intellectually reflective and politically responsible sociological practice.

In the modernist past, postmodernists argue, our understanding of how science and knowledge were constituted relied upon an assumed polarity and hierarchy between truth and its medium of expression. Foundationalist epistemology and modern scientific method insisted that objective truth existed independently of any symbols that might be used to convey it. In this bifurcation, reason was authoritatively superior to its own external systems of expression. Since the Enlightenment, science has thrived on the self-endorsing assumption that the "rhetorical" is by definition separate from the true, ontologically and epistemologically. By contrast, post-moderns subvert the authority of modernist metatheory with a rhetorical conception of science. They relativize reason radically by conflating the traditionally bifurcated hierarchies of truth and expression, *doxa* and *episteme*, rationality and language, appearance and reality, and meaning and metaphor. They do so by focusing on the *how* rather than the *what* of knowledge, its poetic and political enablements rather than its logical and empirical entailments.

Through such shifts of focus, knowledge is relocated in the act of symbolic construction, and no longer is regarded as that which symbols subserviently convey. Knowledge about social reality is not viewed merely as objective product, but also as symbolic process that is inherently persuasive. Humans *enact* truth not by legislating it scientifically, but by performing it rhetorically. Our knowledge of truth is not based on some extralinguistic rationality, because rationality itself is demystified and reconstituted as a historical construction and deployment by human rhetors. Logic and reason are brought down from their absolute, pre-existent heights into the creative, contextual web of history and action (Brown 1987, pp. 64–79). The arena of conversation and contention that logic closed to all but experts is thus prised open by rhetoric, with its emphasis upon audience, narrative, and prudent judgment in the face of historical contingency.

Accordingly, postmodernism shifts the agenda of social theory and research from explanation and verification to a conversation of scholars/rhetors who seek to guide and persuade themselves and each other. Theoretical truth is not a fixed entity discovered according to a metatheoretical blueprint of linearity or hierarchy, but is invented within an ongoing self-reflective community in which "theorist," "social scientist," "agent," and "critic" become relatively interchangeable (Burke 1964; Rorty 1979). This picture of the sociological enterprise suggests that critique of theory and method must be permanently imminent precisely because theories and methods themselves cannot be universalized. This view requires us to acknowledge our own rhetorical constitution – our selves as subjects and our fields as disciplinary objects – and then to maintain and apply the consciousness and the practice of rhetorical awareness.

A postmodern rhetoric for sociological theory

All of these developments illustrate those shifts of discourse that have revived the ancient field of rhetoric. Language, and communicative action more generally, are now seen as the very condition of thought. Similarly, the idea of "text" is no longer restricted to a written representation. Any statement of experience or (more strongly) any lived or imagined experience is a discursive practice that is both culturally embedded and historically situated. A text might be a mathematical model or an archival record, a novel or a myth, a ritual or a public program. Indeed, culture itself is seen as an "ensemble of texts" (Geertz 1973, p. 452). Correspondingly, meaning does not reside autonomously within a text but is created in the process of transforming experience into text in a dialogical relation with other texts and contexts (Todorov 1984, p. 48). Thus a text becomes an intertextual network, "a kind of juncture, where other texts, norms and values meet and work upon each other" (Iser 1987, p. 219). As a result, there is not one privileged meaning but many meanings and many voices. Necessarily, then, we are all engaged in textual problems and production. Society becomes a text, and sociological theory becomes an authorial voice of significant power.

In this view, what a social theoretical text says may be less the product of its own "inherent" properties than of the predispositions brought to the text by the reader (Suleiman and Crossman 1980). Theoretically, then, a given text is open to as many different interpretations as there are articulate readers. Writers in the destructionist mode push this line of thinking to its limits. As Derrida (1974), de Man (1973), and others propose, writing, and by extension sociological theory, are not mimetic. Writing does not describe a world independent of itself. Rather, critical or expository writing is self-referential, governed by rules for its own construction. Thus "discovery" in science is more an honorific than a descriptive appellation; and it is ideological too because it disguises the very practices of reality projection that postmodernists deconstruct.

The rhetorical construction of social reality

The textualist approach also illuminates how selves and societies are constructed and deconstructed through rhetorical practices. In this view, the creation of meaningful personal or collective reality involves the intersubjective deployment of symbol structures through which happenings are organized into events and experience. Peoples establish repertoires of categories by which certain aspects of what is to be the case are fixed, focused, or forbidden. These aspects are put in the foreground of awareness and become articulated or conscious experience against a background of unspoken existence. The knowledge that emerges from this process takes a narrative form (Brown 1990; Greimas 1987, ch. 6). Reciprocally, the sequential ordering of a past, a present, and a future enables the structuring of perceptual experience, the organization of memory, and the constructions of the events, identities, and lives that they express (Bruner 1987, p. 15). This rhetorically constructed narrative unity provides models of identity for people in particular symbolic settings or lifeworlds. It also guides individuals and groups in knowing what is real and what is illusion, what is permissible and what is proscribed, what goes without saying and what must not be said. "The construction of a worldview is thus a rhetorical act of creative human agency; it is a practical accomplishment of a human community over time" (Brulle 1988, p. 4).

In so constructing a world, other worlds are foreclosed. There is always a "surplus reality" because existence (potential experience) is always larger than actual experience. Moreover, as shown in Laurence Sterne's *Tristram Shandy* (1940 [1759–67]), there also is always a "surplus of the signified" because we experience more than we know, and we know more tacitly than we can state. Hence the unreflected, signified world is always larger than whatever version of it becomes canonized into formal knowledge. The land is always larger than the maps, and in mapping it in one official way we narrow awareness of alternative ways of experiencing the terrain. Likewise with human conduct: what is mapped as a catatonic seizure in one culture may be seen as a divine trance in another; each is equally real for those who name their world in that way (Foucault 1973).

In articulating experience through categories, discursive practices realize differences and distinctions; they define what is normal and deviant, and hence express and enact forms of domination. Thus the processes of definition and exclusion are not only logical properties of discourse; they also are preconditions of intelligibility, sociation, social order, and social control. To make reality mutually comprehensible in an intersubjective group and to regularize symbolically guided social behavior, some versions of reality must be legitimized at the expense of their competitors. As Robert Brulle (1988) has discussed, such legitimation is an operation of closure. That is, it discounts the value of pursuing further implications and protects established interpretations by means of social sanctions that marginalize or silence dissident voices. Thus legitimation is a rhetorical achievement (Brinton 1985, p. 281; Brulle 1988, p. 4; Stanley 1978, p. 131). In Foucault's phrase (1970, 1972), it establishes a "regime of truth," a metanarrative by which the society lives.

As noted, closure and legitimation also involve the repression of alternative realities. The establishment of an orthodoxy thus creates heterodoxies – subjugated discourses as "a whole set of knowledge that has been disqualified as inadequate to their task or insufficiently elaborated; naive knowledge, located low down on the hierarchy, beneath the required level of cognition or scientificity" (Foucault 1980, p. 82; see Kristeva 1973). In modern Western societies, such alternative realities are different and deviant from the dominant scientific habitus. They include dream time, carnal wisdom, mystic experience, feminine intuition, primal thought, aesthetic perception, hand intelligence, street smarts, lower-class lore, folkways, dopeways, old wives' tales, grace, and other forms of knowing.

These alternative realities are delegitimated by marginalizing the discursive practices through which they are constructed. Such practices become unofficial, extra-institutional, and "backstage," expressed in the "restricted" rather than the "elaborated" code (see Bernstein 1971; Brown 1987; Goffman 1959, ch. 1). From the viewpoint of the dominant habitus, these discourses are linguistically deprived. Their delegitimation also delegitimates the lifeworlds of their users. The official discourse becomes the only one that provides symbolic capital that could be fruitfully invested in institutional relations. This limits the power and autonomy of speakers of marginalized discourses and forces them to adopt the dominant definition of reality and its regime of truth if they are to participate as full members in the collective institutional life. Indeed, compliance and full membership are expressed practically through adequate performance of the dominant mode of speech.

Thus relations of domination are produced through practice and are reified for members as things given by God, Nature, Tradition, History, or Reason. This movement from creative agency to reified structure is enacted through various persuasive strategies that conceal from social members their own rhetorical construction of the social text. Society comes to be seen as a natural fact rather than a cultural artifact. Reification thus allows relations of domination and authority to be seen as natural instead of created; it thereby facilitates conformity and continued reproduction of the social order. This ascription of naturalness inclines agents to accept the social order as it is. It becomes a "realized morality" to its members (Bourdieu 1977, pp. 163–164).

The appearance of society as a moral entity leads individuals to actions designed to maintain their self-image by avoiding shame and exclusion. Everyday interactions therefore are polite exchanges, aimed at avoiding embarrassment. Should the social fabric and persons' moral esteem be torn temporarily, this damage is repaired with excuses and justifications (Gamson 1985; Goffman 1959; Lyman and Scott 1970; Schudson 1984). In everyday life, Goffman tells us, we are occupied with "maintaining the definition of the situation" in order to "cope with the bizarre potentials of social life" (1974, p. 14). "Definitional disruptions . . . would occur much more frequently were not constant precaution taken" (Goffman 1959, pp.

2, 13). The social order, in other words, requires that "others" be "forced to accept some events as conventional or natural signs of something not directly available to the senses" (Goffman 1959, p. 2). Thus the realized morality of everyday interactions makes successful challenges to authority a risky, difficult, and sometimes unimaginable task. In these ways both social structure and personal identity are achieved rhetorically.

Postmodernism, sociological theory, and the political community

What is the relationship between the rhetorical, textualist perspective of postmodernism and the *telos* of nonideological, emancipatory discourse? Can the postmodernist project also contribute to a more reflexive, more enlightened polity? An adequate paradigm for democratic civic communication must join efficiency in managing complex systems with self-understanding and significance in the lifeworld. That is, it must enable us to govern our polities in a rational manner to ensure collective survival while providing us with meaning and dignity in our existential experience of ourselves. Hence such a discourse must be adequate not only on the level of science and technique, but also on the level of ethics and politics. After we have deconstructed traditional humanism and traditional science, we still confront these challenges. But with what intellectual resources, and with what disciplinary strategies? What additional problems are we likely to confront? How might they be usefully framed and addressed? How are analytic and existential truths to be conjoined within one discourse? How can we put ourselves within our scholarly texts?

The metaphor of scientific and social realities as rhetorical construction helps us to address such questions. First, it allows us to abandon the views both of social structures as objective entities acting on individuals and of subjective agents inventing their worlds out of conscious intentions. Instead both structure and consciousness are seen as practical, historical accomplishments, brought about through everyday communicative action, the result of rhetorical (poetic and political) struggles over the nature and meaning of reality.

In such a manner, absolutist dichotomies of structure and agency or of base and superstructure may be dissolved in the metaphor of society as textual enactment. The structure (language) is both a constraint and a resource for performance (speech). The semiotic moment of the rhetorical approach deals effectively with structure; its hermeneutic moment treats of meaning and action. Both these dimensions – syntactics and grammatics, on the one hand, and semantics and pragmatics, on the other – are contained and logically constituted within the rhetorical or textualist metaphor. This metaphor combines in linguistic terms Durkheim's conception of constraining structures with Marx's idea that the system of exchanges is the source of values (Lemert 1990). Yet it also incorporates Mead's and Garfinkel's conceptions of social reality as constructed through communication interaction.

In abandoning the anti-rhetorical rhetoric of positivism, the discursive approach recovers the ancient function of social thought as a moral and political practice. In this new critical rhetorical view, in constructing social theory we should attend not only to logical propositions and empirical contents, but also to linguistic methods and existential functions. We then see the linguistic dimension of social theory as an integral part of its truth or falsity to social life. This is the case for two reasons. First, truth and validity are themselves rhetorically constructed and hence are a part of our civic life. Second, as rhetorical interventions, social scientific theories convey an existential as well as a propositional truth. Sociological theories provide a truth of facts or meanings, an appeal to the *telos* of elegance and precision, predictability or comprehension. Yet when seen rhetorically, such truth is also an implicit call to action. Its existential *telos* is self-understanding, critique, and emancipation. Reductionists have sought to silence this existential dimension of sociological theory by treating it as an object external to society that makes no personal moral claim upon us. But social theories do convey an existential truth. And, unlike propositional truth, existential truth is not merely to be cross-examined. Instead, when it speaks we ourselves become the "object," for it is we who are addressed.

References

Bernstein, Basil. 1971. *Class, Codes, and Control*. London: Routledge and Kegan Paul.
Bourdieu, Pierre. 1977. *Outline of a Theory of Practice*. Cambridge: Cambridge University Press.
Brinton, Alan. 1985. "On Viewing Knowledge as Rhetorical." *Central States Speech Journal* 36(4): 270–281.
Brown, Richard Harvey. 1987. *Society as Text. Essays on Rhetoric, Reason, and Reality*. Chicago: University of Chicago Press.
    1990. "Narrative in Scientific Knowledge and Civic Discourse." *Current Perspectives in Social Theory* 11.
Brulle, Robert J. 1988. "Power, Discourse, and Social Movements." Unpublished paper, Department of Sociology, George Washington University, Washington, DC.
Bruner, Jerome. 1987. "Life as Narrative." *Social Research* 54(1): 11–32.
Burke, Kenneth. 1964. *Perspectives by Incongruity*. Bloomington: Indiana University Press.

de Man, Paul. 1973. "Semiology and Rhetoric." *Diacritics* 3(3): 27–33.

Derrida, Jacques. 1974. *Of Grammatology*. Baltimore: Johns Hopkins University Press.

Foucault, Michel. 1970. *The Order of Things: An Archaeology of the Human Sciences*. New York: Pantheon.

 1972. *The Archaeology of Knowledge*, translated by A. M. Sheridan. New York: Harper.

 1973. *Madness and Civilization: A History of Insanity in the Age of Reason*, translated by R. Howard. New York: Vintage.

 1980. *Power/Knowledge*, ed. Colin Gordon. New York: Pantheon.

Gamson, William A. 1985. "Goffman's Legacy to Political Sociology." *Theory and Society* 14(5): 605–622.

Geertz, Clifford. 1973. *The Interpretation of Cultures*. New York: Basic Books.

Gergen, Kenneth J. 1982. *Toward a Transformation of Social Knowledge*. New York: Springer-Verlag.

Goffman, Erving. 1959. *The Presentation of the Self in Everyday Life*. Garden City, NY: Doubleday.

 1974. *Frame Analysis: An Essay on the Organization of Experience*. New York: Harper.

Greimas, Algirdas Julien. 1987. *On Meaning: Selected Writings in Semiotic Theory*. Minneapolis: University of Minnesota Press.

Iser, Wolfgang. 1987. "Representation: A Performative Act." In Murray Kreiger (ed.), *The Aims of Representation: Subject/Text/History*. New York: Columbia University Press, pp. 217–232.

Kristeva, Julia. 1973. "The System and the Speaking Subject." *Times Literary Supplement*, October 12 (3, 736): 1249–1250.

Kuhn, Thomas. 1972. *The Structure of Scientific Revolutions*. Chicago: University of Chicago Press.

Lemert, Charles. 1990. "Social Theory? Theoretical Play after Difference." In Steven Seidman and David Wagner (eds.), *General Social Theory and Its Critics*. London: Basil Blackwell.

Lyman, Stanford M. and Marvin B. Scott. 1970. "Accounts." In *A Sociology of the Absurd*. New York: Appleton-Century-Crofts.

McKeon, Richard. 1971. "The Uses of Rhetoric in a Technological Age: Architectonic Productive Arts." In Lloyd F. Bitzer and Edwin Black (eds.), *The Prospect of Rhetoric*. Englewood Cliffs, NJ: Prentice-Hall, pp. 44–63.

Rorty, Richard. 1979. *Philosophy and the Mirror of Nature*. Princeton: Princeton University Press.

Schudson, Michael. 1984. "Embarrassment and Erving Goffman's Idea of Human Nature." *Theory and Society* 13(5): 633–648.

Shapiro, Michael J. 1988. *The Politics of Representation: Writing Practices in Biography, Photography, and Policy Analysis*. Madison: University of Wisconsin Press.

Stanley, Manfred. 1978. *The Technological Conscience. Survival and Dignity in an Age of Expertise*. Chicago: University of Chicago Press.

Sterne, Laurence. 1940 [1759–67]. *The Life and Opinions of Tristram Shandy*. New York: Odyssey.

Suleiman, Susan R. and Inge Crossman (eds.). 1980. *The Reader in the Text: Essays on Audience and Interpretation*. Princeton: Princeton University Press.

Todorov, Tzvetan. 1984. *Mikhail Bakhtin: The Dialogal Principle*, translated by Wead Godzich. Minneapolis: University of Minnesota Press.

2

The computer as sacred and profane*

Jeffrey C. Alexander

The gradual permeation of the computer into the pores of modern life deepens what Max Weber called the "rationalization of the world." The computer converts every message – regardless of its substantive meaning, metaphysical remoteness, or emotional allure – into a series of numerical bits and bytes. These series are connected to others through electrical impulses. Eventually these impulses are converted back into the media of human life.

Can there be any better example of the subjection of worldly activity to impersonal rational control? Can there be any more forceful illustration of the disenchantment of the world that Weber warned would be the result? Much depends on the answer to this portentous question, for discourse about the meaning of advanced technology demarcates one of the central concerns of social theory. If the answer is yes, we are not only trapped inside of Weber's cage of iron but also bound by the laws of exchange that Marx asserted would eventually force everything human into a commodity form.

This query about the rationalization of the world poses theoretical questions, not just existential ones. Can there really exist a world of purely technical rationality? Although this question may be ideologically compelling for critics of the modern world, I will argue that the theory underlying such a proposition is not correct. Because both action and its environments (Alexander 1982–1983, 1988a) are indelibly interpenetrated by the nonrational, a pure technically rational world cannot exist. Certainly the growing centrality of the digital computer is an empirical fact. This fact, however, remains to be interpreted and explained.

---

* First published in 1992 as "The promise of a cultural sociology: technological discourse and the sacred and profane information machine," in N. Smelser and R. Munch (eds.), *Theory of Culture*, Berkeley, University of California Press, pp. 293–323.

Taking meaning seriously

Contemporary sociology is almost entirely the study of social elements from the perspective of their place in the social system. The promise of a cultural sociology is that a more multidimensional perspective can be attained. From this multidimensional perspective, social elements would no longer be seen naturalistically, as things that can exist, in and of themselves, without the mediation of cultural codes. Events, actors, roles, groups, and institutions, as elements in a concrete society, are part of a social system; they are simultaneously, however, part of a cultural system that overlaps, but is not contiguous with, the society. I define culture as an organized set of meaningfully understood symbolic patterns. It is because of their location in such an organized set that every social interaction can also be understood as a text (Ricoeur 1971).

Only if these analytical transformations are made, can the thickness of human life (Geertz 1973), its dimensionality and nuance, enter into the language of social science. Dilthey (1976) prepared us to respect this density by insisting that all social action rests upon the reservoir of our inner experience of life. Because we experience the world rather than simply behave in it, the world is meaningful. As social scientists, we must describe the world's inner life or we will fail to describe "it" at all. We cannot, moreover, handle the problem of meaning cavalierly, taking its character for granted as something obvious and shifting our attention to this meaning's cause or effects. Rather, we must willingly inhabit the world of meaning itself.

To try to inhabit this world does not mean orienting ourselves to the idiosyncratic attitudes of individuals. This is the "getting into the actor's head" approach advocated by microtheorists such as symbolic interactionists. Because culture is an environment of every action, to inhabit the world of meaning is, rather, to enter into the organized sets of symbolic patterns that these actors meaningfully understand.

If we begin with the notion that culture is a form of language, we can make use of the conceptual architecture provided by Saussure's semiotics, his "science of signs." Though they perhaps are not as tightly organized as real languages (but see Barthes 1983), cultural sets have definite code-like properties. They are composed of strongly structured symbolic relationships that are largely independent of any particular actor's volition or speech. Cultural codes, like linguistic languages, are built upon signs, which contain both signifier and signified. Technology, for example, is not only a thing, a signified object to which others refer, it is also a signifier, a signal, an internal expectation. The relation between signifier and signified, Saussure insists, is "arbitrary." When he writes (1964) that the former "has no natural connection with the signified," he is suggesting that the meaning or nature of the sign – its name or internal dimension – cannot be understood as being dictated by the nature of the signified, that is, by the sign's external, material dimension.

If the meaning of the sign cannot be observed or induced from examining the signified, or objective, referents, then how is it established? By its relation to other signifiers, Saussure insists. Systems of signs are composed of endless such relationships. At their most primitive, these relationships are binary. In any actual system of cultural sets, they become long strings, or webs, of interwoven analogies and antitheses, what Eco (1979) calls the "similitude of signifiers" that compose the "global semantic field." Structural anthropology has illustrated the usefulness of this architecture, most famously in the work of Lévi-Strauss (1967) and most usefully in the work of Sahlins (1976, 1981).

Yet, even at its most socially embedded, semiotics can never be enough. By definition it abstracts from the social world, taking organized symbolic sets as psychologically unmotivated and as socially uncaused. By contrast, for the purposes of cultural sociology, semiotic codes must be tied into both social and psychological environments and into action itself. I will term the result of this specification *discourses*, in appreciation of, though not identification with, the phenomena conceptualized by Foucault. Discourses are symbolic sets that embody clear references to social system relationships, whether defined in terms of power, solidarity, or other organizational forms (cf. Sewell 1980; Hunt 1984). As social languages, they relate binary symbolic associations with social forms. In doing so, they provide a vocabulary for members to speak graphically about a society's highest values, its relevant groups, its boundaries *vis-à-vis* conflict, creativity, and internal dissent. Discourse socializes semiotic codes and emerges as a series of narratives (Ricoeur 1984) – myths that specify and stereotype a society's founding and founders (Eliade 1959; Bellah 1970), its critical events (Alexander 1988b), and utopian aspirations (Smith 1950).

In their theories of premodern cultures, classical sociologists constructed powerful models of how this social construction of semiotic codes can proceed. They did so in terms of their theories of religion. Thus, drawing from primitive totemism, Durkheim (1963) argued that every religion organizes social things into both binary relations and deeply felt antitheses between sacred and profane. Because sacred objects have to be protected, the "society" maintains a distance between them and other objects, either routine or profane. Actors not only try to protect themselves from coming into contact with polluted (Douglas 1966) or profane (Caillois 1959 [1939]) objects, but also seek a real, if mediated, contact with the sacred. This is one primary function of ritual behavior (Turner 1969; cf. Alexander 1988c).

While Weber's better-known theory of religion overlaps with Durkheim's, it is historically and comparatively specific. Given the emergence of a more formal and rationalized religion, the goal of believers becomes salvation from worldly suffering (Weber 1946a). Salvation creates the problem of theodicy, "from what" and "for what" one will be saved. Theodicy involves the image of God. If the gods or God is immanent, worshipers seek salvation through an internal experience of mystical contact. If God is transcendent, salvation is achieved more ascetically, by correctly divining God's will and following his commands. Each of these mandates can be pursued, moreover, in either a this-worldly or an other-worldly direction.

While Durkheim and Weber generally limited the application of these cultural theories to premodern religious life, it is possible to extend them to secular phenomena. This possibility is clarified when we define religions as types of semiotic systems, as discourses that reveal how the psychological and social structuring of culture proceeds.

In this section I have briefly sketched a model for examining the cultural dimension of social life. I hope merely that this discussion provides an introduction to what follows. Before examining the construction of the computer as a cultural object in the postwar world, however, I look at a range of earlier sociological treatments of technology to sense the difficulties that a more culturally sensitive approach must overcome.

Sociological accounts of technology: the dead hand of the social system

Considered in its social system reference, technology is a thing that can be touched, observed, interacted with, and calculated in an objectively rational way. Analytically, however, technology is also part of the cultural system. It is a sign, both a signifier and a signified, from which actors cannot entirely separate their subjective states of mind. Social scientists have not usually considered technology in this more subjective way. Indeed, they have not typically considered it as a cultural object at all. It has appeared as the material variable *par excellence*, not as a point of sacrality, but as the most routine of the routine; not a sign, but an antisign, the essence of a modernity that has undermined the very possibility for cultural understanding itself.

In the postmodern era, Marx has become infamous for his effusive praise in the Communist Manifesto of technology as the embodiment of scientific rationality. Marx believed that modern industrial technique, as the harbinger of progress, was breaking down the barriers of primitive and magical thought. Stripped of its capitalist integument, Marx predicted, advanced technology would be the mainspring of industrial communism, which he defined as the administration of *things* rather than *people*. Despite the central role he gives to technology, for Marx it is not a form of knowledge, even of the most rational sort. It is a material variable, a "force of production" (Marx 1962). As an element of the base, technology is something actors relate to mechanistically. It is produced because the laws of the capitalist economy force factory owners to lower their costs. The effects of this incorporation are equally objective. As technology replaces human labor, the organic composition of capital changes and the rate of profit falls; barring mitigating factors, this falling rate causes the collapse of the capitalist system.

While neo-Marxism has revised the determining relationship Marx posits between economy and technology, it continues to accept Marx's view of technology as a purely material fact. In Rueschemeyer's recent work on the relation between power and the division of labor, for example, neither general symbolic patterns nor the internal trajectory of rational knowledge are conceived of as affecting technological growth. "It is the inexorability of interest and power constellations," Rueschemeyer (1986, pp. 117–18) argues, "which shape even fundamental research and which determine translations of knowledge into new products and new ways of production." We would expect modern functionalism to view technology very differently, but this is true in an only limited sense. Of course, Parsons (1967) criticized Marx for putting technology into the base; functionalists have always been aware that technology belongs in a more intermediate position in the social system. They have, however, never looked at it as anything other than the product of rational knowledge, and they have often conceived of its efficient causes and specific effects in material terms.

In *Science, Technology, and Society in Seventeenth-Century England*, Merton emphasizes the role that Puritanism played in inspiring scientific inventions. Within the context of this inventive climate, however, the immediate cause of technology was economic benefit. The "relation between a problem raised by economic development and technologic endeavor is clear-cut and definite," Merton argues (1970, p. 144), suggesting that "importance in the realm of technology is often concretely allied with economic estimations." It was the "vigorous economic development" of the time that led to effective inventions, because it "posed the most imperative problems for solution" (p. 146). In Smelser's (1959) later account of the Industrial Revolution, the perspective is exactly the same. Methodist values form a background input to technological innovation, but they are not involved in the creation or the effects of technology itself. Innovation is problem driven, not culture driven, and the immediate cause is economic demand. The effect of technology is also concrete and material. By resolving strain at the social system level, innovation allows collective behavior to leave the level of generalized behavior – wish fulfillment, fantasy, utopian aspirations – and return to the more mundane and rational attitudes of the everyday (Smelser 1959, pp. 21–50).

Critical theory, drawing from Weber's rationalization theme, differs from orthodox Marxism in its attention to the relation between technology and consciousness. But whereas Weber (for example, 1946b) viewed the machine as the objectification of discipline, calculation, and rational organization, critical theorists reverse the causal relation, asserting that it is technology that creates rationalized culture by virtue of its brute physical and economic power. "If we follow the path taken by labour in its development from handicraft [to] manufacture to machine industry," Lukács writes (1971, p. 88), "we can see a continous trend toward greater rationalization [as] the process of labour is progressively broken down into abstract, rational, specialized operations." This technologically driven rationalization eventually spreads to all social spheres, leading to the objectification of society and the "reified mind" (p. 93). Lukács insists that he is concerned "with the *principle* at work here" (p. 88, original italics), but the principle is the result of technology conceived as a material force.

This shift towards the pivotal ideological role of technology, without giving up its materialist conceptualization or its economic cause, culminates in Marcuse's later work. To explain the reasons for "one-dimensional society," Marcuse actually focuses more on technological production *per se* than on its capitalist form. Again, that technology is a purely instrumental, rational phenomenon Marcuse takes completely for granted. Its "sweeping rationality," Marcuse writes (1963, p. xiii), "propels efficiency and growth." The problem, once again, is that this "technical progress [is] extended to a whole system of domination and coordination" (p. xii). When it is, it institutionalizes throughout the society a purely formal and abstract norm of rationality. This technological "culture" suppresses any ability to imagine social alternatives. As Marcuse states (p. xvi), "technological rationality has become political rationality."

New class and postindustrial theories make this critical theory more nuanced and sophisticated, but they do not overcome its fatal anti-cultural flaw. Gouldner accepts the notion that scientists, engineers, and government planners have a rational worldview because of the technical nature of their work. Technocratic competence depends on higher education, and the expansion of higher education depends in the last analysis on production driven by technology. Indeed, Gouldner finds no fault with technocratic competence in and of itself; he takes it as a paradigm of universalism, criticism, and rationality. When he attacks the technocrats' false consciousness, he does so because they extend this rationality beyond their sphere of technical competence: "The new ideology holds [that] the *society's* problems are solvable on a technological basis, with the use of educationally acquired technical competence" (1979, p. 24, italics added). By pretending to understand society at large, the new class can provide a patina of rationality for the entire society. Gouldner also emphasizes, of course, that this very expansion of technical rationality can create a new kind of class conflict and a "rational" source of social change. This notion, of course, is simply the old contradiction between (technological) forces and relations of production, dressed in postindustrial garb. When Szelenyi and Martin (1987) criticize Gouldner's theory as economistic, they have touched its theoretical core.

This is not to deny that technological production has become more central with the advent of postindustrial society. There has been a quickening in the substitution of information for physical energy, which Marx described as a shift in the organic composition of capital, with dramatic consequences. The shift from manual to mental labor has transformed the class structure and the typical strains of capitalist and socialist societies. The increased capacity for storing information has strengthened the control of bureaucracy over the information that it constantly needs. But the sociological approaches to technology, which we have examined in this section, extend much further than such empirical observations. The stronger version of Marxist and critical theory describes a technologically obsessed society whose consciousness is so narrowed that the meaningful concerns of traditional life are no longer possible. The weaker versions of functionalist and postindustrial theory describe technology as a variable that has a merely material status and orientations to technology as cognitively rational and routine. From my point of view, however, neither of these positions is correct. The ideas that inform even modern society are not cognitive repositories of verified facts; they are symbols that continue to be shaped by deep emotional impulses and molded by meaningful constraints.

Technological discourse and salvation

We must learn to see technology as a discourse, as a sign system that is subject to semiotic constraints and responsive to social and psychological demands. The first step to this alternative conception of modern technology is to reconceptualize its introduction so that it is open to metaphysical terms. Ironically, perhaps, Weber himself provided the best indication of how this can be done.

Weber argued that those who created modern industrial society did so in order to pursue salvation. The Puritan capitalists practiced what Weber (1958) called *this-worldly asceticism*. Through hard work and self-denial they produced wealth as proof that God had predestined them to be saved. Weber (1963) demonstrated, indeed, that salvation has been a central concern of humankind for millennia. Whether it be heaven or nirvana, the great religions have promised human beings an escape from toil and suffering and a release from earthly constraints – only if humans conceived of the world in certain terms and strove to act in certain ways. In order to historicize this conception of salvation and to allow comparative explanation of it, Weber developed the typology of this-worldly versus other-worldly paths to salvation, which he interwove with the distinction between ascetic and mystical. The disciplined, self-denying, and impersonal action upon which modernization depended, Weber argued, could be achieved only by acting in a this-worldly, ascetic way. Compared to Buddhist or Hindu holy men, the Puritan saints focused their attention much more completely on this world. Rather than allowing themselves the direct experience of God and striving to become vessels of his spirit, they believed that they would be saved by becoming practical instruments for carrying out his will. This-worldly salvation was the cultural precursor for the impersonal rationality and objectivism that, in Weber's view (1958, pp. 181–183), eventually dominated the world.

While Weber's religious theory is of fundamental importance, it has two substantial weaknesses. First, Weber conceived the modern style of salvation in a caricatured way. It has never been as one-sidedly ascetic as he suggests. This-worldly activity is permeated by desires to escape from the world, just as the ascetic self-denial of grace is punctuated by episodes of mystical intimacy. In an anomalous strain in his writing about modernity (Alexander 1986), Weber acknowledged that industrial society is shot through with "flights from the world," in which category he included things such as the surrender by moderns to religious belief or ideological fanaticism and the escape provided by eroticism or aestheticism. Although Weber condemned these flights as irresponsible, however, he was never able to incorporate them into his sociology of modern life. They represented a force with which his historicist and overly ideal-typical theory could not contend.

In truth, modern attempts to pursue salvation in purely ascetic ways have always short-circuited, not only in overtly escapist forms but also in the everyday world itself. We would never know from Weber's account, for example, that the Puritans conceived of their relationship to God in terms of the intimacies of holy matrimony (Morgan 1958); nor would we be aware that outbursts of mystical "antinomianism" were a constant, recurring danger in Puritan life. The post-Puritan tradition of evangelical Protestantism, which developed in Germany, England, and the United States in the late eighteenth and early nineteenth centuries, was distinguished by its significant opening to mystical experience. One of its cultural offshoots, the modern ideology of romantic love (Lewis 1983), reflected the continuing demand for immediate, transformative salvation in the very heart of the industrial age.

This last example points to the second major problem in Weber's religious theory, its historicism. Weber believed that a concern with salvation could permeate and organize worldly experience only so long as scientific understanding had not undermined the possibility of accepting an extramundane, divine telos for progress on earth. As I suggested previously, this mistaken effort to rationalize contemporary discourse can be corrected by incorporating the more structural understandings of Durkheim's religious sociology. Durkheim believed that human beings continue to divide the world into sacred and profane and that even modern men and women need to experience mystical centers directly through ritual encounters with the sacred. In the modern context, then, Weber's salvation theory can be elaborated and sustained only by turning to Durkheim. The fit can be made even tighter if we make the alteration in Durkheim's theory suggested by Caillois (1959 [1939]), who argued that alongside sacred and profane there was a third term, *routine*. Whereas routine life does not partake of ritual experience, sacred and profane experiences are both highly charged. Whereas the sacred provides an image of the good with which social actors seek community and strive to protect, the profane defines an image of evil from which human beings must be saved. This conception allows us to be more true to Weber's understanding of theodicy, even when we shift it onto the modern state. Secular salvation "religions" provide escape not only from earthly suffering in general but also more specifically from evil. Every salvation religion has conceived not only God and death, in other words, but also the devil.

The sacred and profane information machine

While there were certainly "routine" assessments of the computer from 1944 to 1975 – assessments that talked about it in rational, scientific, and "realistic" tones – they paled in comparison to the transcendental and mythical discourse that was filled with wish-fulfilling rhetoric of salvation and damnation. In a *Time* magazine report on the first encounter between computer and public in 1944, the machine was treated as a sacred and mysterious object. What was "unveiled" was a "bewildering 50-foot panel of knobs, wires, counters, gears and switches." The connection to higher, even cosmic, forces immediately suggested itself. *Time* described it as having been unveiled "in the presence of high officers in the Navy" and promised its readers that the new machine would solve problems "on earth as well as those posed by the celestial universe" (T8/44).[1] This sacred status was elaborated in the years that followed. To be sacred, an object must be sharply separated from contact with the routine world. Popular literature continually recounted the distance that separated the computer from the lay public and the mystery attendant on this. In another report on the 1944 unveiling, for example, *Popular Science*, a leading lay technology magazine, described the first computer as an electrical brain whirring "behind its polished panels" secluded in "an air-conditioned basement" (PS10/44). Twenty years later the image had not changed. In 1965, a new and far more powerful computer was conceptualized in the same way, as an "isolated marvel" working in "the air-conditioned seclusion of the company's data-programming room." In unmistakable terms, *Time* elaborated this discourse of the sacred technology.

Arranged row upon row in air-conditioned rooms, waited upon by crisp young white-shirted men who move softly among them like priests serving in a shrine, the computers go about their work quietly and, for the most part, unseen from the public (T4/65).

Objects are isolated because they are thought to possess mysterious power. The connection between computer and established centers of charismatic power is repeated constantly in the popular literature. Occasionally, an analogy is made between the computer and sacred things on earth. Reporting on the unveiling of a new and more sophisticated computer in 1949, *Newsweek* called it "the real hero" of the occasion and described it, like royalty, as "holding court in the computer lab uptstairs" (N11/49). Often, however, more direct references to the computer's cosmic powers and even to its extrahuman status were made. In an article about the first computer, *Popular Science* reported that "everybody's notion of the universe and everything in it will be upset by the columns of figures this monster will type out" (PS10/44). Fifteen years later, a famous technical expert asserted in a widely circulated feature magazine that "forces will be set in motion whose ultimate effects for good and evil are incalculable" (RD3/60).

As the machine became more sophisticated, and more awesome, references to godly powers were openly made. The new computers "render unto Caesar by sending out the monthly bills and . . . unto God by counting the ballots of the world's Catholic bishops" (T4/65). A joke circulated to the effect that a scientist tried to stump his computer with the question: is there a God? "The computer was silent for a moment. Then it answered: 'Now there is'" (N1/66). After describing the computer in superhuman terms – "infallible in memory, incredibly swift in math [and] utterly impartial in judgment" – a mass weekly made the obvious deduction: "This transistorized prophet can help the church adapt to modern spiritual needs" (T3/68). A leader of one national church described the Bible as a "distillation of human experience" and asserted that computers are capable of correlating an even greater range "of experience about how people ought to behave." The conclusion that was drawn underscored the deeply established connection between the computer and cosmic power: "When we want to consult the deity, we go to the computer because it's the closest thing to God to come along" (T3/68).

If an object is sacred and sealed off from the profane world, gaining access to its power becomes a problem in itself. Priests emerge as intermediaries between divinity and laity. As one leading expert suggested, while there were many who appreciated the computer, "only specialists yet realize how these elements will all be combined and [the] far-reaching social, economic, and political implications" (RD5/60). Typically, erroneous predictions about the computer were usually attributed to "nonspecialists" (BW3/65). To possess knowledge of computing, it was emphasized time and again, requires incredible training and seclusion. Difficult new procedures must be developed. To learn how to operate a new computer introduced in 1949, specialists "spent months literally studying day and night" (N8/49). The number of people capable of undergoing such rigorous training was highly restricted. The forging of "links between human society and the robot brain" (N9/49) called for "a new race of scientists." The "new breed of specialists [which] has grown up to tend the machines," *Time* wrote sixteen years later, "have formed themselves into a solemn priesthood of the computer, purposely separated from ordinary laymen [and] speak[ing] an esoteric language that some suspect is just their way of mystifying outsiders" (T4/65). The article predicted: "There will be a small, almost separate society of people in rapport with the advanced computer. They will have established a relationship with their machines that cannot be shared with the average man. Those with talent for the work will have to develop it from childhood and will be trained as intensively as the classical ballerina." Is it surprising that, reporting on computer news ten years later, *Time* (1/74) decided its readers would be interested in learning that among this esoteric group of programmers there had emerged a new and wildly popular computer game called "the game of life"? The identification of the computer with God and of computer operators with sacred intermediaries signifies culture structures that had not changed in thirty years.

The contact with the cosmic computer that these technological priests provided would, then, certainly transform earthly life. Like the revolutionary technologies that preceded it, however, the computer embodied within itself both superhuman evil and superhuman good. As Lévi-Strauss (1963) emphasized, it is through naming that the cultural codes defining an object are first constructed. In the years immediately following the introduction of the computer, efforts to name this new thinking machine were intense, and they followed the binary pattern that Durkheim and Lévi-Strauss described. The result was a "similitude of signifiers," an amplified series of sacred and profane associations that created for technological discourse a thick semantic field. One series revealed dreadful proportions and dire implications. The computer was called a "colossal gadget" (T8/44, N8/49), a "figure factory" (PS10/44), a "mountain of machinery" (PS10/44), a "monster" (PS10/44, SEP2/50), a "mathematical dreadnought" (PS10/44), a "portentous contrivance" (PS10/44), a "giant" (N8/49), a "math robot" (N8/49), a "wonder-working robot" (SEP2/50), the "Maniac" (SEP2/50), and the "Frankenstein-monster" (SEP2/50). In announcing a new and bigger computer in 1949, *Time* (9/49) hailed the "great machines that eat their way through oceans of figures like whale grazing on plankton" and described them as roaring like "a hive of mechanical insects."

In direct opposition to this profane realm, journalists and technicians also named the computer and its parts through analogies to the presumptively innocent and assuredly sacred human being. It was called a "super-brain" (PS10/44) and a "giant brain" (N8/49). Attached to an audio instrument, it was described as "a brain child with a temporary voice" and as "the only mechanical brain with a soft heart" (N10/49). Its "physiology" (SEP2/50) became a topic of debate. Computers were given an "inner memory" (T9/49), "eyes," a "nervous system" (SEP2/50), a "spinning heart" (T2/51), and a "female temperament" (SEP2/50) in addition to the brain with which they were already endowed. It was announced that they were to have "descendants" (N4/50), and in later years "families" and "generations" (T4/65) emerged. Finally, there were the developmental phrases. "Just out of its teens," *Time* announced (T4/65), the computer was about to enter a "formidable adulthood." It might do so, however, in a neurotic way, for its designers had "made a pampered and all but adored child" out of him (or her).

The period of compulsive naming quickly abated, but the awesome forces for good and evil that the names symbolized have been locked in deadly combat to this day. Salvation rhetoric overcomes this dualism in one direction, apocalyptic rhetoric in another. Both moves can be seen in structural terms as overcoming binary opposition by providing a third term. But more profound emotional and metaphysical issues are also at stake. Computer discourse was eschatological because the computer was seen as involving matters of life and death.

At first, salvation was defined in narrowly mathematical terms. The new computer would "solve in a flash" (T9/49) problems that had "baffled men for years" (PS10/44). By 1950, salvation had already become much more broadly defined. "Come the Revolution!" read the headline to a story about these new predictions (T11/50). A broad and visionary ideal of progress was laid out: "Thinking machines will bring a healthier, happier civilization than any known heretofore" (SEP2/50). People would now be able to "solve their problems the painless electronic way" (N7/54). Airplanes, for example, would be able to reach their destinations "without one bit of help from the pilot" (PS1/55).

By 1960, public discourse about the computer had become truly millennial. "A new age in human relations has opened," a reigning expert announced (RD3/60). Like all eschatological rhetoric, the timing of this promised salvation is imprecise. It has not yet occurred, but it has already begun. It is coming in five years or ten, its effects will be felt soon, the transformation is imminent. Whatever the timing, the end result is certain. "There will be a social effect of unbelievable proportions" (RD3/60). "By surmounting the last great barrier of distance," the computer's effect on the natural world will be just as great (RD3/60). Most human labor will be eliminated, and people will finally be set "free to undertake completely new tasks, most of them directed toward perfecting ourselves, creating beauty, and understanding one another" (Mc5/65).

The convictions were confirmed in still more sweeping tones in the late 1960s and early 1970s. The new computers had such "awesome power" (RD5/71) that, as God was recorded to have done in the Book of Genesis, they would bring "order out of chaos" (BW7/71). That "the computer age is dawning" is certain. One sign of this millennium will be that "the common way of thinking in terms of cause and effect [will be] replaced by a new awareness" (RD5/71). That this was the stuff of which "dreams are made" (USN6/67) cannot be denied. Computers would transform all natural forces. They would cure diseases and guarantee long life. They would allow everyone to know everything at all times. They would allow all students to learn easily and the best to learn perfectly. They would produce a world community and end war. They would overturn stratification and allow equality to reign. They would make government responsible and efficient, business productive and profitable, work creative, and leisure endlessly satisfying.

As for apocalypse, there was also much to say. The machine has always embodied not only the transcendental hopes but also the fear and loathing generated by industrial society. *Time* once articulated this deep ambiguity in a truly Gothic way. Viewed from the front, computers exhibit a "clean, serene dignity." This is deceptive, however, for "behind there hides a nightmare of pulsing, twitching, flashing complexity" (T9/49).

Whereas contact with the sacred side of the computer is the vehicle for salvation, the profane side threatens destruction. It is something from which human beings must be saved. First, the computer creates the fear of degradation. "People are scared" (N8/68) because the computer has the power to "blot or diminish man" (RD3/60). People feel "rage and helpless frustration" (N9/69). The computer degrades because it objectifies; this is the second great fear. It will "lead to mechanical men who replace humans" (T11/50). Students will be "treated as impersonal machines" (RD1/71). Computers are inseparable from "the image of slavery" (USN11/67). It is because they are seen as objectifying human beings that computers present a concrete danger. In 1975, one popular author described his computer as a "humming thing poised to rip me apart" (RD11/75). More typically the danger is not mutilation but manipulation. With computers "markets can be scientifically rigged . . . with an efficiency that would make dictators blush" (SEP2/50). Their intelligence can turn them into "instruments for massive subversion" (RD3/60). They could "lead us to that ultimate horror – chains of plastic tape" (N8/66).

Finally, there is the cataclysm, the final judgment on earthly technological folly that has been predicted from 1944 until the present day. Computers are "Frankenstein (monsters) which can . . . wreck the very foundations of our society" (T11/50). They can lead to "disorders [that may] pass beyond control" (RD4/60). There is a "storm brewing" (BW1/68). There are "nightmarish stories" about the "light that failed" (BW7/71). "Incapable of making allowances for error," the "Christian notion of redemption is incomprehensible to the computer" (N8/66). The computer has become the Antichrist.

The discussion so far has taken the computer story to 1975. This was the eve of the "personal computer," the very name of which demonstrates how the battle between human and anti-human continued to fuel the discourse that surrounded the computer's birth. In the decade of discussion that followed, utopian and anti-utopian themes remained prominent (for example,

Turkle 1984, pp. 165–196). Disappointment and "realism," however, also became more frequently expressed. In the present day, computer news has passed from the cover of *Time* to advertisements in the sports pages of daily newspapers. This is routinization. We may, indeed, be watching this latest episode in the history of technological discourse pass into history.

Conclusion

Social scientists have looked at the computer through the framework of their rationalizing discourse on modernity. For Ellul (1964, p. 89), it represented a phase of "technical progress" that "seems limitless" because it "consists primarily in the efficient systematization of society and the conquest of the human being." In the analysis of Lyotard, who proposes a postmodern theory, the same kind of extravagant modernizing claims are made. "It is common knowledge," according to Lyotard (1984, p. 4), "that the miniaturization and commercialization of machines is already changing the way in which learning is acquired, classified, made available, and exploited." With the advent of computerization, learning that cannot be "translated into quantities of information" will be abandoned. In contrast to the opacity of traditional culture, computerization produces "the ideology of communicational 'transparency'" (p. 5), which signals the decline of the "grand narrative" and will lead to a crisis of legitimation (pp. 66–67).

I have tried to refute such rationalistic theorizing, first by developing a framework for cultural sociology and second by applying it to the technological domain. In theoretical terms, I have shown that technology is never in the social system alone. It is also a sign and possesses an internal subjective referent. Technology, in other words, is an element in the culture and the personality systems as well; it is both meaningful and motivated. In my examination of the popular literature about the computer, I have shown that this ideology is rarely factual, rational, or abstract. It is concrete, imagistic, utopian, and satanic – a discourse that is filled, indeed, with the grand narratives of life.

Let us return, in conclusion, to the sociological understandings of technology I have recounted above. Far from being empirical accounts based on objective observations and interpretations, they represent simply another version of technocratic discourse itself. The apocalyptic strain of that discourse fears degradation, objectification, slavery, and manipulation. Has not critical theory merely translated this evaluation into the empirical language of social science? The same goes for those sociological analyses that take a more benign form: they provide social scientific translations of the discourse about salvation.

At stake is more than the accuracy or the distortion of social scientific statements. That the rationalization hypothesis is wrong does not make technology a benign force. The great danger that technology poses to modern life is neither the flattening out of human consciousness nor its enslavement to economic or political reality. To the contrary, it is because technology is lodged in the unreal fantasies of salvation and apocalypse that the dangers are real.

For Freud, psychoanalysis was a rational theory of the irrational, even while it did not promise an ultimate escape from unconscious life. Psychoanalysis aimed to provide a distance from irrationality, if not the high ground of conscious rationality itself. Cultural sociology can provide a similar distance and some of the same cure. Only by understanding the omnipresent shaping of technological consciousness by discourse can we hope to gain control over technology in its material form. To do so, we must gain some distance from the visions of salvation and apocalypse in which technology is so deeply embedded.

Note

1 The data are samples from the thousands of articles written about the computer from its introduction in 1944 up until 1984. I selected for analysis ninety-seven articles drawn from ten popular American mass magazines: *Time* (T), *Newsweek* (N), *Business Week* (BW), *Fortune* (F), *The Saturday Evening Post* (SEP), *Popular Science* (PS), *Reader's Digest* (RD), *U.S. News and World Report* (USN), *McCall's* (Mc), and *Esquire* (E). In quoting or referring to these sources, I cite first the magazine, then the month and year; for example, T8/63 indicates an article in *Time* magazine that appeared in August 1963. These sampled articles were not randomly selected but chosen by their value relevance to the interpretive themes of this work. I would like to thank David Wooline for his assistance.

References

Alexander, Jeffrey C. 1982–1983. *Theoretical Logic in Sociology*, 4 vols. Berkeley and Los Angeles: University of California Press.
  1986. "The Dialectic of Individuation and Domination: Max Weber's Rationalization Theory and Beyond." In Sam Whimster and Scott Lash (eds.), *Max Weber and Rationality*. London: Allen and Unwin.
  1988a. "Action and Its Environments." In Jeffrey C. Alexander (ed), *Action and Its Environments: Toward a New Synthesis*. New York: Columbia University Press, pp. 301–333.
  1988b. "Culture and Political Crisis: 'Watergate' and Durkheimian Sociology." In Alexander (1988c), pp. 187–224.

(ed.) 1988c. *Durkheimian Sociology: Cultural Studies*. New York: Cambridge University Press.

Barthes, Roland. 1983. *The Fashion System*. New York: Hill and Wang.

Bellah, Robert. 1970. "Civil Religion in America." In R. Bellah (ed.), *Beyond Belief*. New York: Harper and Row, pp. 168–189.

Caillois, Roger. 1959 [1939]. *Man and the Sacred*. New York: Free Press.

Dilthey, Wilhelm. 1976. "The Construction of the Historical World in the Human Studies." In *Selected Writings*. New York: Cambridge University Press, pp. 168–245.

Douglas, Mary. 1966. *Purity and Danger*. London: Penguin.

Durkheim, Emile. 1963. *The Elementary Forms of Religious Life*. New York: Free Press.

Eco, Umberto, 1979. "The Semantics of Metaphor." In U. Eco (ed.), *The Role of the Reader*. Bloomington: Indiana University Press.

Eliade, Mircea. 1959. *The Sacred and the Profane*. New York: Harcourt, Brace, and World.

Ellul, Jacques. 1964. *The Technological Society*. New York: Vintage.

Geertz, Clifford. 1973. "Thick Description: Toward an Interpretive Theory of Culture." In C. Geertz (ed.), *The Interpretation of Cultures*. New York: Basic Books, pp. 3–32.

Gouldner, Alvin. 1979. *The Future of Intellectuals and the Rise of the New Class*. New York: Seabury.

Hunt, Lynn. 1984. *Politics, Culture, and Class in the French Revolution*. Berkeley and Los Angeles: University of California Press.

Lévi-Strauss, Claude. 1963. *Structural Anthropology*. New York: Basic Books.
    1967. *The Savage Mind*. Chicago: University of Chicago Press.

Lewis, Jan. 1983. *The Pursuit of Happiness: Family and Values in Jefferson's Virginia*. New York: Cambridge University Press.

Lukács, Georg. 1971. "Reification and the Consciousness of the Proletariat." In G. Lukács (ed.), *History and Class Consciousness*, Cambridge, MA: MIT Press.

Lyotard, Jean-François. 1984. *The Postmodern Condition: A Report on Knowledge*. Minneapolis: University of Minnesota Press.

Marcuse, Herbert. 1963. *One-Dimensional Man*. Boston: Beacon.

Marx, Karl. 1962. "Preface to a Contribution to the Critique of Political Economy." In K. Marx and F. Engels, *Selected Works*, vol. I. Moscow: International Publishing House, pp. 361–365.

Merton, Robert K. 1970. *Science, Technology, and Society in Seventeenth-Century England*. New York: Harper and Row.

Morgan, Edmund. 1958. *The Puritan Dilemma*. Boston: Little, Brown.

Parsons, Talcott. 1967. "Some Comments on the Sociology of Karl Marx." In T. Parsons (ed.), *Sociological Theory and Modern Society*. New York: Free Press.

Ricoeur, Paul. 1971. "The Model of a Text: Meaningful Action Considered as a Text." *Social Research* 38: 529–562.
    1984. *Time and Narrative*, vol. I. Chicago: University of Chicago Press.

Rueschemeyer, Dietrich. 1986. *Power and the Division of Labor*. Stanford: Stanford University Press.

Sahlins, Marshall. 1976. *Culture and Practical Reason*. Chicago: University of Chicago Press.

1981. *Historical Metaphors and Mythical Realities: Structure in the Early History of the Sandwich Islands Kingdom*. Ann Arbor: University of Michigan Press.

Saussure, Ferdinand de. 1964. *A Course in General Linguistics*. London: Owen.

Sewell, William, Jr. 1980. *Work and Revolution in France*. New York: Cambridge University Press.

Smelser, Neil. 1959. *Social Change in the Industrial Revolution*. Chicago: University of Chicago Press.

Smith, Henry Nash. 1950. *Virgin Land*. Cambridge, MA: Harvard University Press.

Szelenyi, Ivan, and Bill Martin. 1987. "Theories of Cultural Capital and Beyond." In R. Eyerman, L. G. Svensson, and T. Soderquist (eds.), *Intellectuals, Universities, and the State in Western Modern Societies*. Berkeley and Los Angeles: University of California Press, pp. 16–49.

Turkle, Sherry. 1984. *The Second Self: Computers and the Human Spirit*. New York: Simon and Schuster.

Turner, Victor. 1969. *The Ritual Process*. Chicago: Aldine.

Weber, Max. 1946a. "Religious Rejections of the World and Their Directions." In H. Gerth and C. W. Mills (eds.), *From Max Weber*. New York: Oxford University Press pp. 323–359.

1946b. "The Meaning of Discipline." In H. Gerth and C.W. Mills (eds.), *From Max Weber*. New York: Oxford University Press, pp. 253–264.

1958. *The Protestant Ethic and the Spirit of Capitalism*. New York: Scribners.

1963. *The Sociology of Religion*. Boston: Beacon Press.

3

AIDS and the discursive construction of homosexuality[*]

Steven Seidman

AIDS appeared during a period of significant change in Western sexual conventions. A series of movements in the sixties and seventies pointed in the direction of expanded erotic choice and tolerance for diversity. The women's movement struggled for women's erotic autonomy. Feminists demanded that women be able to define and control their own sexuality, and that included choosing a lesbian alternative. Less visible were the struggles by sexually disenfranchised groups like the elderly or the disabled to be accepted as full sexual beings. The counterculture made a more open and expressive eroticism a prominent part of its social rebellion. Furthermore, changes in our sexual norms that reflected long-term trends became evident. For example, the norm that sex is legitimate only as an act of love or a sign of relational fidelity was challenged. Sex discourses and representations (e.g., pornography, sex manuals, and radical sex ideologies) appeared that constructed sex as an autonomous sphere of pleasure and self-expression with its own intrinsic value and justification. A libertarian sex ethic accepted sex for its pleasurable qualities in any context of mutual consent and respect. This has expanded the types of relationships in which sex is permitted. Indeed, the exclusivity of marriage as the proper site for sex has given way to a more flexible convention that tolerates sex in varied relational settings. In short, while it would be misleading to assert that a revolution occurred, there did transpire important changes in our sexual norms and behavior during this period.

Indicative of this more liberal sexual culture was the increased tolerance for homosexuality. By the mid-seventies gay sub-cultures were visible in virtually every major urban center (Altman 1983; D'Emilio 1983). These pro-

---

[*] First published in 1988 as "Transfiguring sexual identity: AIDS and the contemporary construction of homosexuality," *Social Text* 9(20): 187–206.

vided gay people with institutional protection, a source of social support, and a mass base for a politics of civil rights reform and gay liberation. Within these gay spaces a cultural apparatus emerged that included gay-oriented publications (books, magazines, and newspapers), theatre groups, movies, and so on. Of particular importance is that this new gay intelligentsia articulated affirmative images of homosexuality. Constructions of "the homosexual" as a morally perverse, deviant, or pathological figure were assailed. Homosexuality was reconceived to refer to a morally neutral need or behavior that is not indicative of a distinctive personality type. New models viewed the homosexual as a person with merely an alternative sexual or affectional preference or as a member of an oppressed minority. In fact, some gays endorsed the notion of homosexuals as different but reconceived this in affirmative ways. Finally, gay people made important gains in political empowerment and social inclusion. For example, by the mid-seventies more than half the states in the USA had repealed their sodomy laws; dozens of cities had passed anti-discrimination ordinances; the civil service commission had eliminated its ban on hiring homosexuals, and so on.

The trend towards sexual liberalization and, in particular, the tolerance of homosexuals, encountered a lot of resistance and hostility. In the late seventies this tolerance narrowed considerably as anti-gay themes became integral to a revived conservative politics. The explanation for this lies perhaps in social developments that paralleled sexual liberalization. Specifically, the conjunction of a series of events, including an economic recession, political legitimation problems stemming from Watergate, military setbacks in Vietnam and Iran, and social disturbances arising from the various civil rights, protest and liberation movements, produced a pervasive sense of social crisis and decline. Although social and political responses to this situation were varied, it is not coincidental that a series of purity crusades swept across the country (Rubin 1984). This was one way people responded to feelings of social danger and sought to gain control over social events. Different groups or phenomena, from pornography to paedophiles, were targeted. However, gay people in particular were singled out. This was not entirely fortuitous. The trend towards the acceptance or at least tolerance of homosexuality challenged the exclusive legitimacy of a heterosexual and marital norm. Moreover, the visibility and political assertiveness of homosexuals, coupled to their symbolic association with social dissolution in a context perceived by many Americans as one of family breakdown and national decline, made them easy prey for scapegoating.

The anxiety and hostility many Americans felt towards recent developments were displaced onto homosexuality. Homosexuals were portrayed as a public menace, as a threat to the family, and as imperiling the national security by promoting self-centered, hedonistic, and pacifist values. An anti-gay backlash crystallized that was initially centered around local and state campaigns to repeal gay rights ordinances. Gradually, it expanded to include national legislation, the resurgence of anti-homosexual discourses, and escalating discrimination and violence towards homosexuals (Altman 1983). Its aim was to deny legitimacy to homosexuality; to dismantle gay sub-cultural institutions; to return homosexuals to a condition of invisibility and marginality; and to reassert a discourse of the dangers of homosexuality.

I argue that AIDS has provided a pretext to reinsert homosexuality within a symbolic drama of pollution and purity. Conservatives have used AIDS to rehabilitate the notion of "the homosexual" as a polluted figure. AIDS is read as revealing the essence of a promiscuous homosexual desire and proof of its dangerous and subversive nature. The reverse side of this demonization of homosexuality is the purity of heterosexuality and the valorization of a monogamous, marital sexual ethic. To be sure, the discourse of homosexuality occasioned by AIDS is not uniform. Liberal segments of the heterosexual media have, in the main, repudiated a politics aimed at the repression of homosexuality. Instead, they have enlisted AIDS in their campaign to construct an image of the "respectable homosexual" and to legitimate a sexual ethic of monogamy and romance. Similar themes are conspicuous in the gay media. In fact, many gays have used AIDS to articulate their own redemptive drama. In imagery that oscillates between the apocalyptic and the millennial, AIDS is seen as marking the failure of a way of life; as signaling, like Stonewall, another critical turning point in the coming of age of homosexuals; and, finally, as the beginnings of a new maturity and social responsibility among homosexuals.

AIDS and heterosexual constructions of homosexuality

In the heterosexual media the identification of AIDS as a gay disease was made early and has proved persistent despite overwhelming evidence to the contrary. Initially, the appearance of Kaposi's sarcoma and other rare cancers among young homosexual men led researchers to designate the term GRID (gay related immune deficiency) for this new syndrome. Taking its cue from medical researchers, the mass media referred to this disease as the "homosexual cancer," the "gay epidemic." These terms suggest an intrinsic tie between homosexuality and AIDS. The causal link was identified as homosexual behavior.

The two most prominent epidemiological theories directly joined AIDS to homosexual acts. The so-called "overload theory" held that "the gay lifestyle" (the combination of drug use, poor health habits, and a history of sexually transmitted diseases resulting from sexual promiscuity) is responsible for the collapse of the immune system. The currently more accepted theory asserts the existence of a virus which combined with other factors breaks down the body's resistance to disease. The introduction of semen into the body during sex releases the virus into the blood stream. The typical scenario that is postulated holds that repeated anal intercourse tears the delicate tissue of the anus. This allows the semen and therefore the virus of the infected person to pass into the blood circulation of the unsuspecting other. Both theories underscore the association between sexual behavior and AIDS among homosexuals. They highlight sexual "promiscuity" as the intermediary or connecting link. The overload theory posits a more direct, ironic, and insidious dynamic: the immediate sensual pleasures of "promiscuous" sex set in motion a hidden telos of disease and death. The very act of sexual union – with its cultural resonances of love and the production of life – is turned into an act of death as bodily defenses collapse. Although the viral hypothesis does not view AIDS as the very signature of homosexual behavior, it asserts an indirect tie between promiscuity and AIDS among homosexual men. It is, after all, only under conditions of non-monogamy that sex can threaten viral infection. Both the overload and the viral theory, then, represent medical frameworks that center on the causality between sexual promiscuity, disease, and death.

In the heterosexual media's response to AIDS, promiscuity became the defining property of gay sexuality. Headlines and feature stories in all the major national media dramatized a gay lifestyle, a fastlane life of indiscriminate casual sex. A piece in the *San Francisco Examiner* (Oct. 24, 1982, p. 14) found in AIDS confirmation of the conventional wisdom that gays are "a population whose lifestyle is based on a freewheeling approach to sex," John Fuller in *Science Digest* observed that AIDS is simply further evidence of what science has told us about homosexual men. "Sociologists and psychologists had long noted that the constant search for new sexual partners is a persistent pattern among many gay males" (Fuller 1983). Some commentators underlined the paradoxical aspects of homosexuality. "Ironically, the freedom, the promiscuity . . . that many gays declared an integral part of their culture have come to haunt them" (Cuppola 1983). I want to here underscore a key point regarding this discourse: the promiscuity of homosexual men is not considered incidental or a historically specific behavioral property of homosexuality. Rather, it is viewed as essential to homosexuality. In other words, this discourse resurrects an older notion of the male homosexual as a type of person with unique physical, emotional, and behavioral traits. His essence is that of a hypersexual human type. Homosexual men sexualize themselves and others; they reduce persons to eroticized bodies; they frame sex as mere physical release or pleasure-seeking. Promiscuity manifests the lustful, amoral nature of the homosexual. Homosexual desire symbolizes pure sexual lust or unrestrained desire subject only to the quantitative limitations of physical exhaustion. It is this compulsive, hyperactive, insatiable desire that compels homosexuals to eroticize the forbidden and to transgress all moral boundaries, rendering themselves dangerous. Homosexuality is constructed as the very antithesis of the heterosexual marital ideal where sex is joined to romance, love, and relational permanence and fidelity.

The AIDS discourse on homosexuality is a moral one. The juxtaposition of homosexuality and heterosexual romantic love carries a moral distinction between the dangers of homosexual promiscuity and the purity of heterosexual love and monogamy. From this vantage point, AIDS reveals not only the truth of homosexuality but is its just punishment. Some commentators have seen in AIDS proof of the unnaturalness or perversity of homosexuality. "The poor homosexuals – they have declared war upon nature, and now nature is exacting an awful retribution," writes President Reagan's former aide Patrick Buchanan (1983). Reverend Charles Stanley, head of the 14.3 million-member Southern Baptist Convention remarked: "It [homosexuality] is a sinful lifestyle, according to the scripture, and I believe that AIDS is God indicating his displeasure and his attitude towards that form of lifestyle" (*Times Union*, Jan. 18, 1986). Finally, arriving at the same moral judgment but framed within a medical-scientific discourse, Dr. James Fletcher writes in the *Southern Medical Journal*: "If we act as empirical scientists can we not see the implications of the data [AIDS and STDs among homosexual men] before us? Might not these 'complications' be 'consequences' [of homosexuality]? Were it so a logical conclusion is that AIDS is a self-inflicted disorder . . . Indeed from an empirical medical perspective alone current scientific observation seems to require the conclusion that homosexuality is a pathologic condition" (quoted in E'Eramo 1984).

In the above moral rhetorics, AIDS represents a just punishment for homosexuals since they have violated a basic law of God, Nature and Society. There is, however, another more subtle logic of moral judgment presented in the AIDS phenomenon. AIDS is seen as the homosexual's death-wish turned upon himself. In modern mythology, homosexuality indicates an unconscious will to subvert and destroy society. Images of subversion surround the homosexual. The ubiquitous association of homosexuals with the corruption of children – the very symbol of purity and social order – is indicative of their link to death. It is, I believe, precisely because in our symbolic universe homosexuality is constructed as a social danger evoking resonances of decline and chaos, that AIDS is seen not only as the truth of homosexuality but as its just punishment. AIDS signals the wish for the annihilation of "the other" being turned inward, back against the homosexual himself. It's because homosexuality symbolizes a threat to life and society that even in the face of the mass suffering and death among homosexuals the public reaction has often been complacent, indifferent, and vengeful. For threatening social existence and "killing the innocent," homosexual men have received their just desert in AIDS. This, at least, appears to be a perhaps unconscious moral sentiment conveyed in the heterosexual response to AIDS.

AIDS has contributed to reviving a notion of the homosexual as a dangerous and polluted figure. Moreover, the revitalization of a dis-credited image of homosexuality structured the public response to AIDS. As the principal victim of AIDS but also identified as its chief perpetrator, homosexual men were doubly victimized: by the disease and by society's response to it. Blamed for their own affliction, accused of spreading disease and death to innocent people, criticized as a drain upon scarce national resources, homosexual AIDS victims felt socially scorned and shunned (Starr and Gonzalez 1983; Lee 1983). Stories circulated of hospi-tal staff, police, and criminal justice personnel refusing physical contact with AIDS victims, and of AIDS victims left unattended in hospitals, leaving friends and family responsible for their care. Feature stories told of AIDS victims being fired from their jobs, evicted from their homes, ejected from public places. Numerous reports narrate how homosexual AIDS victims had to manage, often alone, a social death in anticipation of their physical one.

AIDS served as an ideal pretext for upgrading the surveillance and oppression of homosexuals. By the end of 1985 demands were being made for stepped-up state regulation of homosexual AIDS cases through admin-istering an "AIDS" test as a condition of employment, military service, health and life insurance, blood donation, and so on. Quarantining AIDS cases was seriously discussed and in some states statutes were amended to give the government the power to implement a quarantine. Suggestions were heard of empowering the state to rehabilitate sexually promiscuous homosexual men through drugs or confinement. Beyond the repressive measures sought in response to AIDS, backlash forces held that the AIDS crisis rendered homosexuals a public health threat. By claiming that AIDS had produced a national health crisis, backlash forces tried to enlist the state to dismantle gay sub-cultural institutions. Efforts to close gay bars and baths were part of a broader strategy of withdrawing public tolerance for homosexuals. There were renewed efforts to press for the remedicalization and recriminalization of homosexual behavior. For example the Dallas Doctors Against AIDS issued the following declaration: "Such a sexual public health concern must cause the citizenry of this country to do everything in their power to smash the homosexual movement in this country to make sure these kinds of acts are criminalized" (quoted in Patton 1985, pp. 3–4). Movements in support of gay rights ordinances were frustrated and efforts to reinstitute or endorse anti-sodomy laws were given a fresh impetus. At a more immediate level, gay men felt the intensification of oppression through an increase of reported acts of discrimination, harassment, and physical assault (Greer 1986).

Although the liberal media have sought to avoid the politicizing of AIDS, liberals have seized on AIDS, no less than conservatives, to propagate their own sexual morality. They have used AIDS to reaffirm the morality of monogamy and romantic love. In fact, the liberal media have sought to rehabilitate a pre-gay liberation ideal of the "respectable homosexual": discreet, coupled, monogamous, and cohabiting.

The *New York Times*, for example, has virtually campaigned to create and legitimate this ideal of the respectable homosexual (see Lyons 1983a, b, c; 1985). Its coverage of AIDS has regularly included interviews with prominent figures in the gay community or relevant "experts" who uniformly criticize the immature and irresponsible promiscuous lifestyle accepted in the gay sub-culture of the 1970s. Articles appeared that reported changes in the behavior of homosexuals. Key indicators of the fastlane gay lifestyle, e.g., number of sex partners, STDs, and bathhouse attendance were scrutinized to detect indications of a retreat from promiscuity. Reports of a new emphasis upon dating, courting, and nonsexual attendance were given prominence. The *Times* did more than report these developments; it clearly endorsed them. In fact, by virtue of its prestige and its enlisting of experts and community leaders, the *Times* became a major social force in promoting these changes. It ran pieces on homosexual couples who were obviously intended to serve as role models to a crisis-ridden and anomic gay community. One such piece, entitled "Homosexual Couple Finds a Quiet Pride," focuses on two professional men who have lived together for some forty years. They are, in appearance, indistinguishable from conventional heterosexuals. In other words, there is no trace of a more unconventional gay sub-cultural style to their self-presentation. There is an implied discreetness to their homosexuality and their demeanor exudes an almost exaggerated sense of staid respectability. They are described as preoccupied with typical heterosexual concerns such as career, family, domestic affairs, hobbies, and anniversaries. The "success" or longevity of their relationship is summed up by the remark, "You have to work at it." Quite clearly, the *Times* is offering them, or its construction of them, as a model of what is an acceptable homosexual style. With moral codes and identity-models in flux, and with homosexuality itself assailed by backlash forces, this image of a discreet, monogamous, coupled, and conventional homosexual life is endorsed as an alternative to more unconventional gay socioerotic models. In fact, the principal thesis of the article is that a "heterosexual model" is now being adopted by homosexuals. "In recent years, some homosexual couples have begun to adopt many of the traditions of heterosexual marriage. Besides having wedding and anniversary parties, couples are exchanging vows . . . in religious services known as 'gay unions'. They are drawing up contracts, wills . . . to provide legal protections for themselves and their partners. They are adopting children . . ." (Dullea 1984). Setting aside for the moment the credibility of this argument, the message seems indisputable: AIDS is a positive catalyst encouraging homosexual men to adopt heterosexual relational patterns. Because of AIDS homosexual men are rediscovering the charm, civility, security, and safety of romance and monogamy. Liberals, no less than conservatives, have exploited AIDS for their own moral purposes. Whereas the latter enlist AIDS as part of their backlash politics, the former use AIDS to relate a moral tale of the virtues of romantic love and monogamy.

AIDS and the crisis of homosexuality in the gay community

Sexual promiscuity stands at the center of the gay media's response to AIDS. It is seen as a product of an historically unique gay sub-culture. It is, moreover, seen as having a direct causal relation to the current epidemic and to the anti-gay backlash. For homosexual men with a traditional cultural background, for older homosexuals who came of age in a milieu emphasizing heterosexual models, for those men uncomfortable with their sexuality, or for gay liberationists whose ideals are perceived to have faded behind a wave of self-indulgence, AIDS has functioned as an appropriate symbol of the failure of current gay life. AIDS provides an ideal opportunity for gays to vocalize their discontents. I am suggesting, to be perfectly clear, that for heterosexuals and homosexuals, AIDS has served as a pretext to speak critically about homosexuality and to advocate reforms of the gay sub-culture. Perhaps gay men felt that the suffering and intensified oppression they have experienced in the AIDS crises could be somewhat neutralized or even made self-confirming by reconceiving AIDS as a moral drama. AIDS comes to signify the beginnings of a great reformation in gay life.

The notion that AIDS has ushered in a time of trial and marks a turning point for gays is neatly captured in the apocalyptic imagery of Larry Kramer's eloquent and moving piece "1112 and Counting." Kramer frames the AIDS phenomenon as a test of collective survival. "Our continued existence as gay men . . . is at stake . . . In the history of homosexuality we have never been so close to death and extinction before" (Kramer 1983). Survival hinges on a shift from the current hedonistic preoccupations of gay men to a new social consciousness and a responsible erotic ethic. Where Kramer is somewhat pessimistic, other gay men speak in an oddly defiant and upbeat tone of AIDS initiating a new era of maturity and respectability. Toby Marotta observes that "most gays share my view – that [AIDS] is the most profound, maturing incident for the gay community in its history" (quoted in Morgenthau 1983, p. 33). David Goodstein couples a critical view of pre-AIDS gay life to the prospects for renewal and reform initiated by AIDS. "During the last half of the 1970s, it wasn't chic in gay male circles to place a high value on life-companions or close friendships. Now [i.e., with AIDS] we have another chance for progress: to acknowledge the value of intimate relationships" (Goodstein 1985). Stephen Harvey is even more direct in acknowledging the redemptive possibilities of AIDS. "It's a perverse and maybe [!] tragic irony that it took the AIDS outbreak . . . to at last . . . integrate [our] sexual natures with the rest of what [we] are" (Harvey 1982). A central feature of this emerging gay maturity is the appropriation of the behavioral models and rituals of heterosexual interpersonal patterns. Arthur Bell comments: "Indiscriminate sex with phantom partners in backrooms is beginning to diminish. The grudge and filth bars are losing their appeal. Fistfucking is fading. Barbarity is on the way out. Romance [is] . . . on the way in" (Bell 1982). Stories abound in the gay press of homosexual men rediscovering the quiet joys and healthy lifestyle of romantic love and monogamy. Typically, such narratives set off a pre-AIDS period which is now described as one of immaturity and indulgence. AIDS marks the great turning point where after a protracted period of soul-searching one is reborn: the profligate, self-destructive ways of the past are given up for the new morality of monogamy and romance. Typical is the piece by Arnie Kantrowitz: "Till Death Us Do Part." He begins by recalling the liberating experience of sexual promiscuity. "My experiment in sexual anarchy was a rare delight, a lesson in license, an opportunity to see both flesh and spirit glaringly naked. I will never apologize to anyone for my promiscuity." Yet, that is exactly what he does as he narrates his odyssey of personal growth. From the standpoint of a post-AIDS sexual morality his early sensual delights now appear to him as compulsive and narcissistic. The endless cycle of excitement, release, and exhaustion left him jaded and

empty. "I decided to trade self-indulgence for self-respect." Having personally witnessed the guilt-ridden, self-destructive ways of his pre-AIDS days,
he "decided to get healthy." Exercise and proper diet replaced drug abuse
and sleepless nights. With health and self-respect intact, there could be only
one proper dramatic finale. "Finally, I rediscovered the difference between
lust and love and began an affair" (Kantrowitz 1983). The transfiguration
of AIDS into a moral and mythic drama of reformation and renewal has
allowed some gays to be so emotionally distanced from the enormity of
suffering it has brought that the current period is defined as one of optimism. One gay writer observes in what is a common motif that "the energy
formerly reserved for the sexual hunt [can now be] channeled into the community in other ways [such as] . . . the growth of gay community centers,
sports clubs, choruses, and a host of other groups." He concludes by
remarking: "all of which I believe makes 1983 a time for optimism and joy"
(Martz 1983).

AIDS and homosexuality: the limits of a discourse

The public heterosexual and gay responses to AIDS share a common moral
theme: the dangers of promiscuity which are asserted to be a defining
feature of homosexuality today. The former frequently derives promiscuity
from the very essence of homosexual desire. The latter traces promiscuity
to the contemporary gay sub-culture. In both the heterosexual and gay
media, promiscuity is taken as the decisive link between homosexual men
and AIDS. It is moreover, considered the essence of a universal or more historically specific homosexual desire. Yet, one looks in vain for a definition
or a serious analysis of its meaning. Its sense, however, is conveyed by
references to having many sex partners. This, however, is misleading.
Promiscuity cannot be defined by the sheer number of one's sex partners.
For example, a serial monogamous pattern which involves a sequence of
changing partners is not promiscuous behavior. Similarly, promiscuity is
not synonymous with nonmonogamy. We would not consider, say, an extra-
marital affair as promiscuous behavior. In general, we must distinguish promiscuity from polygamy or "sexual pluralism." The latter involves multiple
sex partners but there may also be established relationships of intimacy and
responsibility with each partner. Promiscuity involves a sexually active
person whose sex partners change frequently and with each there is an
absence of personal intimacy and extended responsibilities. Furthermore,
the line between serial monogamy, polygamy, and promiscuity cannot
always be drawn in a hard and fast way. A serial monogamous pattern
involving a sequence of short-lived, emotionally distant relationships has a

promiscuous aspect. A polygamous pattern involving one primary long-term relationship and sex with anonymous others suggests a more salient promiscuous element.

At stake is more than a matter of conceptual clarification. The categories used to describe homosexuality carry moral and practical implications. Homosexual behavior cannot be characterized as promiscuous in some generic or essential way. The available studies of current behavior highlight a diversity of homosexual patterns ranging from a monogamous, marital model to promiscuity (Bell and Weinberg 1970). Any attempt to frame homosexual desire as some abstract, universal, and homogeneous entity whose essence is promiscuity will not find much empirical support in behavioral research. Researchers agree that a more typical pattern for gay men – at least in the seventies – has been to combine an on-going love relationship with secondary affairs centered on sex (Harry and Duvall 1978; Peplau and Gordon 1983; Tripp 1975; White 1980). The pattern of these secondary involvements ranges from having a few erotically centered relationships involving extended responsibilities to having high numbers of changing, anonymous sex partners. To the extent that the latter is more common then the line between polygamy and promiscuity is blurred. In fact, according to some observers, this more promiscuous style characterized a segment of the urban gay population in the 1970s. Indeed, surveys of sexual behavior show that during this period gay men had, on the average, a much higher number of sex partners – many of whom were anonymous – than heterosexuals and lesbians (Bell and Weinberg 1970; Blumstein and Schwartz 1983). It is reasonable to assume *some* connection between this behavior and AIDS among homosexual men. The error is to assume a generic causal tie between homosexuality, promiscuity, and disease or to take AIDS as evidence of the pathological nature of homosexuality.

There is a series of wrong moves here. Promiscuity is *not* the cause of AIDS but a risk factor. To be even more precise, it is a risk factor *if* one engages in high-risk sex and *if* one does so in circumstances where the HTLV-III virus is widely circulated. Homosexuals do *not* have to be promiscuous or nonmonogamous to acquire AIDS. It is *not* legitimate to take AIDS as indicative of a particular type of sexual pattern or lifestyle. Furthermore, given its appearance among heterosexuals, who in some nations are primarily afflicted, it is wrong to interpret AIDS as a homosexual disease. There is no evidence that AIDS is congenital or that it is produced by homosexual behavior or that it favors homosexual men. The only statement that can be endorsed unequivocally is that *specific homosexual acts* are today high-risk. This fact does not, however, require that homosexual men adopt any particular lifestyle or sexual ethic. It mandates only safe-sex practices, but how these are incorporated into a lifestyle or pattern of intimate relationships is open to diverse possibilities.

Conclusion

Foucault has shown how the original intent and political purpose of a discourse on sexuality can be reversed. For example, the scientific-medical discourse of "the homosexual" as a perverse or pathological human type promoted new forms of social control. Yet, taking the issue of homosexuality out of a religious context and placing it in a scientific one has allowed an appeal to empirical evidence to challenge stereotypes and, ultimately, to contest the medical model itself. Moreover, this medical discourse contributed to creating a common homosexual consciousness and culture that eventuated in a politic aimed at legitimating homosexuality.

It is, then, possible that AIDS may have a long-term beneficial effect. AIDS requires credible empirical knowledge of homosexuality. This will stimulate and legitimate research on homosexuals, much of which will challenge stereotypes. Finally, this knowledge will be disseminated throughout society and will be taken seriously because of its link to a health crisis. This could provide a favorable setting for legitimating homosexuality and gaining the social inclusion of homosexuals. In the end, this will not result merely from a process of mass enlightenment. Rather, it will require gay people, in particular, to mobilize in order to play a greater role in shaping public discussions. Homosexuals must have a political presence if they expect to shape public policy decisions emerging from the AIDS crisis.

References

Altman, Dennis. 1983. *The Homosexualization of America*. Boston: Beacon Press.

Bell, Alan, and Martin Weinberg. 1970. *Homosexualities*. New York: Simon and Schuster.

Bell, Arthur. 1982. "Where Gays Are Going." *The Village Voice*, Jun. 29.

Blumstein, Philip, and Pepper Schwartz. 1983. *American Couples*. New York: Morrow.

Buchanan, Patrick. 1983. "AIDS Disease: It's Nature Striking Back." *New York Post*, May 24.

Cuppola, Vincent. 1983. "The Change in Gay Life Style." *Newsweek*, Apr. 18.

D'Emilio, John. 1983. *Sexual Politics, Sexual Communities*. Chicago: University of Chicago Press.

Dullea, Georgia. 1984. "Homosexual Couple Finds a Quiet Pride." *New York Times*, Dec. 10.

E'Eramo, James. 1984. "The New Medical Journal Homophobia." *The New York Native*, May 21.

Fuller, John. 1983. "AIDS: Legacy of the '60s?" *Science Digest*, Dec.

Goodstein, David. 1985. Editorial. *The Advocate*, Aug. 6.

Greer, William. 1986. "Violence Against Homosexuals Rising." *New York Times*, Nov. 23.

Harry, Joseph, and William Duvall. 1978. *The Social Organization of Gay Males*. New York: Praeger.

Harvey, Stephen. 1982. "Defenseless: Learning to Live with AIDS." *The Village Voice*, Dec. 21.

Kantrowitz, Arnie. 1983. "Till Death Us Do Part." *The Advocate*.

Kramer, Larry. 1983. "1112 and Counting." *The New York Native*, Mar. 14.

Lee, John. 1983. "The Real Epidemic: Fear and Despair." *Time*, Jul. 4.

Lyons, Richard. 1983a. "Homosexuals Find a Need to Reassess." *New York Times*, May 29.

   1983b. "Homosexuals Confronting a Time of Change." *New York Times*, Jun. 16.

   1983c. "Sex in America: Conservative Attitudes Prevail." *New York Times*, Oct. 4.

   1985. "AIDS Education Takes on Urgency." *New York Times*, Sept. 22.

Martz, Steve. 1983. "A Quick Look Back and Some Thoughts on the Year Ahead." *Washington Blade*, Jan. 7.

Morgenthau, Tom. 1983. "Gay America in Transition." *Newsweek*, Aug. 8.

Patton, Cindy. 1985. *Sex and Germs*. Boston: South End Press.

Peplau, Letitia, and Steven Gordon. 1983. "The Intimate Relationships of Lesbians and Gay Men." In Elizabeth Allgeier and Naomi McCormick (eds.), *Gender Roles and Sexual Behavior*. Palo Alto: Mayfield.

Rubin, Gayle. 1984. "Thinking Sex." In Carole Vance (ed.), *Pleasure and Danger*. Boston: Routledge.

Starr, Mark, and David Gonzalez. 1983. "The Panic over AIDS." *Newsweek*, May 4.

Tripp, C. A. 1975. *The Homosexual Matrix*. New York: McGraw-Hill.

White, Edmund. 1980. *States of Desire*. New York: E. P. Dutton.

4

Fundamentalism and liberalism in public religious discourse[*]

Robert Wuthnow

Every community is awash in words. Religious communities are no exception. Sermons, prayers, singing, creedal recitations, and discussion groups make up the very being of such communities.

In recent years the flow of religious discourse has spilled into the public arena with increasing intensity. Religious broadcasts fill the airwaves and direct-mail solicitations fill our mailboxes. Bishops issue statements on social issues such as nuclear disarmament and economic justice. A pope stumps the country delivering homilies. Preachers become presidential candidates. And media specialists try to make sense of it all.

Social scientists have in recent decades developed a fairly standard way of studying the relations between religion and public affairs. Opinion polls are the method of choice, supplemented by occasional applications of content analysis, in-depth interviews, and discussion of broader social developments to provide context. As a result of this often valuable research, we have a good sense of the public's tolerance for religious leaders making statements about various kinds of social issues. We also have some evidence on the issues clergy say they speak about. And we have many studies of the ways in which religious beliefs and attitudes towards social issues correlate: fundamentalism and bigotry, parochialism and conservatism, conservatism and views of the priesthood, moralism and attitudes towards abortion, religious preference and voter orientation. We even have frequency counts of the kinds of themes that are expressed on religious television shows or in religious books.

But on religious discourse *as discourse* we have virtually nothing. It is as if our standard methods have trained us to think of religious communities (and not just religious communities) as silent worlds. People have religious

[*] First published in 1988 as "Religious discourse as public rhetoric," *Communication Research* 15(3): 318–338.

beliefs, convictions, and sentiments. They harbor predispositions, orientations, and commitments. They behold religious symbols that give meaning
to their lives, help them to construct reality, and provide them with security and a sense of belonging. But they do not speak.

Of if they do speak, our standard methods register only the surface features of their discourse. For instance, we may work through the transcripts
of religious broadcasts to see how many of them touched on abortion,
school prayer, the Supreme Court, or politics in general. We may scan the
titles of religious books to see how many fall into various preconceived categories: theology, family, self-improvement, sexual relations. Or we may ask
church and synagogue members or clergy whether they have discussed
topics such as personal crises, moral issues, politics, and the federal budget
with fellow parishioners. But none of this gives us any indication of the
ways in which religious discourse is actually put together.

Of course, it may require more than a leap of religious faith to argue that
the actual composition of religious discourse is itself important. To
someone trained in the social psychology of opinion research, discourse is
likely to be relevant only as a means of tapping into the deeper attitudinal
predispositions that supposedly govern behavior. Discourse is in this view
ephemeral, unpredictable, and superficial – only the underlying mind-sets
are meaningful. We want to discover how personalities are put together, in
this view, not to invest time in the study of meaningless chatter.

Discourse rediscovered

There has for some time been a movement in the social sciences to bring
discourse back in. Besides the small coteries of ethnomethodologists and
conversation analysts who have always studied discourse, we now have the
formidable (and often forbidding) legacy of Foucault's decentered post-
structuralism, Habermas's borrowings from speech-act theory, Derrida's
language-focused deconstructionism, and a more scattered array of empirical investigations focusing on public discourse.

We need not become camp followers of esoteric theoreticians, however,
to appreciate the importance of understanding religious discourse. Much
of it is highly codified in sacred traditions. Its practitioners gain competence through long years of training and experience. Homiletics and
hermeneutics are required features of most pastoral educations. How-to-
books for preaching, leading discussions of religious texts, and proselytiz-
ing abound. Even the sacred traditions themselves recognize the
importance of the word, the *kerygma*, as the vehicle of creation, reconciliation, and community.

This much we could discern by immersing ourselves in a religious tradition: any competent practitioner of the faith could testify to the importance of discourse. But when religious discourse enters the public sphere – when it becomes public rhetoric – we confront another compelling reason for trying to understand it: some of it seems to affront common sensibilities so deeply that we find it difficult even to focus on what is being said.

For example, I have had students look at direct-mail solicitations from religiopolitical organizations in a course I teach on sociology of religion. Sometimes I also ask students to sample a few religious broadcasts on television or to watch a short video of fundamentalist dialogue in class. Generally the reaction from my mostly privileged, sophisticated, tolerant, upper-middle-class white juniors and seniors is repulsion. They find fundamentalist discourse so alien to what they are used to thinking that their processing capacity breaks down. Why?

Put the same students in an upper-middle-class white Episcopal church or Jewish synagogue and the response, of course, is quite different. But why "of course"? Close inspection of the content of the discourse in these different settings may reveal a great deal of overlap, including talk of God, love, forgiveness, and faithfulness. Apparently the discourse is packaged – or framed or structured – in a more meaningful way in one context than in the other.

This becomes the heart of the matter when we consider religious discourse as public rhetoric. Is it that Jerry Falwell's ideas are so alien to the American democratic tradition that thoughtful intellectuals dismiss them on rational grounds after careful consideration? Or does the structure of Falwell's discourse itself cause his ideas to be dismissed out of hand? We may be correct in saying that Falwell's ideas are indeed alien to the ways in which most academics think, but I suspect there is more to it than that. The fact that we find them alien, depends, at least in part, on the way Falwell's discourse is put together. By the same token, if we find the US Catholic bishops' statement on nuclear disarmament much more compelling (my students do), probably part of the reason is that this statement has a discursive structure with which we are more comfortable.

Communication about social goals

The issue is not really whether academics can better appreciate Falwell's or the bishops' discourse, although that may be important. The issue is whether different segments of society can speak effectively to one another about broad issues of societal importance. At present, much evidence (including some from the kinds of opinion surveys I have just criticized) indicates that religious conservatives and religious liberals in the United States are deeply divided on nearly everything. The two groups are also about equal in number, each comprising about 40 percent of the adult population, at least according to ways people categorize *themselves*. And each side expresses enormous hostility and misgiving towards the other (for details, see Wuthnow 1988).

The reasons for this hostility and misunderstanding are of course, extremely complex. They include historic precedents, different organizational trajectories, and even class differences. But they also reflect different styles in the use of public discourse. Like my students, religious conservatives can walk into a church and sense almost instantly that it is "too liberal" for them, and the converse holds for religious liberals. But how?

Here, I wish to focus on the possibility of mining recent work in literary criticism for insights into the structure of religious discourse. An ample tradition exists here as well, especially because religious texts have been fair game for literary analysis for a long time. Two works of fairly recent origin, however, seem particularly valuable.

Literary models: Frye and Suleiman

Northrop Frye's *The Great Code: The Bible and Literature* (1982) is a masterful analysis of the biblical canon by one of the foremost literary analysts of our time. It is an attempt to say, from a literary standpoint, what is distinctive about the biblical texts. Frye focuses on language, myth, metaphor, typology, imagery, narrative, and rhetoric. In so doing, he demonstrates the importance of discursive structure to the communication of religious meaning. He also supplies some general concepts – as well as numerous substantive hints – about how to analyze religious discourse. Although his book deals specifically with the Bible as a written text, the analytic framework is sufficiently broad to be applied to many other kinds of religious discourse as well.

Susan Rubin Suleiman's *Authoritarian Fictions: The Ideological Novel as a Literary Genre* (1983) is quite different. With the exception of a rich, twenty-page section on "exemplary narratives" that focuses on biblical parables, the book is not about religious discourse at all. Its examples are drawn primarily from the works of nineteenth- and twentieth-century French novelists: Balzac, Arago, Bourget, and Nizan, among others. Suleiman is concerned with a particular kind of novel, the novel that attempts to persuade readers of the validity of a doctrine, and in this her work is of immediate relevance to the study of religious discourse.

The two studies also complement one another: Frye's creates a stage,

Suleiman's fills in the props. From Frye we learn some of the ways in which the arrangement of words in religious texts influences their meaning; from Suleiman we discover some of the particular strategies that writers and speakers may use to shape that meaning. Both are concerned with the restriction of meaning, that is, with the ways in which the relationships among words influence the variety of interpretations that can be drawn from those words. Together, the two books give us clues about the ways in which religious discourse may function in public settings.

Suleiman includes religious discourse within a larger set of communication that she describes as "ideological" or "authoritarian," the kind of communication that attempts to persuade readers or listeners of the correctness of a particular way of interpreting the world. Usually it explicitly refers to – and identifies itself with – a recognized body of doctrine or a system of ideas. This, of course, is a very broad category, including philosophical as well as religious discourse. But apparently it does exclude many other kinds of communication, for example, conversation that is not aimed at persuading someone of a particular point of view or discourse oriented solely towards description or entertainment (although all of these might have some ideological overtones).

Frye sets the stage

For Frye, in contrast, religious discourse is more distinctly differentiated. At least biblical discourse (Frye does not attempt to generalize to, say, primitive myths) makes use of poetic and metaphoric imagery but also purports to tell an historic story. And yet these stories are not merely descriptions of the past but stories told to convey specific ideas about the sacred and its relation to society. It is, Frye claims, extremely important that biblical stories be regarded as "historically true," even though external sources of validation are generally lacking. Thus a distinctive feature of religious discourse is that it presents itself as truth through the ways in which the discourse itself is internally arranged. This means a biblical text must avoid making certain kinds of claims that would render it subject to external verification and must also demonstrate certain kinds of internal coherence.

For example, no evidence (Frye claims) exists for the life of Jesus outside the New Testament. Consequently, the writings that refer to Jesus must follow certain criteria to avoid making this a problem: "Evidence, so called, is bounced back and forth between the testaments like a tennis ball; and no other evidence is given us. The two testaments form a double mirror, each reflecting the other but neither the world outside" (Frye 1982, p. 78). Frye stops short of trying to capture these criteria in any simple formula. But his view that religious discourse depends heavily on its own internal arrangement constitutes the basis for one of the central themes of his analysis.

This theme is expressed metaphorically. Religious discourse, Frye asserts, revolves around itself, creating both centripetal and centrifugal motion. The centripetal aspect refers to the "primary" or "literal" meaning of the text. It depends on not questioning the words and on not looking for deeper meanings or applications or connections, but simply taking the story at face value as, for example, in reading the Exodus story as an account of an historical episode. The centripetal aspect is also illustrated by the foregoing quotation about the two testaments forming double mirrors. Centripetal meaning derives from what other biblical scholars have called its "intertextual coherence." One text within the biblical canon refers to another, and that one refers to another, thereby providing a kind of closed system – a system that reinforces itself.

Centrifugal meaning, in contrast, refers to the more numerous connotations and layers of interpretation that "spin off" from a religious text. The Exodus story may be taken not simply as an historical account but as a message of hope, an illustration of redemption, and a metaphor of new life – even of revolutionary possibilities. Frye suggests that religious discourse invites both centripetal and centrifugal meaning: it encourages both a closed reading and an open horizon of broader meaning and functions effectively only when these two forces are held in tension.

Another basic point to be gleaned from Frye comes from his final chapter: religious discourse tends to evoke either the centripetal orientation or the centrifugal orientation as a kind of overarching *gestalt* from which all its internal content is viewed. Because (in Frye's view) religious discourse has both of these tendencies inherent within it, its practitioners have generally gravitated towards one pole or the other. Some have felt more comfortable emphasizing the closed aspect of biblical meaning, that is, whereas others have stressed its more open, expansive interpretations.

Frye believes that religious faith can never be reduced to simple doctrinal statements, but requires re-creative action and thought to the point that it becomes too complex to understand, and thus produces an inevitable degree of inherent doubt. Those who regard religious discourse in this manner, Frye suggests, emphasize its polysemousness, its centrifugality. In their view, the proper approach to religious discourse is one that says, "There is more to be got out of this" (p. 220).

There is, however, the opposing tendency as well. Religious discourse does fold back on itself. It does exclude many interpretations. It damns heresy, hypocrisy, and wrongdoing. It begs for a literal reading. And this, coupled with the uncertainties inherent in its centrifugal interpretations, encourages some to emphasize only the centripetal orientation and to find security in delimiting the range of biblical interpretations. As Frye puts it: "Man is constantly building anxiety-structures, like geodesic domes, around his social and religious institutions" (p. 232). This orientation de-emphasizes freedom, variety, and multivalency. It seizes on those metaphors that are most conducive to exact, literal renderings. To some, of course, this itself is heresy. But to Frye it is a normal reaction to religious discourse. As he concludes, "The normal human reaction to a great cultural achievement like the Bible is to do with it what the Philistines did to Samson: reduce it to impotence, then lock it in a mill to grind our aggressions and prejudices" (p. 233).

Suleiman supplies the props

Frye fulfils a kind of general stage-setting function for thinking about religious discourse; Suleiman is more helpful for supplying the specific props. Her book is replete with examples of the ways in which texts restrict possible interpretations in order to drive home the validity of a particular ideological position. She helps us understand, in Frye's terms, the centripetal forces at work in religious discourse. We can also appreciate, by contrast, how different structures may reinforce centrifugal tendencies. There is, in fact, a striking resemblance between Suleiman's interest in meaning and that of Frye (although Suleiman cites Frye only once, and then in a different context). Suleiman contrasts two kinds of novels, one that exhibits centrifugal tendencies, the other in which centripetal forces predominate. "Modernist" novels, she says, seek to "multiply meaning" (or even, as Barthes observed, to pulverize it). The *roman à thèse*, in contrast, "aims for a single meaning and for total closure" (Suleiman 1983, p. 22). Suleiman's concern is with the latter.

One of the ways in which certain kinds of texts or discourse close down the array of possible meanings, we learn from Suleiman, is through sheer repetition. By saying things over and over, texts reveal the way in which we should interpret them. If there is confusion or ambiguity the first time around, by the *n*th time we should be clear. Although this sounds like an obvious and simple point, Suleiman demonstrates that the study of repetition in texts is anything but obvious or simple. If something is repeated exactly the same way at different points in a text, it actually fails to achieve its goal of creating greater clarity. There has to be redundancy, but in different settings – and across different features of a text – for us to get the point.

Exemplary narrative and apprentices

Other chapters of Suleiman's book deal less formalistically, but nevertheless effectively, with particular patterns of discourse that seem to be employed frequently in ideological texts. For example, many such texts contain what she refers to as an "exemplary narrative," that is, a story – embedded within the larger text – that reveals by example how we are supposed to think, act, or feel. Suleiman examines religious parables as one illustration of these kinds of narratives. Her purpose is not to show, as others have, that parables lend themselves to multiple interpretations. Rather, it is to show that the capacity of parables to make any point at all depends on a particular style of construction.

Suleiman asserts the whole purpose of a parable is to set up a situation in which an interpretation is needed. Often the audience in the text actually asks the narrator to supply an interpretation, thereby speaking for the listener outside of the text. For example, Jesus' disciples routinely ask him to explain what his stories meant. Typically the narrator supplies an interpretation.

The examplary narrative works because it conforms to this identifiable construction. It establishes a relation between a sender and a receiver within the text that evokes a similar relation between the text and its actual reader or listener. It tends to be sufficiently general to allow for a wide range of identification: Jesus' parables are about "a sower," "a woman," or "a father" who had "two sons." It occurs within a larger textual context that invests it with intentionality. It also tends to be interpreted by an authoritative narrator who experiences little or no challenge to his authority from other characters or voices in the larger text.

Another specific literary device that Suleiman discusses is the use of apprentices and stories about apprentices to help drive home an author's ideological intent. As Suleiman defines an apprenticeship story, it is "two parallel transformations undergone by the protagonist: first, a transformation from *ignorance* (of self) to *knowledge* (of self); second, a transformation from *passivity* to *action*" (p. 65). Or, more simply, an apprenticeship story is about a hero who goes forth into the world to find himself and achieves this goal by undergoing a series of adventures or tests. Religious discourse is, of course, replete with such stories – from the biblical stories of Jacob, Joseph, Jesus, and Paul to modern equivalents about religious converts to such fictionalized variants as Luke Skywalker and Indiana Jones.

Like the exemplary narrative, apprenticeship stories work because they conform to certain rules of construction. In addition to the apprentice himself (or herself), various antagonists must be introduced to provide contrasts and to present hurdles to overcome. Often there is a guide or mentor who functions not only to help the apprentice but to make explicit the lessons the apprentice has learned. Above all, a virtual identification must be created between the reader and the protagonist. This is often accomplished by dialogue between the guide and the apprentice that parallels the dialogue going on between the narrator of the text and the reader. For instance, Jesus counsels his disciples and receives questions from them in a way that permits the reader of the text to ask the same questions and receive the same answers. It is also accomplished by creating the apprentice as a figural actor who exemplifies general characteristics of a certain social class or a particular time. Bunyan's Christian in *Pilgrim's Progress* evokes images of the Puritan artisan more generally, for example, just as the communist heroes of the twentieth-century fiction that Suleiman analyzes typify broader themes.

Applications to ordinary discourse

All Suleiman's examples come from formal texts – novels, fables, parables – and all of Frye's examples come from the biblical canon itself. The question thus arises: does any of this have validity for the analysis of more ordinary kinds of religious discourse?

The pastor of a liberal Protestant church preaches a sermon on the story of the Prodigal Son called "Intolerable Love"; across town, a preacher at a small fundamentalist church delivers a sermon called "The Meaning of Life." If we had not been told one was given in a liberal church and the other in a conservative church, could we have placed them correctly merely from examining the two transcripts? Or, perhaps more importantly, what do the two texts reveal about the differences between liberal religious discourse and conservative religious discourse?

This is not the place to examine the two texts in detail, but we can illustrate how some of the foregoing points might be applied. From the surface content of the titles alone, we would get little clue as to the underlying differences between the two. Both speak of broad existential, psychological themes; neither focuses specifically on a religious or biblical phrase. Moreover, when we consider the structural arrangement of the words in each title, we also see similarities: both are quite brief, both contain a primary noun and modifier of that noun, and both relate the noun and its modifier in a way that seems sufficiently paradoxical or contradictory to evoke a question: how can love be intolerable, how can life have meaning (specifically, something singular, referred to as "*the* meaning of life")? With a little sleight of hand that comes from peeking ahead and thinking of

Frye's basic distinction, we can already sense that one text is going to emphasize centrifugal meanings; the other, centripetal meanings. We sense this from the fact that "intolerable love" genuinely opens up all sorts of questions and possible answers, whereas "the meaning of life" implies that something as vague and complex as "life" is going to have a simple interpretation that can be called "the meaning" (consider the quite different implications that would be evoked by the phrase "meaning in life").

Pushing into the body of each text, we find further similarities and differences. For example, both employ some of the devices Suleiman discusses for creating an identification between the audience and either the narrator or characters in the story. In one, the speaker begins: "Who of us can read the story of the Prodigal Son nowadays without a catch in our throats?" The pronouns are all plural; they categorize the narrator and his audience together. In the other, all the pronouns are singular, but they occur in a sequence of questions that collectively encompasses everyone in the audience: "How can I handle death? How can I overcome my feeling of loneliness? How can I better manage my time?"

As the sermons progress, we increasingly see two different patterns in the relations suggested between narrator and audience. In the sermon about intolerable love, the narrator seldom refers to himself; he consistently uses plural pronouns, and when he does refer to himself, he refers to someone who is himself struggling, learning, uncertain, weak. He objectifies the story and relates it to himself and to the collective "we" with phrases that make the latter dependent: "like a resentful child," "broken," "caught." In the other sermon, the narrator tells numerous anecdotes about himself and becomes a much more intrusive object in his own narrative, stories in which his authority is never challenged. Indeed, they are often apprentice stories in which the speaker as apprentice encounters other people and then observes their confusion and supplies them with answers. But they are not genuine apprentice stories of the kind Suleiman analyzes. They show the speaker as one who has already found the answers, or who instantly recognizes them, or sees their applicability to others' problems. In short, the role of the narrator in the text proves to be a key to the relatively more "ideological" or "authoritarian" tone of the second sermon in comparison with the first.

More interesting is the manner in which the two sermons move between simple, univocal meanings and complex, multivocal meanings. The narrator of the sermon on love observes near the outset that the story of the Prodigal Son is a "simple little story." And in retelling the story, his sentence structure underscores its simplicity: "First we have the younger son, the prodigal. We remember him most vividly. He is hungry for life. He acts. . . . He is the experimenter." These are simple, short, declarative statements.

They reinforce the story's surface simplicity. The same sentence structure is present as the narrator continues his description of the other characters in the story, the elder brother and the father.

But then the narrator of the sermon on love switches to interpretation. He announces the switch by stating that "we learn some things" from the story and that this was Jesus' point in telling the story. Now the meanings conveyed become more complex. The story, it turns out, is not so simple after all. It is a story about envy, alienation, forgiveness, searching, the self, grace, reconciliation. And now the very complexity of the sentences forces the listener to abandon any conception of simple, straightforward interpretations. Here is the key sentence that summarizes the main point of the sermon: "The biblical notion of the Wrath of God is not so much that of the anger of a just God, but it has to do with God's passionate intolerance towards all forms of sin and what sin does to the world which is loved." Forty-four words! Delivered orally, it is little wonder that the story evokes, as the narrator said it would, "a catch in our throats." Meaning is not straightforward. One probably cannot even grasp it on one hearing. The sentence does not invite clarity but a sense of mystery to be probed, re-examined, and experienced.

Contrast this movement from the simple to the complex with that in the other sermon. Here the flow moves in the opposite direction. As noted previously, the text begins with some simple questions that draw the audience into their orbit. Each question is short and beguilingly simply. But there are nineteen of them! And they are delivered as a single unbroken chain. Together they signify the complexity of life – the problems of stress, decision making, communication, fear, pain. Then there is a series of short narratives, each describing its answer with statements that typify confusion, mystery, openness, searching: "He does not know real answers"; "You don't know where you're going"; "We find ourselves never getting anywhere"; "Knowledge does not contain answers"; "There are no answers in power."

The words themselves open up the complexity of the subject. But, as in the other sermon, so does the sheer length of many of the sentences. For example, here is a sentence that describes the confusion among the followers of Jim Jones's People's Temple: "Every one of them was steeped in traditional religion, and they left it because they found a group of people that loved them, that gave them more answers, that cared for them, that generated warmth – when all they did was sit in pews and have meaningless things told to them so they could go out and live meaningless lives." Fifty-nine words. The very fact of the run-on sentence places the listener in a situation of openness: the specific clauses of the sentence could go on endlessly.

Finally, however, the narrator asks directly, "Where's the answer?" And then gives the answer: "Jesus is the answer." Note the simplicity of the sentence, one actually framed and set apart from all other sentences in the text: the narrator reveals that he saw the answer on a billboard along the highway when he was driving home from his grandmother's funeral. Lest there be any confusion on the audience's part, he makes explicit towards the end of the text – just as the other narrator did at the beginning – that things are really quite simple: "Does life ever seem mysterious?" he asks. The answer, he says, "is simply found," and he underscores the point by saying it is "not hard to understand," is "so simple," and is "profound in its simplicity." Again he relies on slogans to underscore the point, including simple refrains from well-known hymns and short biblical quotations. Twice he puts these statements in the mouths of children.

The two sermons illustrate strikingly the contrast between Frye's centrifugal and centripetal tendencies in religious discourse. In the sermon on intolerable love, the movement runs from simplicity to complexity, from a restricted literal reading to a figurative multivocal reading. In the sermon on the meaning of life, in contrast, the direction of movement is from complexity and searching in many directions to simple, succinctly codified answers. The one "opens out" into broader meanings, the other "closes down" possible meanings to a single answer.

Is it perhaps this contrast that lies beneath the chasm separating religious liberals and religious conservatives? Had we considered both sermons in full, we would have observed that the liberal sermon actually devoted more time to quoting and paraphrasing the Bible than did the conservative sermon. We would have also noted that the scriptural text spoke more directly and objectively in the liberal sermon, whereas the narrator himself was more intrusive in the conservative sermon. We would have observed, too, that the conservative sermon did not contain a rigid set of "thou shalt nots" and did not go ahead to spell out in propositional statements what it meant to assert that "Jesus is the answer." In other words, the two sermons did not differ in many of the ways we might have expected them to on the basis of preconceived notions about liberalism and fundamentalism. The main contrast was in style, and in the openness or restrictedness of meaning that was connoted by that style.

Broader implications

What does this imply about religious discourse in the public sphere? Perhaps it is the style of discourse that causes it to communicate in some contexts and fail utterly to communicate in others. Perhaps clues are buried in the structure of discourse itself that say to us, "Life is really too confusing and here are some simple answers," or "The answers we have are really too simple and we need to recognize the complexity of it all." As in the sentence structure of the two sermons, there may be an implicit emphasis on the priority of centripetal meaning or of centrifugal meaning. The two emphases may also be spelled out explicitly, as the two ministers did when they employed the word "simple" itself.

More generally, issues of redundancy and methods of drawing an identification between readers and characters in the text also boil down to questions about distinctions and connections, contrasts and parallels – the structural features of discourse. These, I suggest, are what we need to give greater attention. Religious discourse in the public arena is not simply talk about the gods in an otherwise secular context. It is the use of a certain rhetorical style, a style that conforms to certain rules of underlying structure, but that communicates only to the extent that this structure is appropriate for the application in question.

References

Frye, Northrop 1982. *The Great Code: The Bible and Literature*. New York: Harcourt Brace Jovanovich.

Suleiman, Susan 1983. *Authoritarian Fictions: The Ideological Novel as a Literary Genre*. New York: Columbia University Press.

Wuthnow, Robert 1988. *The Restructuring of American Religion: Society and Faith since World War II*. Princeton: Princeton University Press.

5

Analytic and concrete forms of the autonomy of culture*

Anne Kane

As the field of sociology renews its interest in culture, the role of cultural analysis in historical explanation has become a growing issue of contention. Traditionally, historical sociologists have fallen into two main theoretical camps when dealing with culture. Cultural reductionists have been instructed by Marx's famous utterance that "it is not the consciousness of men that determines their being, but, on the contrary, their social being that determines their consciousness" (in Tucker 1972, p. 4). Cultural determinists may have interpreted Weber's observation that "ideas have, like switchmen, determined the tracks along which action has been pushed by the dynamic of interest" (1958, p. 280) to mean that the ideal realm of social being is determinative in the last instance.

Recent progress in the fields of both cultural analysis and historical sociology has redefined the classic debate of material vs. ideal determination as an issue of cultural autonomy. Although this could be a positive theoretical step towards greater understanding of the role of culture in historical explanation, theoretical and methodological confusions about the autonomous nature of culture abound. In clearing the way for a historical sociology that incorporates cultural factors into explanation, many questions must be addressed. If autonomy is an attribute of structures, how is culture structural? Because culture has to do with subjective meaning, how can we recognize historical structures of culture? What is the relationship of material and ideational structures to each other and to the historical events in which they are situated?

Beginning with the most fundamental point, I define autonomy strictly in terms of independence. The theoretical question then seems clear

* First published in 1991 as "Cultural analysis in historical sociology: the analytic and concrete forms of the autonomy of culture," *Sociological Theory* 9(1): 53–69.

enough: is culture independent? Now comes the murky element: independent of what? Independent in relation to other social structures and material conditions? The answer hinges on another question: is culture a structure in the same sense as an economic or a political system? Does it have discrete elements, institutions, processes, and the capacity to reproduce itself independently of the rest of the social system? The answer is both yes and no. Yes, cultural forms are autonomous structures; no, they are not independent of the rest of the social system.

This is the paradox that hampers development of cultural theory in historical sociology and leads to analytical confusion in substantive works. On the one hand, the "idealists" (e.g., Hunt 1984; Prager 1986; Zelizer 1985) demonstrate successfully the structure of the cultural form they are studying. Then, however, they conflate that independent quality to be both complete in itself and determinative of other social spheres. On the other hand, the "materialists" (e.g., Clark 1979; Zaret 1985), maintaining that economic and political conditions determine cultural formations, refuse to recognize the structure of culture, therefore denying its independent contribution to historical processes.

My solution to this confusion is to recognize that there are two forms of cultural autonomy – analytic and concrete. Analytic autonomy, termed as such because of the definitional implication of separation, posits the complete and independent structure of culture; it is conceptualized through the theoretical, artificial separation of culture from other social structures, conditions, and action. To find the analytic autonomy of culture, "we must bracket contingency . . . and treat action as if it were a written text" (Alexander 1987, p. 296). This text, with its intrarelational logic of symbolic elements, patterns, and processes, is the structure of culture.

Concrete autonomy, referring to historical specificity, establishes the interconnection of culture with the rest of social life. Whereas analytic autonomy of culture is sought apart from material life, concrete autonomy must be located within, and as part of, the whole of social life. In this sense the autonomy of culture is relative. This relativity, however, does not diminish the independent nature of culture because just as culture is conditioned materially, in turn it "inform[s] the structure of institutions, the nature of social cooperation and conflict, and the attitudes and predispositions of the population . . . [Culture] is constitutive of social order" (Sewell 1985, p. 161).

Analytic autonomy

There are three steps to fleshing out the analytic autonomy of culture: (1) specifying the elements and internal logic of a culture structure, (2) establishing how the symbolic processes work, and (3) reconstructing the development of culture – that is, how it reproduces and/or transforms itself.

Internal elements and logic of culture

The basic element of the "culture structure" and of its internal logic is the symbol, the vehicle through which meaning is expressed. As explained by Durkheim (1965) and by Saussure (1966), the meaning of symbols cannot be deduced from the social system: they are arbitrary constructs based on the common experience of group members and shared collectively. Organization of the culture structure is based on symbolic classification; symbols are classified and have significance in terms of each other. Symbolic classification is based primarily on binary opposition (Lévi-Strauss 1966). The classic example is Durkheim's division of the world into the sacred and the profane; more recent renditions are pure/polluted (Douglas 1966), good/evil (Alexander 1988), virtuous/nonvirtuous (Mann 1993), breaking with the past/tradition (Hunt 1984), and edible/inedible (Sahlins 1976). The demarcations of these classifications, and the categories within them, serve as boundaries for social action. Hermeneutically speaking, the "parts" of culture are the symbols. The "whole," or what social theorists call the structure, is the pattern of relationships among the symbols.

In this first step we see how culture functions at the individual level. People will understand and interpret their experience in terms of the classifications of a symbol system, and will "act upon circumstances according to their own cultural presuppositions, the socially given categories of persons and things" (Sahlins 1981, p. 67). Yet how are symbolic categories "socially given"? And how does culture operate on the social level?

Symbolic process

For the purposes of this argument, it is useful to simplify cultural systems into two basic components – beliefs and practices. Beliefs, as discussed above, are the intellectual concepts for which symbols have meaning. Rituals are the practice, the acting out of those symbolic meanings. Through the ritual process, symbolic categories are given social significance. For the participants, the believers, rituals are the "enactments, materializations, realizations of . . . the particular [cultural] perspective . . . Rituals are not only models of what they believe, but also models for the believing of it" (Geertz 1973, pp. 113–114). Through the drama of ritual, people acquire, and to some degree create, the cultural system in the act of portraying it.

Rituals are often enactments of the myth. In turn, the myth encompasses and recounts the belief system. It is the means by which the belief and the action that it prescribes are transmitted historically. Through the transmission, beliefs are perpetuated and the system is maintained.

Ritual has two consequences in which we can see the autonomy of culture. First, by making meaning evident, rituals infuse members of the group with an understanding of experience, a prescription for action in life, and a bond of solidarity to the group. The functional power of ritual therefore provides the culture structure with autonomy. Although ritual is seen here, in the analytic form of autonomy, as internal to the culture structure, it is a process that connects analytic with concrete autonomy, as will be discussed below.

Reproduction of the cultural system

The second consequence of ritual is that it maintains the symbolic system, and transmits it through myth from generation to generation. This process of self-regulation and reproduction is evidence of cultural autonomy. It renews the system and people's commitment to it, both in times of social stability and in crisis.

Yet reproduction of a system implies transformation. As theorized by Durkheim and other structuralists, change in the culture structure is systemic: it occurs within the boundaries of the symbolic classifications of the culture. Factors that normally are regarded as forces of change – for example, impinging external events – are subsumed by the culture structure. Through ritual, culture orders the event in terms of the received pattern of categorical relationships. In other words, people understand new experience and its meaning in terms of the given symbolic classification system, and they act accordingly. The event is reproduced in the image of the structure.

Analytic autonomy of culture and the French Revolution

In *Politics, Culture, and Class in the French Revolution* Lynn Hunt (1984) sees political culture as providing the logic of revolutionary action. The political culture consisted of the "values, expectations, and implicit rules that expressed and shaped collective intentions and actions" (p. 10); the structure of the culture came from the underlying patterns of language, images, and ritual activities.

Hunt explains the revolutionary culture in terms of beliefs and practices. The basic belief was "that the French were founding a new nation" (p. 26). Proceeding from this belief, the pattern of symbolic classification was based on the opposition between tradition and innovation (breaking with the past). The symbols that expressed and continually created this collective belief were rich with rhetoric and imagery.

Rhetorically, "the nation" became the most sacred of terms on the revolutionary side of the dichotomy. Other important words were "*patrie*," "constitution," "law," and, more radically, "regeneration," "virtue," and "vigilance." The relationship of these words to each other and to words on the side of tradition "were the means by which people became aware of their positions" (p. 53) in the revolutionary struggle. Moreover, the revolutionary symbols shaped people's perception of themselves and of their interests. For example, "*procureurs* and *avocats* (Old Regime legal types) became *hommes de loi* (simple 'men of the law')" (p. 20).

The images of the revolution – embodied in seals, engravings, and statuary – indicate the arbitrary nature of symbolic representation and creation. The symbolic meaning of the ancients as the revolutionary model of society, of female images of the republic, and of Hercules on the revolutionary seal cannot be deduced from social structural conditions. They must be interpreted in terms of collectively created and increasingly patterned beliefs. In this way Hunt demonstrates the autonomous – that is, the culturally determined – nature of symbols.

Rituals were the means by which revolutionary beliefs became manifest. Ritual created, for instance, the appearance of cockades on the hats of the revolutionary-minded. In the creation of symbols some rituals, such as the debates over the choice of revolutionary seals, became arenas for working out factional conflict. This process in turn strengthened collectively held beliefs. Furthermore, rituals such as the planting of liberty trees allowed people to take a political stand: "they made adherence, opposition, and indifference possible" (p. 53).

Evidently some rituals were simple and almost everyday activities. Others were very elaborate and ceremonious. In either case, participation was the key to the symbolic and revolutionary process. "Ordinary activities . . . taking minutes, sitting in a club meeting, reading a republican poem . . . became invested with extraordinary significance" (p. 72). Participating in a ritual, whether as simple as wearing garb deemed revolutionary or as elaborate as the festivals of Federation, infused people with the sentiment needed to understand the revolutionary experience, and it strengthened the bond of solidarity among participants.

Although the revolutionary culture was in constant flux, the symbolism of the "mythic present, the instant of the new community, the sacred moment of the new consensus" was the structural mechanism by which it renewed, regulated, and reproduced itself. "The ritual oaths . . . sworn *en masse* during the many revolutionary festivals commemorated and recreated the moment of social contract; the ritual words made the mythic present come alive, again and again" (p. 27).

This thumbnail sketch of Hunt's structural analysis of French revolutionary culture demonstrates the components of a culture structure that I contend make it autonomous. In any particular historical situation, analytic autonomy posits a culture's independence in relation to other social structures. In order to understand how culture figures into historical processes – that is, to determine the degree of its causality – we must explain both cultural transformation and the strength of culture structures. To this end we must reposition culture in relation to other social structures.

Concrete autonomy

Precisely within this relationship we find concrete cultural autonomy. History is a structuring process; therefore the relationship between culture and social structure is one of mutual formulation, both between each other and with society as a whole. Furthermore, this formulation is a continual process, and in constant motion. Accordingly, we need to identify the historically specific ingredients and processes of the formula. The basic ingredients in historical events are conditions, actors, contingent events, and arenas of action.

Conditions, such as existing social, economic, political, and cultural structures, are of both the ideal and the material variety. It is important to recognize that conditions are the result of previous structuring processes: a structure may be distinctly material, but both cultural and material elements contributed to its formation.

We need first to ascertain actors' *interests*, keeping in mind Weber's (1946) admonition that both ideal and material interests govern people's conduct directly. For example, the ideal and the material interests of the people with whom Weber deals in *The Protestant Ethic* (1958) – urban business people, small landowners, craftsmen, and artisans – are respectively salvation and maintaining economic independence. Second, we must determine how actors' *experience* of conditional factors directs their intentional action. This experience is mediated by cultural understandings; yet if these understandings are ineffective in explaining conditions, the culture is subject to change. Catholicism no longer offered a path to salvation in the changing economic and political climate of early modern England; hence the religious system of the people who were to become capitalists began to change.

Contingent events can impinge both practically and culturally on the given circumstances of the event under study. For example, subsidizing the American Revolution added to the French monarchy's already troubled financial situation. At the same time, the American Revolution demonstrated to the French people that the civil society path to social reform and progress was possible (Mann 1993).

Arenas of action are the social historian's entrée to the actual formulation of the culture structure. In these arenas, historically specific conditions, interests, experiences, and contingencies meet, interact, and culminate in cultural formations through "the often contradictory or antagonistic action of a large number of actors or groups of actors" (Sewell 1985, p. 61). Arenas may seem to be one-dimensional. When workers strike for higher wages, for example, their action is obviously based on material interests. Yet the act of striking provides ideal benefits: it raises consciousness and builds solidarity among the workers.

Concrete autonomy of culture and the French Revolution

Michael Mann (1993) properly analyzes the French Revolution as an historical process. The actors in the sequences of revolutionary events are members of the *ancien régime* and of the revolutionary groups. The conditions launching the revolution are fourfold. (1) The political condition is a decaying absolutist government and a society based on privilege. (2) Economically, France is feudal; capitalism is emerging, but is held back by traditional social structure. (3) The military has been occupied with geopolitical war excursions; the last straw was the American Revolution. (4) Finally, the cultural realm is dynamic: the Enlightenment is underway, literacy is growing, and the presence of the Catholic church is strong.

All of these conditions were critical to the French Revolution. To understand how the revolution began and eventually developed, we need to explain what these conditions meant to the French people. Then, keeping in mind that interpretation of experience is mediated through the cultural structure (ideology in formulation), we can begin to understand the collective, revolutionary action.

Mann contends that ideology did not cause the revolution, but he argues strongly that it was a major factor in how the revolution began and how it unfolded. The revolution began because of the fiscal crisis of the state, brought to a head by involvement in the American Revolution, and by the internal division and the "unconsciousness" in the regime, which prevented it from dealing effectively with the crisis. Mann, however, shows that the transformation was furthered by ideological power – the old regime losing it and revolutionaries gaining it.

How was this revolutionary ideology formulated and how was its power seized? According to Mann, the revolutionary ideology began in the old regime: the court supported and encouraged the Enlightenment *philosophes*; the government swelled the ranks of lawyers; and the Church, wanting people to be able to read sacred texts, promoted literacy among the general populace. While these groups were enjoying a cultural awakening, the *ancien régime* lost control over the fiscal crisis. People, especially the *philosophes* and members of the legal profession, began to look critically at the state and society on the basis of new cultural understandings.

Ironically, this reinterpretation of material conditions was structured by ideas that had begun to take shape within the structure of the old culture – that is, the moral principles of the Enlightenment. The *philosophes*' language changed from defense of privilege to appeals to fundamental laws and customs, especially the "imprescriptible" rights of (propertied) citizens. Likewise the lawyers' language went from defense of privilege to defense of general liberties. United, the *philosophes* and the lawyers produced a movement of principle led by ideologists.

Not only had the old regime inadvertently encouraged new revolutionary ideas; the medium for spreading the message, namely the circulation of the *cahiers* (registers of grievances), was begun by the regime in its desperate effort to reform itself. Thus the movement begun by the *philosophes* and the lawyers was joined by the rest of society, primarily the petty bourgeoisie, the upper peasants, and the lower clergy. Through local literary networks, people began to express their needs and discontents; this action can be seen as a form of ritual. Political consciousness expanded as the *cahiers* were discussed in local communication networks.

As Mann describes this formative stage of the revolution, he demonstrates the proposition that action is determined both materially and culturally. Mann sees in the content of the *cahiers* a gradual universalization and modernization of political discourse as well as a growth of capitalist economic rationality. In other words, both the ideal and the material interests of revolutionary-minded people were addressed in the emerging ideology; the revolutionary process was one of "escalating appeals to principle." When we look at Mann's description of the principles behind the ideology, we can see again its multidimensionality. He says, "'Principle' . . . carries its double meaning of both a general and a moral rule – for the revolutionaries became obsessed with 'virtue' and 'purity' [i.e., cultural] as well as with schemes of rational reconstruction [i.e., material]" (Mann 1993, p. 169).

This early revolutionary ideology was a symbol system that resulted from collective experience and served as a guide for action. Mann demonstrates that much of the content of the revolutionary ideology emerged from discourse generated through the communication networks between intellectuals, the petty bourgeoisie and the upper peasants, and the lower clergy. Furthermore, the leaders of the revolution, the "ideologists," emerged from this communication process. Looking at the ideologists multidimensionally, we see that they were leaders not only because they were able to express the will of the people (*la parole*), but also because they represented class interests. Moreover, although the leaders believed in the ideals they expressed, instrumentally they discovered the power invoked by proclaiming principles, which could forge emotional links (solidarity) between disparate political actors.

This synopsis shows how Mann's work approximates successful analysis of the autonomy of culture in the concrete form. By interrelating the state, the economy, classes, and cultural institutions in an historically specific manner – and in doing so, revealing the structure and the structuring of revolutionary ideology – Mann makes evident the causal power of culture in the French Revolution.

The causal power of culture: analytic and concrete autonomy

How does this idea of analytic and concrete autonomy contribute to understanding the causal power of culture in history?

There are two generally accepted explanations of the causal power of culture. The first finds causality in the social structural nature of the cultural system: culture is a component of the social system, so that culture is a *possible* causal factor, one among many, in any historical event. The second posits culture as constitutive of the social order: because culture is basic to and informs all social relations and institutions, it is always causal. I contend that both types of causality should be recognized. Culture is always a causal factor in historical processes, but the degree of causality is different; in some situations it carries more weight than in others. Although many historical sociologists might agree with this proposition, nobody has offered a theoretical explication of why it is true.

Theoretically, the structural nature of culture must be recognized. This is accomplished by demonstrating analytic autonomy, the empirical identification of specific culture structures. Without reconstructing the cultural system and actually showing its elements and processes, the social historian has no basis for claiming that culture is a determinative structure in its own right. At the same time, the structuring of a cultural system must be examined in its concrete interrelationship with other structures in historical processes: without positioning culture in its historically specific context and showing its interaction and formulation in relation to other structures, the analyst cannot determine its importance as a causal factor in a particular historical process.

I have shown that Hunt is successful in demonstrating analytic autonomy and that Mann comes close to revealing concrete autonomy. Yet, because each writer explicates only one type of autonomy, neither offers a complete cultural analysis. To demonstrate the consequences of ignoring either the structure or the social embeddedness of culture, I will compare the analyses of Hunt and Mann as they deal with two phenomena of the revolution – aristocratic plots and the Terror.

According to Mann, plots came to dominate consciousness because they "contrasted . . . with the genuine openness and 'morality' of the Revolution's own infrastructures" (1993, p. 198) and demonstrated symbolically the contrast between the honest virtue of the "people" and the corruption of the old regime. The plots led directly to the Terror because they were real; and the expressed intransigence of the king and his supporters forced pragmatic, moderate revolutionaries into extreme positions and strategies.

Hunt states that the "Terror followed logically from the principles enunciated in revolutionary rhetoric," of which conspiracy had become "the central organizing principle" (1984, p. 48). She explains that in opposition to conspiracy and interests, the notion of "transparency" became a revolutionary ideal: nothing should separate or hinder communication between citizens. Furthermore, the "true patriot could have nothing to hide" (p. 46). Political transparency necessitated public vigilance and denunciation, which became institutionalized in the Terror.

In Mann's rendition we see how concrete events of the revolution influenced the formulation of the revolutionary ideological structure. Yet we are led to believe that the ideological constructs reflected conditions directly: the people's reaction to the king's duplicity was reflected in the ideological concept of open virtue vs. secret evil. We gain little sense of an ideological *system* that influences the way in which people react to unfolding events, mediating their interpretations through its own structural formulations.

Hunt, on the other hand, elevates the concept of conspiracy to the symbolic level. By placing it in the political culture structure, she reveals the relationship of conspiracy to other symbolic concepts such as transparency, virtue, and vigilance. Moreover, in terms of the social context, Hunt recounts both aristocratic plots and the historical French fear of conspiracy, based on threats of hunger and starvation. In Hunt's interpretation, however, the revolutionary political culture structure has become so inviolate that no mutual transformation occurs between people's reactions to events and the political culture. As concrete events in the revolution, the aristocratic plots are interpreted and given meaning only in terms of the now-static political culture of the revolution. Yet, as Mann demonstrates, these plots greatly influenced further formulation and transformation of that culture.

Furthermore, in Hunt's vision, the culture structure takes on a life of its own and becomes the guiding force of the revolution. During the Terror,

> Revolutionary rhetoric was . . . defeated by its inherent contradictions. While being political, it refused to sanction factional politicking. While showing the power of rhetoric, it denied the legitimacy of rhetorical speech. While representing the new community, is pushed toward the effacing of representation . . . In short . . . [the] text was constantly subverting its own basis of authority (1984, p. 49).

Of course, the rhetoric did not constrain factional politicking, deny the right of speech, or efface representation – *people* did these things. At the precise juncture where the cultural system should be placed in relation to the social context, Hunt abstracts it further, making it completely autonomous and thus completely determinative. Ideology by itself did not produce the Terror, any more than ideological contradiction determined the tragic latter stages of the revolution. To understand the concrete role of ideology in both these processes, compare the above passage to a section from Mann's analysis:

> France was further centralized as the war added government economic intervention. Armies had to be provisioned, as did their main recruiting bases, the towns. The remaining ideological elite still wished to avoid popular wrath. The Committee of Public Safety, led by Robespierre, organized economic intervention and the Terror while still fudging class divisions. Robespierre declared: "The state must be saved by whatever means and nothing is unconstitutional except what can lead to its ruin." The Republic of Virtue controlled "purity" and purged "corruption" but policy was less principled . . . They succeeded well enough, but by varied tactics, here by Terror, there by conciliation, according to local exigencies and their predilections (1993, p. 206).

Here we see the interconnected formulation of revolutionary ideology, state policy, and emerging class struggle; all of this took place, as Mann narrates, in the complicated context of war and the *Levée en Masse* (mass mobilization).

Though I have argued that Mann's demonstration of the concrete form of cultural autonomy is successful, his accomplishment is inadvertent.

Granted, his plan of research and analysis is sound: "By exploring ideological infrastructures . . . [we can] assess the causal significance of ideological power" (1993, p. 170). Mann even recognizes that in order to identify causal significance, one must emphasize the role of "ideological institutions, symbolic and ritual practices and the content of ideologies" (1993, p. 168). Yet, in the otherwise correct effort to distance himself from an idealism "eschewing specific causal analysis and instead redescribing an entire social process in cultural terms" (1993, p. 168), Mann refuses to recognize an analytically autonomous structure of culture. The complex pattern of symbols and rituals elaborated by Hunt is mere form (or text) to Mann; in his analysis he divorces this pattern from the ideological content.

True, Mann discusses many of the elements of the ideological structure – symbols such as the "nation" and the ritualistic nature of the *cahiers* and the meeting of the Estates General. In the case of the revolutionary principles, he even examines their semantic interrelations. Yet because Mann does not recognize, much less attempt to identify, the analytic independence of the revolutionary cultural system, the cultural elements *appear* as reflections of material and political conditions – for example, principled resistance in reaction to the fiscal crisis, and the ideas of the ideological elite as representing the interests of the emerging bourgeoisie. I emphasize "appear" because a close reading of Mann reveals that culture is not a mere reflection of material structure. His analysis demonstrates both the independent nature and the causal power of ideology. Unfortunately, however, much of the theoretical import of Mann's work in cultural analysis is lost because of his denial of the analytic autonomy of culture.

Hunt has reconstructed a cultural system, one that she claims is the political culture of revolutionary France. Clearly, Hunt believes that culture is constitutive of society and is always causal, and that its structure always can be found. Following her methodology of abstracting culture analytically from the social system, one can find the structure of culture at any time, in any place. So far, this is fine.

Yet, because Hunt ignores explicitly the formulation of revolutionary political culture – through specific actors, their interests, and the historical conditions and development of the revolution – our only proof of the actual causal significance of the culture is the abstract correlations she draws between cultural structures and events, as expressed by the cultural text she has shown us. Identification of a symbolic system does not mean that the latter is a determinative structure in the specific historical process being examined. How do we know that a specific belief system helped to determine the course of the revolution unless we know which groups of people collectively constructed that system and were motivated to action by it? Furthermore, because Hunt does not relate the culture structure to specific actors and conditions that we know existed before and during the French Revolution, we do not know whether the text that Hunt has shown us was the political culture of revolutionary France. Thus, although Hunt gives us an elegant structure, we do not know its ultimate social meaning because it is removed from its social context.

Conclusion

In overreacting to functionalist determinism (Bellah 1957; Lipset 1967; Smelser 1959), historical sociology has become dominated by a materialist perspective (Moore 1966; Skocpol 1979; Tilly 1964; Zeitlin 1984) that relegates culture to the marginal role of reflecting social structural processes. In turn, sociologists who attempt to apply cultural analysis to historical explanation have reacted to material determinism and recognize that cultural systems are crucial to how people formulate their understandings of the world. These sociologists often have gone to extremes in their culturally deterministic explanations (Alexander 1988; Furet 1978; Little 1969; Walzer 1965).

The dual nature of cultural autonomy must be recognized; otherwise cultural analysis in historical sociology will continue to be incomplete, and either reductionist or determinist. Both Durkheimian and Weberian theories support this claim, and it is no coincidence that my outlines for finding analytic and concrete autonomy respectively resemble their theoretical approaches. Durkheim is concerned with understanding sociologically the internal structure of culture – what symbol systems and ritual processes do in social life. Weber is concerned with connecting that internal structure to transcendental interests, which are rooted in historically specific political, economic, and normative conditions. Though amalgamating Durkheimian with Weberian theory is tricky at best, cultural analysis in historical sociology must draw on both theories. Social historians need to abandon their disdain for what they see as the opposing camp – whether materialist or idealist – and to try to understand the relationship between cultural and structural analysis in historical sociology. To this end, the notion of analytic and concrete cultural autonomy provides a conceptual starting place.

References

Alexander, Jeffrey C. 1987. *Twenty Lectures: Sociological Theory since World War II*. New York: Columbia University Press.
    1988. "Culture and Political Crisis: Watergate and Durkheimian Sociology." In

Jeffrey C. Alexander (ed.), *Durkheimian Sociology* New York: Columbia University Press, pp. 187–224.

Bellah, Robert. 1957. *Tokugawa Religion*. Glencoe, IL: Free Press.

Clark, Samuel. 1979. *Social Origins of the Irish Land War*. Princeton: Princeton University Press.

Douglas, Mary. 1966. *Purity and Danger*. London: Penguin.

Durkheim, Emile. 1965. *The Elementary Forms of Religious Life*. New York: Free Press.

Furet, François. 1978. *Penser la Revolution Française*. Paris: Gallimard. (Translated as *Interpreting the French Revolution*. Cambridge: Cambridge University Press [1981].)

Geertz, Clifford. 1973. *The Interpretation of Cultures*. New York: Basic Books.

Hunt, Lynn. 1984. *Politics, Culture, and Class in the French Revolution*. Berkeley and Los Angeles: University of California Press.

Lévi-Strauss, Claude. 1966. *The Savage Mind*. Chicago: University of Chicago Press.

Lipset, S. M. 1967. *The First New Nation*. Garden City, NY: Basic Books.

Little, David. 1969. *Religion, Order and Law*. Chicago: University of Chicago Press.

Mann, Michael. 1993. "The French Revolution and the Bourgeois Nation." In *The Sources of Social Power*, vol. II. Cambridge: Cambridge University Press, pp. 167–213.

Moore, Barrington. 1966. *Social Origins of Dictatorship and Democracy*. Boston: Beacon.

Prager, Jeffrey. 1986. *Building Democracy in Ireland: Political Order and Cultural Integration in a Newly Independent Nation*. New York: Cambridge University Press.

Sahlins, Marshall. 1976. *Culture and Practical Reason*. Chicago: University of Chicago Press.

1981. *Historical Metaphors and Mythical Realities*. Ann Arbor: University of Michigan Press.

Saussure, Ferdinand de. 1966. *Course in General Linguistics*, translated by Wade Baskin. New York: McGraw-Hill.

Sewell, William H., Jr. 1985. "Ideologies and Social Revolutions: Reflections on the French Revolution." *Journal of Modern History* 57: 57–85.

Skocpol, Theda. 1979. *States and Social Revolutions*. Cambridge: Cambridge University Press.

Smelser, Neil. 1959. *Social Change in the Industrial Revolution*. Chicago: University of Chicago Press.

Tilly, Charles. 1964. *The Vendee*. Cambridge, MA: Harvard University Press.

Tucker, Robert (ed.). 1972. *The Marx–Engels Readers*. New York: Norton.

Walzer, Michael. 1965. *The Revolution of the Saints: A Study in the Origins of Radical Politics*. Cambridge, MA: Harvard University Press.

Weber, Max. 1946. *From Max Weber: Essays in Sociology*, translated and edited by H. Gerth and C. Wright Mills. New York: Oxford University Press.

1958. *The Protestant Ethic and the Spirit of Capitalism*, translated by Talcott Parsons. New York: Scribner.

Zaret, David. 1985. *The Heavenly Contract: Ideology and Organization in Pre-Revolutionary Puritanism*. Chicago: University of Chicago Press.

Zeitlin, Maurice. 1984. *The Civil Wars in Chile*. Princeton: Princeton University Press.

Zelizer, Viviana. 1985. *Pricing the Priceless Child*. New York: Basic Books.

PART II

The production and reception of culture

The essays presented in the first part of this book were primarily concerned with uncovering the meanings and structures of culture. Issues related to the social constraints on the production and reception of culture were given somewhat less attention. This is not to say that they were neglected entirely. The work by Brown suggested that the production of discourses is related to the distribution of power, whilst those of Seidman and Alexander pointed to the critical role of the mass media as a communicative institution. Similarly, Wuthnow dealt with the issue of reception in suggesting that the messages of religious fundamentalists and liberals would be interpreted differently by divergent audiences. Finally, Kane's contribution indicated the need to explore the distribution of cultural practices and beliefs across different social groups. Yet in the main, the research questions driving these scholars focused around how best to conceptualize meaning rather than exploring the circumstances under which it is "manufactured" and "consumed."

The investigation of the production and reception of culture is an area which has recently generated a good deal of scholarship. In part this is the result of a backlash against the monolithic "dominant ideology" and "value systems" theorizing of radicals and functionalists respectively. It also reflects a substantial body of research in the field of mass communications which showed that messages were always mediated in some way by pre-existing prejudices and beliefs, social networks, and a variety of standard socio-demographic variables. Finally, it can also be considered to eventuate from the tradition of empirically grounded, middle-range organizational and institutional analysis in American sociology.

Scholars who focus on the production and reception of culture usually argue that simply decoding cultural texts and discourses is inadequate. What we need to do, they suggest, is to investigate how and why particular discourses are produced and institutionalized and why and how they are received. Prevalent understandings of this process invoke social structural factors, focusing in particular on social (e.g., status, cultural capital) and material (e.g., money, power) rewards, social location (e.g., class), or organizational constraints and imperatives (e.g., newsroom realities and routines). Despite its somewhat one-sided nature, this tradition has at least had some methodological dividends. Difficult questions relating to the measurement of emotions and symbolic motivations can be bypassed, allowing quantitative research to take place. This in turn has had a significant payoff for the legitimacy of cultural sociology within the discipline as a whole. Yet, although it provides for methodological clarity, the focus on production and reception as products of social structure often leaves a delimited domain for cultural sociology. Studies in the genre almost invariably study forms of culture – such as news broadcasts and television programs – which are relatively simple to measure and understand as being produced and consumed. Generally excluded from this kind of analysis are the more amorphous and pervasive manifestations of culture as are captured by ideas like social text, zeitgeist, ethos, forms of life, and solidarity. These might infuse social life in the elusive manner illustrated by Geertz's Balinese ethnographic material. Such understandings of culture make it difficult to differentiate from everyday life, difficult to define operationally, difficult to understand as produced or received by anyone.

So a space still remains for a fully worked understanding of this process, one which would look to the personal and emotive processes and the symbolic resonances and rewards involved in the production and consumption of cultural forms. The essays presented here are perhaps the closest to producing such a model.

Michèle Lamont's study of the popularity of Derridean ideas remains one of the most sophisticated contributions in this genre thanks to the deft articulation of cultural and social structural factors. Lamont takes up a traditional topic from the sociology of knowledge (viz. the dissemination and legitimation of ideas) and explains it in partly cultural, partly institutional terms. Derrida and his deconstruction theory are essentially treated as symbolic goods. Their success has less to do with their intellectual qualities (viz. an ability to illuminate, inform, discover some "truth") than with their value as a commodity in a marketplace of ideas. This marketability was constrained in both France and the United States by the dynamics of potential audience groups and institutions and by the partly studied, partly felicitous "fit" between Derrida's ideas and the cultural requirements of ongoing academic debates. Such an approach is a long way from traditional, normative, cultural sociology which emphasized the role of deeply internalized beliefs in patterning action and generating belief and commitment in the subject. Indeed, the approach taken by Lamont is only a short step away from the theories of Bourdieu with their emphasis on cultural consumption as a slightly dishonest game in which taste communities vie for power and individuals use culture strategically to advance their own interests in and through particular fields.

Nicola Beisel's work on censorship and the interpretation of art shares many features of Lamont's paper, arguing that the reception of art depends upon the characteristics of the taste community. Yet, Beisel's argument is subtly different. By introducing the concept of "identity" into the argument Beisel brings existential questions relating to self and collective self-images back into the analytic frame. In Beisel's account honour, shame, deep cultural norms about moral behavior, and a vision of the good society are knitted up with the reception, consumption, and interpretation of cultural products. Moreover, these cultural criteria are relatively autonomous in the concrete in that they divide members of the same social class. As Beisel neatly points out, the inclusion of identity issues into aesthetic interpretation enables her theory to transcend the structural determinism which lies at the heart of Bourdieu's theory of taste.

Wendy Griswold's chapter on Jacobean drama makes a rather different case for the autonomy of culture. Whereas Beisel shows that social location under-determines interpretation, Griswold's argument for the autonomy of culture hangs upon demonstrating an enduring structure within culture. Her point is that Jacobean drama was populated by archetypal figures (heroes, villains, etc.) whose particular manifestation in this instance was sculpted by the structural location of audience segments and their need for legitimacy in the context of a rapidly changing social structure. In this way the form and messages of signifiers are shown to be the result of a complex interplay between suppliers, consumers, cultural needs, and social structural forms. By spinning this yarn around the spindle of legitimacy Griswold is able to provide a hard-headed, plausible account of the process through which cultural texts are produced. The concept of legitimacy can often lead to images of a furtive, instrumental conspiracy between culture producers and culture consumers. It is a credit to Griswold's text that this issue is treated with some delicacy with the "gallant" appearing genuinely attractive to young men entering the world of commerce whilst simultaneously operating as the benign face of capitalist enterprise.

For purposes of contrast it is useful to imagine what a hermeneutically inspired decoding of gender bias in Victorian novels might look like, or a study of the textual consequences of increasing male dominance in the field of the novel. Such a study might explore the divergent character traits of heroes and heroines, or the way that patriarchal institutions like marriage are depicted as solutions to women's problems. Such an essay might have been well suited to the first part of this book. However, Gaye Tuchman and Nina Fortin are concerned with a different question, in particular the issue of who is producing cultural goods and who controls the processes through which they are reproduced. The emphasis here on competition for space and prestige within cultural spheres and the role of gatekeepers is reminiscent of Lamont's essay on Derrida. But whereas Lamont tends to stress the role of instrumental motivations (the pursuit of status and legitimacy) amongst gatekeeping elites, Tuchman and Fortin foreground the role of beliefs, in particular the subtle biases of a patriarchal culture on the perceptions of the gatekeepers and the shifting meanings of the novel within the field of cultural production.

The essay by Robin Wagner-Pacifici and Barry Schwartz is the most deeply hermeneutical study in this part, its mood reflecting the tidal pull of Durkheim's sociology of the sacred. The text embodies the various ways that Durkheimians have responded to persistent criticisms over idealism, collectivism, and consensus theorizing. The production and reception of the Vietnam Veterans Memorial is shown to be the result of a complex and multidimensional interplay of forces: moral entrepreneurship, struggles between social groups, and personal negotiations of significations. With this double emphasis on both meaning and agency the paper points back to the previous part of this collection and forwards to the next.

6

The reception of Derrida's work in France and America[*]

Michèle Lamont

The successful introduction of Jacques Derrida's work to American literary criticism raises interesting sociological questions. The evaluation of cultural goods is highly dependent on contextual cultural norms. How then does a cultural good gain legitimacy in two cultural markets as different as France and the United States? Or, how can a French philosopher gain acceptance in the land of empiricism? More generally, what are the conditions under which a cultural product becomes defined as important? This paper analyzes the cultural, institutional, and social conditions of interpretive theories by analyzing the legitimation of Jacques Derrida's work in France and the United States.

I argue that the intellectual legitimation of a theory in different settings depends on its *adaptability* to specific environmental requirements, which permits a fit between the work and specific cultural and institutional features of various markets. I show that the legitimation of Derrida's work in the United States was made possible by its adaptation to an existing intellectual agenda and by a shift in public from a general audience to a specialized literary one. Also, Derrida benefited from the concurrent importation of a number of other French authors, which created an American market for French interpretive theories.

I proceed by reconstructing the intellectual, cultural, institutional, and social conditions of the intellectual legitimation of Derrida's work. These conditions refer to (1) the construction, assessment, and institutionalization of deconstruction theory as an important theory by Derrida, his peers, and the intellectual public and (2) the structured cultural and institutional system of environmental constraints on the construction process, that is,

[*] First published in 1987 as "How to become a dominant French philosopher: the case of Jacques Derrida," *American Journal of Sociology* 93(3): 584–622.

the rules of the game, the structural requirements that Derrida's work and personal trajectory had to meet in order for his theory to be defined as important.

Derrida's work and French intellectual environments

Academic and cultural requirements

Derrida describes his writing style in the following terms: "To be entangled in hundreds of pages of a writing simultaneously insistent and elliptical, imprinting as you saw, even its erasures, carrying off each concept to an interminable chain of differences, surrounding or confusing itself with so many precautions, references, notes, citations, collages, supplements – this 'meaning-to-say-nothing' is not, you will agree, the most assured of exercises" (1981*b* [1972], p. 14).

Some have described this style as a game, a "pleasure without responsibility," and others, as a deliberate attempt to confuse the reader, a "technique of trouble" (Watson 1978, p. 13). Derrida, like other French intellectuals, is renowned for writing in a sophisticated and somewhat obscure style (Lemert 1981, p. 10). Moreover, most contemporary French philosophers share Derrida's highly dialectical style of argument. Postwar French intellectuals were strongly influenced by Hegel and Marx, who shaped their basic cultural framework (Descombes 1980). To write and argue within the dialectical framework shared by intellectuals is to capitalize on the established thinking and reading habits of the French public and to increase, *ipso facto*, one's potential for diffusion (Bourdieu 1975, p. 110). In contrast, Jacques Bouveresse, one of the few French analytic philosophers, writes, in his "Why I Am So Very UnFrench": "I have been told that my own works were practically unreadable by the French philosophical public because they were concerned essentially with 'logic' (which meant in addition that they were not in any event worth reading, inasmuch as they contained nothing that was properly philosophical)" (1983, p. 10).

A sophisticated rhetoric seems to be a structural requirement for intellectual legitimation in the French philosophical community: rhetorical virtuosity contributes to the definition of status boundaries and maintenance of stratification among French philosophers. To participate in the field, one has to play the rhetorical game, and this environmental characteristic is present in Derrida's work.

A highly rhetorical writing style is shared or emulated by many less successful French philosophers and is therefore not a decisive or automatic criterion of intellectual legitimation. More important is the creation of a *theoretical trademark* framed within an established intellectual tradition

(Bourdieu 1986). Derrida has created a theoretical apparatus that is clearly distinct from other philosophical systems. Deconstruction presents a set of "non-concepts" – to use his term – such as trace, gramme, supplement, hymen, tympan, dissemination, and metaphor, that serve to designate the phenomena studied. Derrida's theoretical apparatus is so clearly packaged and labeled that it can readily circulate in the intellectual community. As Heirich (1976, p. 37) argues, packaging ideas as commodites improves their potential exposure and facilitates their penetration into various intellectual milieus. Sartre's "existentialism," Althusser's "epistemological break," Lefèbvre's "*quotidienneté*," Lacan's "unconscious text" and "mirror stage," Foucault's "archaeology," and Deleuze's "schizo-analysis" (Descombes 1980; Kurzweil 1980) may well have served as theoretical trademarks in the legitimation of their work.

Academic works need to be framed in relation to the major debates of a field and associated with the major authors in order to be legitimated (Adatto and Cole 1981; Bourdieu 1975). Deconstruction resembled other theoretical systems enough to fit and be incorporated into the Parisian intellectual milieu of the 1960s, that is, to be judged sufficiently significant and relevant by the philosophical audience to be included in the system of diffusion. Derrida's references to the transcendence of philosophical discourse and the end of philosophy were central themes of texts widely read in the 1960s (Althusser's *For Marx* and Marx and Engels's *German Ideology* [Ferry and Renaut 1985]). Also central were references to the Saussurian questions and to the multiplicity of meaning and intertextuality, themes that are basic to semiology. He presented his theoretical innovations as a continuation of the writings of Husserl, Heidegger, and Nietzsche, and in opposition to Hegel. Husserl's phenomenology, Heidegger's critique of the logocentrism of the philosophical tradition, and Nietzsche's critique of humanism are explicitly presented as the theoretical antecedents of deconstruction. Derrida's conception of interpretation as a free play of the mind is also borrowed directly from Nietzsche. Derrida defines himself in opposition to Hegel and criticizes the Hegelian ideas of totality and contradiction as the epitomes of the ideas of unity and presence (Derrida 1981*a* [1972], pp. 40–1).

Finally, like Barthes, Foucault, and Lacan, Derrida builds on the established culture of the left-oriented European intellectual public when he focuses on the relationship between power, on the one hand, and culture, knowledge, and rationality, on the other. The Frankfurt school, the Birmingham school, and Italian Marxism all make this issue a central one. This question has historically been important in socialist thought, as seen in the roles of the party and of intellectuals.

Prestige and diffusion

The legitimation of Derrida's work is facilitated by the philosophical tradition in which he situates it: deconstruction gains prestige from its affiliation with Heidegger, Husserl, and Nietzsche, its transcendence of the philosophical tradition, and its application to classics (Boltanski 1975). Also, the ambiguity of this framework and its adaptability to any text favor its reproduction. By enhancing the diffusibility of Derrida's work, these features contribute to its legitimation.

Derrida's focus on implicit meaning and his dialectical arguments create much ambiguity in his writing and generate endless debates on his work. What Searle has called the "heads I win, tails you lose" Derridian argument maintains the reproduction of deconstruction because of the absence of nonrelativist criteria to evaluate the theory. Also, its reproduction is favored by the fact that the same deconstructive operations can be applied to any text. This is an advantage for those who use his technique, in terms both of the accessibility of working material and of the ability to transfer their expertise to new texts or fields.

Finally, Derrida provides his intellectual public with a charismatic image of the avant-garde intellectual. Because he conceives the reader as re-creating the text, he represents his work as a creative enterprise similar to that of an artist or writer – see, e.g., *Positions* (1981*a* [1972]). Like Barthes and Lévi-Strauss before him, Derrida, through his work, presents intellectual life as the adventure of a modern Prometheus whose rationality challenges power. Along with other charismatic intellectuals, Derrida provides a role model for young French intellectuals and has increased the appeal of the humanities.

Social, political, and institutional contexts

We have seen that Derrida meets a number of the cultural and academic requirements of the French intellectual scene, such as having a sophisticated writing style, a distinctive theoretical framework, and a focus on questions defined as both important and concerned with an important philosophical tradition. These requirements are a part of the environment in which Derrida has had to define his work, and his fulfilling these requirements is a *sine qua non* for the legitimation of his work, quite independent of its content. This work, I suggest, also fits the larger French intellectual, political, and professional contexts that facilitated Derrida's diffusion. By contexts, I refer to (1) the intellectual references of French upper-middle-class culture, (2) the political context of the late 1960s, and (3) the institutional changes in philosophy.

(1) The consumption habits of segments of the upper-middle class (professionals in the cultural sectors and human services, teachers, and civil servants) and their patterns of participation in the intellectual culture facilitated the diffusion of Derrida's work. The very limited possibilities for upward economic mobility between and within social classes characteristic of postwar France were compensated for by investments in educational and cultural mobility, especially by the upper-middle class (Marceau 1977). During this period, members of the cultural segments invested greatly in the consumption of sophisticated cultural goods (Bourdieu 1984; Lamont 1987) as a means of maintaining and improving their status. By consuming a cultural *produit de luxe*, one becomes an initiated member of a status group. Among those "products" are sophisticated intellectual goods, including deconstruction itself, which is barely accessible even to the highly educated; it requires considerable investment to be understood and is targeted at an intellectual elite. Along these lines, Lucette Finas, a Parisian proponent of Derrida, notes:

To open to a larger public a work as important and difficult as Derrida's would necessarily create deformities, approximations and impoverishment. The difficulty of the text is not an accident. It is linked to the way knowledge may be transmitted through writing. Jacques Derrida is a writer, and no systematic or didactic presentation of what is called his ideas can reproduce the proliferating complexity of the text (Finas 1973, p. 23).

Packaging deconstruction as a sophisticated cultural good increases its potential for diffusion, given the importance of symbolic status boundaries for the target public. Moreover, it improves the fit between Derrida's work and a large extant market.

(2) The diffusion of Derrida's work peaked at the beginning of the 1970s, a few years after the French political climax of May 1968. After the student insurrection, intellectuals had grown weary of traditional Marxist rhetoric (Judt 1986; Wuthnow *et al.* 1984, p. 135). The post-1968 years were a period of stagnation for the Left, and leftist analyses were in need of rejuvenation. Derrida provided just the theoretical position that met and matched the political climate. Like other structuralist and post-structuralist intellectuals (Roland Barthes, Gilles Deleuze, Michel Foucault), indeed like Sartre before them, Derrida looked at more subtle forms of manifestations of power that had been ignored by classical Marxism. Similar to Marx's theory of ideology, Derrida's work postulated that power and hierarchies are hidden behind the apparent meanings of texts. Deconstructing meant

identifying those hierarchies of meaning. The theoretical goal became a "Nietzschean affirmation, the joyous affirmation of the free-play of the word without truth, without origin, offered to an active interpretation" (1981*a* [1972], p. 43). As Jay (1984, p. 516) and Ryan (1982, p. 213) point out, this framework sustained a form of theoretical anarchism. It fitted the climate of the French cultural market in the late 1960s.

(3) The diffusion of Derrida's work was favored by its connection with the professional interests of philosophers. French philosophy went through a legitimacy crisis in the 1960s and 1970s. The government attempted to reduce the philosophy requirements in *lycées*, and the social sciences launched strong critiques against the philosophical enterprise. Derrida defended philosophy by attacking the logocentrism of these criticisms and by reformulating the philosophical project as the intellectual enterprise that takes the most far-reaching and critical analytical perspective (GREPH 1977). By doing so, he promoted a positive image of philosophy – criticizing, following Barthes, "old academism" and countering simultaneously the decline of the field. He attempted to delegitimate science as a logocentric discourse. His epistemological answer to the crisis spawned a large following in certain circles. The fit between Derrida's conception of philosophy and the disciplinary crisis again favored the diffusion of his work.

In this section, I have been concerned with the effect of a producer's work on the institutionalization of his theory. I have also been interested in delineating the link between Derrida's work and the cultural and institutional environment that it existed in. I will now be concerned with uncovering a second layer of intellectual legitimation, namely, the process through which peers and the intellectual public came to define a theory and its producer as "important."

Derrida's intellectual and institutional trajectory

Institutional supports for intellectual legitimation

The legitimation of cultural products is highly dependent on intellectual collaboration and institutional settings. Derrida participated in institutions that contributed to disseminating his work and defining it as important. Because many French intellectuals have access to the same prestigious institutions, Derrida's participation in those institutions – journals, schools, cultural media, professional associations – can be considered as meeting structural requirements for intellectual legitimation in France.

The schools where Derrida received his philosophical education gave him legitimate cultural codes. He studied philosophy at the Ecole normale supérieure (rue d'Ulm), which is the most prestigious French institution for the study of philosophy and one of the centers of philosophy in France (Clark and Clark 1982). He also studied at the Sorbonne with Hippolyte and Gandillac. The support of these influential professors gave Derrida his first opportunities to publish and helped mark him as a promising beginner. "Ulm" and the Sorbonne provided Derrida with an institutional context for peer assessment of his aspirations and capabilities. Most members of the Parisian intellectual elite attended Ulm and formed circles in this school that played an important role in their careers. Students shared the same intellectual world; therefore, they tended to define the same questions as important (Bourdieu 1969, p. 113).

Two journals were especially influential in the diffusion of Derrida's work and its institutionalization as a significant contribution: *Tel Quel* and *Critique*. Similar to Sartre's *Les Temps modernes*, these journals published essays in literary criticism and philosophy directed towards the Parisian academic public.

The diffusion of Derrida's work to the general intellectual public was the result of its coverage by the main cultural media. Cultural magazines and newspapers have become central to Parisian intellectual life as they define what one has to read in order to be considered "literate" (Debray 1979; Hamon and Rotman 1981). They cater to the intellectual culture of the upper-middle class, and their control over access to that market is a structural feature of the French intellectual scene. It is therefore essential for intellectual producers to fit into the circles of these cultural publications (Pinto 1981).

Derrida joined the full-time faculty of the Ecole normale supérieure in 1967 and started teaching at the Ecole des hautes études en sciences sociales around 1984. Louis Althusser, Michel Foucault, and Jacques Lacan, to name only a few, have also taught at the Ecole normale supérieure, and a large number of important specialists in the *sciences des l'homme* teach at the Ecole des hautes études. Derrida's presence in these prestigious schools further institutionalized his vision of the world and also himself as an important philosopher. It also allowed him to develop a circle of Ulm students who created a journal – *Digraphe* – publishing articles inspired by his work.

Two organizations associated with the defense and promotion of French philosophy also enhanced Derrida's visibility and intellectual legitimacy. In 1974, Derrida and his students created the Groupe de recherche sur l'enseignement de la philosophie (GREPH) in order to resist a governmental reform threatening jobs in philosophy. Derrida's political declaration concerning the "Réforme Giscard-Haby" steered the media's attention to him as a representative of the profession. Around 1981, the Socialist government appointed him as one of the directors of the Collège international de philosophie, whose publicly acknowledged mission is, among other things, to reaffirm the presence of French philosophy internationally (Collège international de philosophie 1982). This appointment reinforced his position in the French intellectual field and legitimized his presence in the United States.

Finally, Derrida's access to institutions was greatly facilitated by his cultural capital. Several features of Derrida's work defined it as a high-status cultural good, particularly its references to a prestigious intellectual tradition and its display of erudition. References to high-status cultural works seem to have great influence on the legitimation of interpretive theories. Also, access to prestigious institutions is facilitated by cultural capital, that is, by cues indicating the sharing of a common high-status cultural background, whether it is the culture of the Ecole normale supérieure, the sharing of a common definition of important questions, or experiencing situations similarly (DiMaggio and Mohr 1985).

The structuralist debate

Derrida defined himself as a poststructuralist by criticizing the structuralist enterprise for being logocentric in its search for structural explanatory principles and for giving priority to language. In "Force et signification" (1963), he had attacked Foucault and Lévi-Strauss, the founding father, through de Saussure. Foucault replied to Derrida in *The Order of Things: An Archaeology of the Human Sciences* and in the second edition of *Madness and Civilization*, criticizing his interpretation of the Cartesian *cogito* (Giovannangeli 1979, pp. 161–171). This debate gave Derrida the opportunity to display his distinctive theoretical trademark publicly and to be identified as a major actor in the structuralist controversy and as one of the main critics of structuralism.

A central theme for structuralists is their ongoing attack on the Western emphasis on humanism. They also look for hidden structures of meaning and the organizational principles of systems (Kurzweil 1980). Derrida recognized the importance of these issues through his work on implicit meaning and his critique of the humanist tradition. His critiques helped to legitimate structuralism and institutionalize it as a school of thought.

Concurrently, by responding to Derrida's objections, structuralists recognized and affirmed him as a significant critic, thus contributing to his intellectual legitimation (Bourdieu 1983, p. 323). Lévi-Strauss, Roland Barthes, and Michel Foucault had well-established reputations in the mid-1960s, and their prestige trickled down to Derrida. As with other participants in this debate, Derrida's personal legitimacy grew through this association, and his legitimacy became linked to the legitimacy of the structuralist circle itself.

In table 1, publications *on* Derrida have been broken down by type of journal (philosophy or literature) and country (France or the United States). The declining diffusion of Derrida's work in French philosophy journals is shown in the decrease of articles on his work published in French journals after 1974. The decline of his popularity among philosophers can be related to Derrida's refusal to respect academic professional norms by choosing not to write a dissertation until 1980. Others, like Althusser and Foucault, had also decided not to pursue their *doctorat d'état*. One of my informants, who also made this choice, observed that this refusal expressed an important feature of the French intellectual ethos: the power of the Cartesian *cogito* is proved by one's ability to win the game without playing by the rules.

As shown in figure 1, publications in specialized philosophy journals on Derrida's work started in 1963 and remained greater than publications in literary criticism journals until 1969. After a 1973 boom, the number of articles was quite irregular in philosophy journals. In contrast, publications in literary journals became important in 1970. A 1972–73 boom was followed by a progressive decline. However, overall, literary criticism articles clearly outnumber philosophical articles after 1972. This figure illustrates that, over time, literary critics constituted a growing part of Derrida's public, while the proportion of philosophers decreased. In the next section, I will argue that Derrida's penetration of the American intellectual market was conditioned by a shift in public.

The American connection

The legitimation of Derrida's work in America results from mechanisms similar to those active in its legitimation in France, that is, (1) the definition of this work as important by Derrida, his peers, and the public, and (2) a fit between Derrida's work and the American intellectual and institutional environment (i.e., its adaptation to already existing intellectual agendas and its diffusion by prestigious universities and journals).

Table 1. *Publications on Derrida's work by country (France/United States) and by type of journal (philosophy/literary criticism), 1963–1984.*

	France		United States	
	Philosophy	Literary criticism	Philosophy	Literary criticism
1963	2	—	—	—
1964	—	—	—	—
1965	—	—	—	—
1966	1	—	—	—
1967	5	2	1	—
1968	5	1	1	2
1969	6	2	1	1
1970	2	4	—	3
1971	1	4	2	1
1972	3	17	—	4
1973	16	13	2	8
1974	5	10	3	7
1975	1	4	1	12
1976	4	—	1	15
1977	2	—	10	10
1978	—	—	8	7
1979	—	—	3	6
1980	—	—	2	22
1981	2	—	—	27
1982	1	—	—	16
1983	1	1	2	26
1984	—	—	3	56

Note: Articles published in specialized journals and literary magazines, reviews and review articles, as well as books. In the case of collected editions, each article is counted as a publication. When the classification of articles by type of journal was impossible, the publications were classified on the basis of (1) the topic of the article and (2) the field of the author, if available. The publications that did not fit in one of the categories were excluded from the sample ($N=51$, including 27 publications published in other countries for the period 1963–78). Belgian publications are included in the French sample, and Canadian publications in the American one. For the period 1963–78, the sample includes all the numbered items of Miller's (1981, pp. 130–166) bibliography, which has been supplemented by Leavey and Allison's (1978) bibliography. For the period 1979–84, data are from the *International Bibliography of Books and Articles on Modern Languages and Literature*, vols. 1, 2, and 4, subsections on deconstructionist literary theory, deconstructionist criticism, poststructuralism, "Derrida" (in categories "subject" and "Literature – 20th Century"). The 1979–84 data are clearly not exhaustive, but sufficient for purposes of the current analysis.

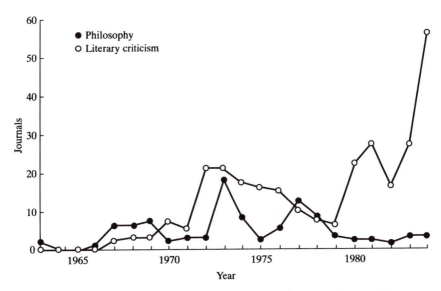

Fig. 1. Publications on Derrida's work by type of journal (philosophy/literary criticism) for France and the United States, 1963–84.

Structuralism in America

The legitimation of Derrida's work was related to the cultural context that predated its importation and that contained conditions favoring its diffusion. New Criticism was among the most influential theories in the field of American literary criticism from the 1940s to the end of the 1950s. In 1957, Northrop Frye published his *Anatomy of Criticism*, launching a powerful attack against the textual emphasis of this approach. In conjunction with other critiques published previously (see Sutton, 1963, pp. 219–267), Frye's critique precipitated a deep crisis in American literary criticism. The extant paradigm was rejected, and new paradigms gained consensus and filled the void. French structuralism was successfully introduced, partly as a response to the vacuum created by the end of New Criticism; it indirectly prepared the ground for the arrival of deconstruction.

An international conference on structuralism was organized at Johns Hopkins in 1966 under the title "The Languages of Criticism and the Sciences of Man" (Macksey and Donato 1970). Many French intellectuals associated with structuralism were invited: Roland Barthes, Jacques Derrida, Serge Doubrovsky, Lucien Goldmann, Jacques Lacan, and Tzvetan Todorov were all present. This was the first large-scale introduction of structuralism to America, and it was followed later that year by the publication of a special issue of *Yale French Studies* on structuralism. However, structuralists did not gain a substantial American following until the beginning of the 1970s, when several books were published introducing structuralism to the American public (e.g., Jameson's *Prison-House of Language*, Boon's *From Symbolism to Structuralism*, and Scholes's *Structuralism in Literature*) (Ruegg 1979). Several further factors favored the diffusion of structuralism in the United States. A limited number that also contributed to the diffusion of deconstruction can be pointed to here: First, comparative literature departments did not have a long intellectual tradition and were in search of a paradigm. French specialists have long enjoyed a high status in comparative literature, which facilitated the spread of their influence. Second, structuralism "epitomized dangerously seductive qualities of style; as intellectual fashion goes, it was flashy, different, ingenious, and slightly exotic" (Ruegg 1979, p. 189). These qualities offered hope of rejuvenation for the traditionally austere and meticulous American literary criticism. Third, some American scholars saw the chance to build their own institutional and intellectual positions by promoting the importation of structuralism, and they organized an impressive number of colloquia. Structuralism was a way for a growing new generation to construct and secure a niche in opposition to older scholars by introducing new theoretical standards. Fourth, like New Criticism itself, structuralism was a *theoretical* approach, and, as such, it could be applied to many kinds of literary products. It constituted a potentially powerful basis of intellectual influence extending across literature departments and bridging the gap between specialists in different periods and national literatures.

The diffusion of deconstruction

Derrida arrived on the American scene in the same period as structuralism. At the Johns Hopkins conference, he presented a vitriolic critique of Lévi-Strauss. The prestige of French literary criticism and of structuralism in particular trickled down to deconstruction, which soon became "*le hip du hip*" as it superseded the trendiest of new theories.

The diffusion of Derrida's work in the United States required the interest of renowned scholars who could incorporate it into their own work, while presenting it to the American audience as something important and worth reading. Paul de Man and J. Hillis Miller attended the Johns Hopkins conference and later became energetic proponents of Derrida's work, as did Harold Bloom and Geoffrey Hartman. They all began to integrate deconstruction into their intellectual agenda and to translate

Derrida's work in terms both accessible and attractive to the larger American audience.

The influence of the Yale Critics on the diffusion of deconstruction is extremely important. Derrida's position in the United States is greatly dependent on this exceptionally strong and concentrated academic support in literature departments. No other French intellectual has as strong an academic base in the United States – for instance, on the average, between 1978 and 1984, twenty-six pieces related to Derrida's work were published in literary journals per year in contrast to fourteen for Foucault. Furthermore, Derrida's support outside literature departments is relatively weak. For instance, his American public is narrower than Foucault's; between 1981 and 1984, on the average, Foucault had 280 citations a year in the *Social Science Citation Index* in contrast to 59 for Derrida, in part because of Foucault's strong support from Marxists in various disciplines. Along with Sartre, Lévi-Strauss, and Barthes, Foucault is more strongly supported by cultural magazines such as *Commentary, New Republic*, the *New Yorker*, and the *New York Review of Books* than Derrida. This suggests that the mechanisms through which Derrida penetrated the French and the American markets differ. In America, professional institutions such as prestigious departments, journals, and associations have been essential. In France, access to the large intellectual public through the cultural media was more important. This illustrates the difference in the structures of the two markets. The general intellectual milieu has more influence on French than on American upper-middle-class culture. In particular high-brow magazines provide the French upper-middle class with the intellectual culture that constitutes an important component of their cultural capital. In contrast, in the United States, intellectual life is not as central to upper-middle-class culture. Thus, cultural capital seems to take expressive rather than cognitive forms and to be expressed through other forms of high culture and through behaviors such as conspicuous consumption, self-reliance, individualism, problem-solving activism, entrepreneurship, and leadership (see, e.g., the analyses of the American middle class by Bellah *et al.* [1985] and Varennes [1977]; see also Lamont and Lareau [1987]).

Derrida's work was largely ignored by American philosophers until the mid-1970s, except for some phenomenologists at Northwestern University for whom his writings offered a new and seductive way of formulating traditional hermeneutic questions. It was only later that it spread to the wider American philosophical public, via Derrida's debate with John Searle in the *New York Review of Books* (1983) and via Richard Rorty's *Philosophy and the Mirror of Nature* (1979). Its reception was necessarily limited because, in the Anglo-American philosophical tradition, the philosophy of language occupies a central place, while phenomenology has been relatively marginal. Moreover, the emphasis that analytic philosophy puts on language is antagonistic to the primary assumption of deconstruction concerning logocentrism. The intellectual operations and style typical of deconstruction are in decided opposition to the ethos of analytic philosophy, which emphasizes precision, clarity of language, and detailed argumentation. The differences between analytic philosophy and deconstruction explain the lesser visibility of Derrida in both American and British philosophy, where its diffusion is also limited by the presence of a strong Marxist tradition. This further demonstrates that cultural environments define and delimit the value and, more important, the scholarly reception of a body of work.

Conclusion

This study has been one step in the development of a grounded structural theory of the process of intellectual legitimation of interpretive theories. I have sought to demonstrate that the legitimation of a theory depends on both the producer's definition of his own work as important and the institutionalization of its importance by peers and the general intellectual public, as well as on a fit between the work and a structured institutional and cultural system. The legitimation of theories results more from a complex environmental interplay than from the intrinsic qualities of theories themselves. Theories cannot thus be considered in isolation, even if they are experienced through their own logic and in their own cultural realm by their producers and consumers.

References

Adatto, Kiku, and Stephen Cole. 1981. "The Functions of Classical Theory in Contemporary Sociological Research: The Case of Max Weber." *Knowledge and Society* 3: 137–162.

Bellah, Robert, Richard Madsen, William W. Sullivan, *et al.* 1985. *Habits of the Heart*. Berkeley and Los Angeles: University of California Press.

Boltanski, Lue. 1975. "Note sur les échanges philosophiques internationaux." *Actes de la recherche en sciences sociales* 5–6: 191–199.

Bourdieu, Pierre. 1969. "Intellectual Field and Creative Project." *Social Science Information* 8(2): 89–119.

   1975. "L'ontologie politique de Martin Heidegger." *Actes de la recherche en sciences sociales* 5–6: 109–156.

   1983. "The Field of Cultural Production, or: The Economic World Reversed." *Poetics* 12: 311–356.

1984. *Distinction: A Social Critique of the Judgement of Taste.* Cambridge, MA: Harvard University Press.

1986. "The Production of Belief: Contribution to an Economy of Symbolic Goods." In Richard Collins *et al.* (eds.), *Media, Culture and Society: A Critical Reader.* Beverly Hills, CA: Sage, pp. 164–193.

Bouveresse, Jacques. 1983. "Why I Am So Very UnFrench." In Alan Montefiore (ed.), *Philosophy in France Today.* Cambridge: Cambridge University Press, pp. 9–34.

Clark, Priscilla P., and Terry N. Clark. 1982. "The Structuralist Sources of French Structuralism." In Ino Rossi (ed.), *Structuralist Sociology.* New York: Columbia University Press, pp. 22–46.

Collège international de philosophie. 1982. *Rapport présenté à Monsieur Jean-Pierre Chevènement, Ministre d'Etat, Ministère de la Recherche et de l'Industrie par François Châtelet, Jacques Derrida, Jean-Pierre Faye et Dominique Lecourt.* Paris.

Debray, Régis. 1979. *Teachers, Writers, Celebrities: The Intellectuals of Modern France.* London: New Left.

Derrida, Jacques. 1963. "Force et signification." *Critique* 15: 483–499.

1981*a* (1972). *Positions.* Chicago: University of Chicago Press.

1981*b* (1972). *Dissemination.* Chicago: University of Chicago Press.

Descombes, Vincent. 1980. *Modern French Philosophy.* Cambridge: Cambridge University Press.

DiMaggio, Paul, and John Mohr. 1985. "Cultural Capital, Educational Attainment and Marital Selection." *American Journal of Sociology* 90: 1231–1261.

Ferry, Luc, and Alain Renaut. 1985. *La Pensée 68, essai sur l'anti-humanisme con-temporain.* Paris: Gallimard.

Finas, Lucette. 1973. "Étude. Jacques Derrida: Le déconstructeur." *Le Monde (des livres)* no. 8838, 14 July, pp. 22–23.

Giovannangeli, Daniel. 1979. *Écriture et répétition: Approches de Derrida.* Paris: Union générale des éditeurs.

GREPH (Groupe de recherche sur l'enseignement de la philosophie). 1977. *Qui a peur de la philosophie?* Paris: Aubier-Flammarion.

Hamon, Herve, and Patrick Rotman. 1981. *Les Intellocrates: Expédition en haute intelligentsia.* Paris: Ramsay.

Heirich, M. 1976. "Cultural Breakthroughs." In Richard A. Peterson (ed.), *The Production of Culture.* Beverly Hills, CA: Sage, pp. 23–40.

Jay, Martin. 1984. *Marxism and Totality.* Berkeley and Los Angeles: University of California Press.

Judt, Tony. 1986. *Marxism and the French Left.* Oxford: Clarendon.

Kurzweil, Edith. 1980. *The Age of Structuralism: Lévi-Strauss to Foucault.* New York: Columbia University Press.

Lamont, Michèle. 1987. "The Influence of Intellectuals on the Production of Culture in France and the United States since WW II." In Alain G. Gagnon (ed.), *The Role of Intellectuals in Liberal Democracies.* New York: Praeger.

Lamont, Michèle, and Annette Lareau. 1987. "Cultural Capital in American Research: Problems and Possibilities." *Working Papers and Proceedings of the Center for Psychosocial Studies*. Chicago: Center for Psychosocial Studies.

Leavey, John, and David B. Allison. 1978. "A Derrida Bibliography." *Research in Phenomenology* 18: 145–160.

Lemert, Charles (ed.), 1981. *French Sociology: Rupture and Renewal since 1968*. New York: Columbia University Press.

Macksey, Richard, and Eugenio Donato. 1970. *The Structuralist Controversy*. Baltimore: Johns Hopkins University Press.

Marceau, Jane. 1977. *Class and Status in France: Economic Change and Social Immobility, 1945–1975*. New York: Oxford University Press.

Miller, J. M. 1981. *French Structuralism: A Multidisciplinary Bibliography*. New York: Garland.

Pinto, Louis. 1981. "Les Affinités électives: Les amis du *Nouvel Observateur* comme 'groupe ouvert.'" *Actes de la recherche en sciences sociales* 36–37: 105–124.

Rorty, Richard. 1979. *Philosophy and the Mirror of Nature*. Princeton: Princeton University Press.

Ruegg, Maria. 1979. "The End(s) of French Style: Structuralism and Post-Structuralism in the American Context." *Criticism* 29(3): 189–216.

Ryan, Michael. 1982. *Marxism and Deconstruction: A Critical Articulation*. Baltimore: Johns Hopkins University Press.

Searle, J. R. 1983. "The Word Turned Upside Down." *New York Review of Books* October 27, pp. 74–78.

Sutton, Walter E. 1963. *Modern American Criticism*. Englewood Cliffs, NJ: Prentice-Hall.

Varennes, Herve. 1977. *Americans Together: Structured Diversity in a Midwestern Town*. New York: Teachers College Press.

Watson, George. 1978. *Modern Literary Thought*. Heidelberg: Carl Winter Universitätsverlag.

Wuthnow, Robert, J. D. Hunter, Albert Bergensen, and Edith Kurzweil. 1984. *Cultural Analysis: The Work of Peter L. Berger, Mary-Douglas, Michel Foucault and Jurgen Habermas*. Boston: Routledge & Kegan Paul.

7

Censorship, audiences, and the Victorian nude*

Nicola Beisel

On November 11, 1887, Anthony Comstock, leader and agent for the New York Society for the Suppression of Vice (NYSSV), entered the Knoedler Gallery on New York's Fifth Avenue and arrested the proprietor, Roland Knoedler, for selling obscenity, specifically, photographic reproductions of female nudes painted by French artists like Bouguereau, Cabanal, Henner, and Lefèbvre (Clapp 1972). This event is notable for several reasons. First, Knoedler's gallery was, and still is, one of New York's leading art galleries. During the nineteenth century, Knoedler's, which was a branch of Goupil's art gallery in Paris, was influential in developing a taste for European Salon art among America's upper class. Several of the prints confiscated by Comstock had been displayed in the Paris Salon, the showcase of the greatest French art. Second, while virtually every New York city newspaper expressed outrage at this act of censorship, Knoedler's arrest was not unprecedented – Comstock had prosecuted numerous dealers of photographic reproductions. The most important precedent was the 1883 conviction of August Muller, a store clerk, for selling photographic reproductions of paintings of nudes, some of which had been displayed in the Paris Salon. On appeal, the New York State Supreme Court and the Court of Appeals upheld the conviction.

The Muller case provoked little commentary, even though the photographs that led to the Muller conviction were the same as those used to indict Knoedler. While Comstock saw the Muller case as a "great victory," the Knoedler case ended quite differently – although two of the thirty-seven pictures that Comstock based his charges on were found obscene by the court, the case was a public relations failure. The public outcry over

---

* First published in 1993 as "Morals versus art: censorship, the politics of interpretation, and the Victorian nude," *American Sociological Review* 58(1): 145–162.

Knoedler's arrest may explain why Comstock abandoned art censorship to pursue other targets for the remainder of the century.

While Comstock is remembered as the quintessential prude ("comstockery" means excessive prudery, particularly in matters of art), his supporters were men at the pinnacle of New York society. Comstock was the leader and agent of the NYSSV, an organization that in its early years arrested pornographers, abortionists, and gamblers. The NYSSV was supported by many members of New York's upper class – over 80 percent of its financial supporters were upper or upper-middle class (Beisel 1990). However, not all of the NYSSV's supporters were antagonistic to art: J. P. Morgan, a founder of the NYSSV, and William E. Dodge, Sr., a generous supporter, were important figures in the history of the Metropolitan Museum of Art (Tompkins 1970).

Knoedler's customers and Comstock's supporters were of the same social class, a fact that challenges prevailing assumptions about censorship. Supporters of modern censorship movements come primarily from the working and lower-middle classes, and sociologists tend to explain such movements as status-group conflicts or defenses of traditional values (Page and Clelland 1978; Wood and Hughes 1984; Zurcher and Kirkpatrick 1976). But the conflict within the upper class represented by the NYSSV's arrest of Knoedler cannot be explained by the status resentments of the lower-middle class. Furthermore, sociologists' focus on the class or status position of participants in censorship movements neglects an essential question: how do participants in a censorship debate construct the meaning of the disputed objects? The conflict over Knoedler's arrest was acrimonious in part because the photographs in question were simultaneously claimed to be "art," signifying the culture and refinement of the upper class, and "obscenity," vehicles of sexual depravity that threatened children's morals. On what basis were these contending meanings imposed on the photographs? Why was one meaning more compelling than another?

Art and the problem of meaning

Most sociologists have neglected the study of censorship, and those who have studied it have usually not focused on conflicts about art (Beisel 1990; Wood and Hughes 1984; Zurcher and Kirkpatrick 1976; for exceptions, see Beisel 1992; Binder 1992). Gans (1974) noted that controversies about art and obscenity tend to arise when "high culture" works are condemned by sexual conservatives who also seek to eliminate pornography, a "low culture" product, from their communities. Gans suggested that the holders of cultural and political power in such communities use controversies about obscenity to bolster their social or political positions, implying that struggles over obscenity in art are covert struggles over class and status.

Dubin (1992), who wrote about controversies over art that erupted in the 1980s and early 1990s, made a similar argument. Dubin argued that censorship emerges when "distinct social cleavages have left individuals estranged from one another" (p. 37), i.e., censorship is the product of intergroup conflict.

The censorship of Knoedler challenges such interpretations. Excepting Comstock, virtually all leaders and most members of the NYSSV were of the same class and status as Knoedler and his clientele (Beisel 1990). Thus, I argue that in the Knoedler controversy the important question is what makes one interpretation of a cultural object more persuasive than another. Cultural sociologists have considered the social construction of the meaning of objects, but have neglected the question of why one interpretation of a cultural object is more compelling than another (Blau 1988; Zolberg 1990). I argue that interpretations of cultural objects gain power by: (1) drawing on cultural schemas that constitute and are constituted by social structures such as family relations and relations between classes, genders, and ethnic groups; and (2) allowing adherents to construct attractive images of themselves.

Constructing compelling interpretations: structure, culture, and identity

Sociologists studying moral reform movements tend to focus on how actors' social positions determine their propensity to participate in such movements. Most studies have concluded that struggles over moral issues emerge to preserve the status group's position against a real or imagined threat. For example, Gusfield (1963) argued that the temperance movement was an attempt by the native-born middle class to assert the superiority of its lifestyle – symbolized by abstinence – to the immigrants' lifestyle. Luker (1984) asserted that abortion controversies are struggles over the meaning of motherhood: pro-choice activists, who have invested in higher education and careers, want to control the timing of reproduction, whereas pro-life activists, who have invested in traditional roles, see career women and abortion as threats that undermine the notion that motherhood is central in women's lives. Thus, both Gusfield and Luker emphasized that the social position of participants in moral battles structures their stands.

Literary critics and sociologists of culture have similarly argued that the meanings readers impose on a text reflect readers' social positions. If cultural schemas from different contexts provide alternative interpretations of

art, how does an individual persuade others of the validity of a new interpretation?

The answer lies not only in what Schudson called rhetorical force, e.g.,
the status of the speaker and the characteristics of the audience, but also in
another aspect of rhetorical appeals – the construction of group and individual identities. Ideologies or cultural schemas reinforce boundaries
between groups, justifying the exclusion of powerless groups from the
social worlds of the powerful. Cultural schemas are thus an essential aspect
of macro-level structures of power (Lamont 1992; Thompson 1990). The
power of interpretations, I argue, is predicated in part on ideologies about
excluded groups. Thus, interpretations of photographic reproductions of
paintings of nudes gained power, in part, from ideologies about consumers
of the photos. This resembles Gusfield's (1981) argument that rhetoric
about the "killer drunk" as a marginal social deviant and a danger to
society gained force by locating the problem drinker at the bottom of the
social class and ethnic hierarchies.

But individuals also use cultural schemas and objects to construct their
personal identities. Shively (1992) found that Native Americans liked a
'Western" film because they identified with the cowboy hero of the film.
Although both Indian and Anglo respondents used aspects of the film to
validate their own ethnic identities, they focused on different character
traits of the cowboy hero. Social movement analysts have argued that
movement leaders must construct an identity for the movement's adherents
(Gamson 1992). Students risked death on Tiananmen Square in part to
fulfill the social role of "intellectuals," but also because they could not
maintain their sense of honor without confronting the violence of the state
(Calhoun 1991). Thus, rhetorical claims are powerful because (1) they
interpret social structures to human actors, and (2) individuals use rhetorical claims to construct a self-image and determine appropriate actions
based on this image.

Identity is relevant to appeals to the powerful as well as appeals to the
powerless. While rhetorical appeals in the Knoedler case referred to images
of socially excluded groups like immigrants and the working class, they also
pointed to competing images of the upper-class art consumers. Thus, the
power of competing interpretations derived not only from images of
groups that the upper class wanted to exclude, but from images of what the
upper class wanted to be. At issue in the Knoedler debate was which interpretation of the photos would prevail: was the Salon nude a symbol of
sophistication and refinement that confirmed the cultural advancement of
Americans, particularly upper-class Americans? Or did the nude incite
sexual arousal and other behaviors that threatened all families and required

eradication? Both interpretations were offered in the Knoedler debate, but the former prevailed. The aesthetic interpretation of the nude succeeded because Comstock's opponents held out the possibility of Europe's scorn if censorship triumphed, while Comstock was unable to convince the public that the photographs threatened their homes. The Knoedler controversy concerned what constitutes art and the meaning of art. Should art be viewed from an aesthetic perspective or a moral perspective? If art is viewed from a moral perspective, what are offending art objects?

The Muller precedent: photographs and social class

Comstock's emphasis on the distinction between photographs and originals, and the sporadic support of the art world for censorship of photographs during the Knoedler controversy, raises the question of whether the definition of "art" was based on characteristics of the object, in this case a photographic reproduction, rather than on the social class of its consumers. My claim that the social class of the viewer was the primary consideration in determining obscenity is strengthened by comparing the press response to Knoedler's arrest with its response in the case of August Muller. The media displayed little interest when Comstock arrested August Muller in 1883 for selling photographs of the same Salon paintings that were targeted in the Knoedler arrest. The *New York Herald*, whose initial headline on the Knoedler case proclaimed Comstock an "autocrat" whose action against Knoedler was an "outrageous abuse of the law," used considerably more sedate language when describing Muller's case. Indeed, the *Herald* did not oppose his conviction. The article announcing Muller's conviction read, "As to Indecency in Art. August Muller Convicted of Selling Improper Photographs. The Paris Salon No Guide for Us" (*New York Herald* Dec. 19, 1883, p. 9). Most coverage of the Muller case did not mention censorship. A brief editorial that appeared in *The World* concerned what social class was competent to determine whether art was obscene. The only issue in the Muller trial that the press deemed controversial was whether art experts would be allowed to testify about whether the photographs were obscenity or art (*New York Herald* Dec. 19, 1883, p. 9; *New York Times* Dec. 18, 1883, p. 8). Judge Brady, who presided in the case, decided that the jury rather than art experts should determine if the photographs were obscene, and forbade expert testimony. *The World* took issue with this decision because of the social class of jury members:

It must be perfectly plain to any man that it is not safe for the owner of a Venus, a Psyche or a Leda to take the opinion of his footman and stable-boy on the worth of his statuary. And it is reasonably certain that a jury in the Court of Oyer and

Terminer can never determine for the community what reproduced works of art
Mr. Anthony Comstock shall have the liberty to destroy. (*The World* Dec. 19, 1883,
p. 4.)

Judge Brady's ruling was appealed through all levels of the New York State
courts and was upheld (*People v. Muller* 1884), but the appeals received no
press coverage. Thus, the Muller case suggests that the press was not particularly outraged when a store clerk from a poor neighborhood was convicted for selling Salon art reproductions – it was the social class of
Knoedler's customers that made his arrest a public sensation.

Interpretation and the problem of artistic authority

Participants in the Knoedler debate cited the social class of the people
viewing pictures of nudes to decide if such pictures were obscene. Both
sides in the debate accepted the ideology that the American art connoisseur
was a genteel person who would not be titillated by artistically portrayed
nudes. In using such rhetoric, Knoedler's defenders and Comstock himself
invoked an image of the upper class as refined, not base. The image of the
cultivated upper-class art consumer appealed to potential elite supporters
of either side of the debate with an implied or explicit contrast with the
unwashed. Knoedler's defenders invoked an image of the upper class as
showing its gentility by bringing culture to the masses. In contrast,
Comstock characterized the upper class as so far above the masses that
their refined culture should be protected from those unable to appreciate
art. In both cases, arguments about art versus obscenity were compelling
because they reflected widely shared beliefs about social classes – upper-
class refinement was contrasted with the unrefined hordes. Comstock predicated his case on the presumed sexual excitability of the masses, which
contrasted with the restraint of the cultured upper class: "Constituted as
society is, with hundreds and thousands who cannot even appreciate the
nude in art at its best, photographs of the nude are a curse to many"
(Comstock 1887, p. 9).

Opponents of censorship invoked another considerably less flattering
image of New York's upper class. While Knoedler and his supporters lured
elite support by invoking the sophistication of the upper class, they warned
that this glow of cosmopolitanism would be tarnished if Comstock were
victorious. Artists in the city cited the supposed cultural superiority of the
French and played freely with the wealthy's fear that they were less refined
than Europeans. By evoking the disdain of French sophisticates, members
of the art world encouraged Americans to adopt French ideologies about
morality in art.

The overriding issue in the Knoedler debate concerned the standards for morality in art. The consensus of the press was that, in Comstock's eyes, nudity was obscenity. This was a tenuous position in a country in which Hiram Power's "The Greek Slave," which depicted a naked and manacled Christian woman being sold into sexual slavery by the Turks, was the country's (and the Metropolitan Museum of Art's) most popular statue, and Bouguereau's nudes were among its most popular paintings. The Fifth Avenue art dealer T. J. Blakeslee explained that "A nude picture . . . might be decent and chaste in its conception and treatment and it might be positively indecent. It behooved Comstock to learn the difference" (*New York Herald* Nov. 13, 1887, p. 4). *The World* wrote that Comstock was "guided entirely in his empiricism by the absence of clothes" (*The World* Nov. 20, 1887, p. 13), and the sculptor St. Gaudens stated that "the decision as to the morality of a work should not be let to a man like Comstock" (*New York Herald* Nov. 15, 1887, p. 4).

Who was, and is, qualified to decide issues of morality in art? The debate over Knoedler's arrest became, in part, a struggle about artistic authority. Artists asserted that they were best qualified to judge whether art was obscene, and the Society of American Artists condemned the arrest. Noting that reproductions of works by some of the foremost living painters were the objects of Comstock's raid, the artists asserted that "the proper representation of the nude . . . is refining and ennobling in its influence." Furthermore, "the popularization of such works of art by photography [is] of the greatest educational benefit to the community." Finally, the artists concluded, "We protest against the actions of the Society for the Suppression of Vice as the work of incompetent persons, calculated to bring into bad repute one of the highest forms of art, and denounce such action as subversive of the best interests of both art and morality" (*The World* Nov. 17, 1887, p. 8).

Newspaper editors and reporters agreed that artists should determine whether art violated morality. The *Evening Post* asserted that the petition from the Society of American Artists, which included leading sculptors and painters, should be honored by "the great number of intelligent people in this city whose cultivation, however advanced it may be in other respects, is deficient in matters involving questions of aesthetics." If questions of morality in art were left to the Society of American Artists, it would exercise a "capable and discriminating censorship" (*Evening Post* Nov. 17, 1887, p. 4).

The NYSSV countered by arguing that art should be judged by moral rather than aesthetic standards, making the NYSSV the best qualified judge. Disdaining the ideal of aestheticism, the leaders of the NYSSV argued that art was beautiful only when it was moral. Furthermore, the promotion of morality created aesthetic pleasure:

The closer art keeps to pure morality the higher its grade. Artistic beauty and immorality are divergent lines. To appeal to the animal in man does not inspire the soul of man with ecstasies of the beautiful. Every canvas which bears a mixture of oil and colors on it is not a work of art. The word "art" is used as an apology for many a daub. (Comstock 1887, p. 6.)

Comstock cited the president of Rutger's College, Merrill E. Gates, who asserted that the "cry of art for art's sake" is made by those who "fail to understand the first principle of all art," that it must suggest "the beauty of holiness" (Comstock 1887, p. 6).

Comstock was angered at his censure by the Society of American Artists, and in response to the claim that public taste was educated by photographic reproductions, Comstock (1887) retorted:

It is said the exposing to public view of the nude figures of women is "an educator of the public mind." It may educate the public mind as to the form of beautiful women, but it creates an appetite for the immoral; its tendency is downward; and it is in many cases a blight to the morals of the young and inexperienced. (p. 9.)

By rejecting aesthetics as the sole criterion for judging art, the NYSSV rejected artists' claims that only artists could determine the morality of art. The Reverend Charles Parkhurst defended the NYSSV against the artists' condemnations: "They can look at a picture that in its very constitution is devilish and nasty, without any sense of the vileness that is in it, being so controlled and mastered by the aesthetical sense, which asserts its absurd authority over all the others" (NYSSV 1888, p. 32).

Parkhurst argued that constant exposure to pictures of nudes had numbed the artists' moral senses. If art should be moral, censors should have a say in artistic content: the leaders of the NYSSV were not qualified art critics but they were qualified moral police. Samuel Colgate, president of the NYSSV, asserted:

It is not Art that is on trial; but Immorality. If the picture is calculated to carry impure ideas, or tends to excite prurient passions, and thus destroy the character of our youth, that picture is condemned, however artistic the work may be. We are not incompetent to judge of the moral quality of the picture, having received a fifteen years education in this work. (NYSSV 1888, p. 28.)

The leaders of the anti-vice society recapitulated a controversy about the nude in art that had raged in elite American periodicals a decade earlier. In 1879, *Appleton's Journal* published an editorial complaining about "certain literary and art folk" who condemned their opponents as "Philistines." The label of Philistinism was virtually assured, *Appleton's* noted, when someone judged a painting by "its motive and story rather than by its *technique*," and particularly when anyone objected to an artistic display of nudity (1879a, p. 183). In a later issue, the editor asserted that artists were particularly incompetent when it came to judging the morality of art – the public could look to artists for education in the principles of art, but it should look to moral experts for standards of artistic morality (*Appleton's Journal* 1879b). The authority of "art folk" was contested on other issues: in 1880, the curator of the Metropolitan Museum of Art, General Di Cesnola, was charged with forging a collection that he had sold to the museum. Although Cesnola was cleared of the charges, the following year the *Art Amateur* printed two articles accusing the trustees of grossly inflating the importance of their collection and their statistics on the number of people who came to see it (Cook 1881a, 1881b). Struggles over artistic authority split New York's cultural elite and adversely affected cultural institutions like the Metropolitan Museum of Art, which throughout the nineteenth century was considered inferior to Boston's Museum of Fine Arts (Jaher 1982). Comstock's censorship, and the arguments he used to justify it, are attributable, in part, to the problem of contested artistic authority.

Interpreting paintings: morality and the French

The central issue in the adoption of French discourses about art was how the American elite would appear in the eyes of Europeans. The Salon origin of Knoedler's photographs was repeatedly cited to threaten supporters of censorship with the scorn of the French. Under the headline "How Paris Will Laugh!" Charles Sedelmeyer, a European collector, noted that men, women, and children from around the world had visited the Salon and admired its art. Parisians would greet the news that American morals were threatened by Salon art with great laughter "at the expense of your institutions here" (*New York Herald* Nov. 13, 1887, p. 4). The curator of the Metropolitan Museum of Art, Di Cesnola, used Knoedler's arrest to deride Americans' artistic knowledge:

It is only another example . . . of a spirit of ignorance and prejudice which I myself have had to contend against for years past in the management of the Metropolitan Museum. It was formerly many times worse than now, but the American public still needs an immense deal of educating in the general principles of art before it will be able, as the most ordinary small shopkeeper in any continental city may, to distinguish between a pure nude and a suggestive nude. (*New York Herald* Nov. 14, 1887, p. 10.)

The scorn of Europe was a potent threat – Americans had often been told that they were deficient in matters of art, particularly by those who wanted to encourage patronage of museums. Elite Americans who wanted to legitimate their social position were particularly vulnerable to the threat of French ridicule, although this threat was somewhat allayed by the stereotype of the French as morally lax (Nead 1988). The *Art Amateur* argued that, although Knoedler's pictures had been displayed in the Paris Salon, this "says little for their decency," and entreated, "Let us hope the Parisian toleration of lewdness under the guise of art will never set the standard of decency in this country" (*Art Amateur* 1888, p. 28). But contempt for the French was far outweighed by admiration for French sophistication: "There is an American variety of vegetable which is indigenous. The *Cabbagensis Comstockius*, or Comstockian cabbage-head, would not thrive in any other soil" (*Evening Telegram* Nov. 15, 1887, p. 2). Although many years would pass before "comstockery" came to denote ludicrous prudery, Comstock and his supporters were clearly under pressure to rebut the claim that they were moral zealots who were ignorant of art and a danger to art.

To show that his own impurity did not cause him to see obscenity where others saw beauty and purity, Comstock borrowed discourses about obscenity in art from the art world, trying, unsuccessfully, to alter their meanings. Comstock's statement that nudity in art might be acceptable in some circumstances highlighted a division among his supporters, some of whom claimed that nudity was inevitably harmful. For example, Comstock argued that nudity might be acceptable, but pictures of nudes that incited sexuality were not; nudity could not be tolerated when "the brow" is "insincere" or "the physical beauty suggests a moral ugliness" (Comstock 1887, p. 7). But one of Comstock's vocal supporters, the Rev. Charles Parkhurst, condemned paintings displayed in the homes of some wealthy families, claiming that the "pictures cultivate the most diabolical animal instincts in the mind of the beholder . . . In them are women stark naked" (NYSSV 1888, p. 33). Comstock was caught in a contradiction: he could not claim, as French and American art experts did, that only paintings of prostitution were unacceptable – his successful prosecution of Muller for selling Salon art showed that his criteria for acceptable art differed from the Salon's. Thus, while Comstock described immorality in art using some of his critics' language, his critics never saw him as a credible judge.

Indictable art: law, children, and censorship

Throughout his crusade against various vices, Comstock cited the need to protect children. To justify art censorship, Comstock (1887) declared that young men might fall prey to prostitutes once they had been aroused by libidinous art. Thus art, rather than symbolizing refinement of the elite, threatened its dissolution.

There is nothing on earth more chaste or beautiful than a modest and chaste woman, unless it be that of innocent childhood, and *that chastity every chivalrous man ought to defend and protect*. The nude in art is a menace upon this chastity. The youth of this country to-day are being cursed by the dissemination of pictures where woman is exposed to vulgar gaze, through the medium of photography and art. There is nothing more repulsive than an unchaste woman; there is nothing more seductive than a beautiful woman. Art has been employed to reproduce and represent all of these characteristics. And when art lends its charms to the seduction of the harlot, the law stretches out its strong arm over the heads of innocent children and says, "You shall not approach these innocent ones to contaminate them." (p. 34.)

Art, Comstock argued, could "fan the flame of secret desires," a particular problem for young men "cursed with secret vices" (Comstock 1887, p. 9). Thus, Comstock relied on arguments against obscenity that had previously gained him the support of the upper class, namely, that the social position of elite children depended on protecting them from debauchery (Beisel 1990).

In his appeals to protect the family, Comstock transposed ideologies about gender and the family to the realm of art. Not only was art a threat to young men of all classes who might respond to nudity with uncontrolled sexual feelings, but such youthful arousal might threaten "respectable" women. Noting that the nude in art "unclothes beautiful women," Comstock argued that such public exposure "is food for impure imaginations, and provokes comment among the evil-minded" (Comstock 1887, p. 10). Thus, Comstock argued that art threatened young men with prostitution, the "social evil," and increased the sexual dangers that women faced in the city (Walkowitz 1992).

Comstock's detractors disputed the significance of the Muller precedent and the presumption that art threatened children. Although Comstock and the NYSSV repeatedly cited the decisions of the New York Supreme Court and Court of Appeals to justify their case against Salon art, the *Evening Post* noted that the higher courts had merely upheld the jury's decision in the Muller case. Thus, the courts had upheld the *procedure* by which Muller was convicted, but did not rule on the pictures themselves. The question remained of whether an "average New York criminal jury" was competent to ascertain the boundary between nudity and obscenity in art, but the *Evening Post* deemed that submitting such a question to a jury was "absurd." Although Comstock fostered the impression that the Court of

Appeals had declared the photographs obscene, the *Post* charged him with exaggerating the legal precedents for censorship (*Evening Post* Nov. 28, 1887, p. 4).

Given that the upper class for years had supported Comstock's crusade against obscenity and accepted his claims about the effects of obscenity on children, why was his argument that art threatened children so ineffective? Comstock lamented the effects of the Knoedler arrest on his organization, noting that even though the NYSSV had been engaged in a fifteen-year crusade against obscenity, it began 1888 with "an empty treasury, a lax support, [and] a questionable sympathy on the part of many good men and women" (Comstock 1888, p. 48). The failure of the elite to support Comstock in the Knoedler case reflects what Knoedler's arrest implied about the culture of the upper class. Although Comstock viewed the arrest as an extension of his crusade against common obscenity and considered Muller's conviction a virtual warrant for Knoedler's arrest, the city's elite had reason to see the Knoedler case as an indictment of their own taste and refinement. Knoedler's arrest represented a dramatic change in the type of people Comstock prosecuted: the crusade against obscenity had been an attack on immigrants and other miscreants, whereas Knoedler could hardly be counted as a member of the menacing masses. In spite of Comstock's assurances that original art in museums was acceptable, when he asserted that he would enforce the obscenity law against rich and poor alike, saying, "Fifth Avenue has no more rights in this respect than Centre street or the Bowery, and the law will be impartially enforced so far as I am an agent in enforcing it," art connoisseurs among his supporters might have feared for their liberty (*The World* Nov. 13, 1887, p. 1). Clement Bowers, a painter, asserted that Comstock, "if left alone . . . will probably take another of his moral fits and walk into the mansions on Fifth Avenue and seize the paintings hung there" (*Evening Telegram* Nov. 16, 1887, p. 1). While Comstock tried to refute the accusation that he was a threat to original works of art, the charge was made more credible by one of Comstock's supporters, the Rev. Dr. Crosby:

Fashionable people buy these pictures because they are nasty. They make a pretence of buying them because of their artistic beauty, but this is all a farce. Fashionable people want to be as nasty as they can and still keep out of prison, and I think that the suppression of all such paintings, or copies of them, is perfectly right, and I hope that all these voluptuous pictures of the last Paris Salon will be among the first to be suppressed. (*Evening Telegram* Nov. 16, 1887, p. 1.)

As Knoedler's brother pointed out, Comstock's supporters owned pictures of nudes – indeed, he claimed, they owned the originals of the pictures

Comstock seized (*Evening Telegram* Nov. 15, 1887, p. 4). While NYSSV supporters were willing to attack pornographers, they certainly were not inclined to view themselves in the same light. During Comstock's campaign against common pornography, ideologies about immigrants and the poor allowed for its construction as a threat to the purity of respectable children. The arrest of Muller for selling cheap photographic reproductions of paintings of nudes in a poor section of the city was a plausible extension of the crusade against the impure. But the arrest of Knoedler, one of the city's leading art dealers, questioned the purity of the upper class itself.

Art and justice: Knoedler in the court

In one sense, Comstock won the Knoedler case – Judge Kilbreth decided that the defendants should be tried for selling obscene material on the basis of two photographs, "Rolla" and "Entre 5 et 6 Heures en Breda Street" (*The Sun* Mar. 24, 1888, p. 1). However, Kilbreth ruled that the other photos, including those used to convict Muller, were not obscene, and he chided Comstock for bringing charges against them, undermining many of Comstock's claims about legal precedent. When Comstock protested that young people might be corrupted by such paintings, Kilbreth retorted: "Oh, the minds of the young haven't anything to do with it . . . If we conduct ourselves only with consideration for the minds of the young we wouldn't do a good many things we do" (*New York Herald* Mar. 24, 1888, p. 3). Comstock won the case, but lost the legal justification for his crusade against art, whereas Knoedler lost the case but won the moral battle; Kilbreth's decision upheld Parisian criteria about morality in art. In Paris, only realistic portrayals of prostitution rendered a painting obscene, and "Entre 5 et 6 Heures en Breda Street" and "Rolla" probably violated this criterion. Although the former painting seems to be lost, Breda Street was the center of Parisian prostitution, so sexual commerce was a likely theme of that painting. Gervex's "Rolla" was thrown out of the 1878 Salon as indecent. The painting depicts Rolla, a debauched son of the bourgeoisie, about to commit suicide after spending his last money on a night of pleasure with Marie, a beautiful young prostitute (Clayson 1991). Although Comstock threatened to again bring charges against dealers who sold the pictures that had convicted Muller, he did not follow through on his threat (*Morning Journal* Mar. 25, 1888, p. 4), and the NYSSV looked elsewhere for things to censor. Its 1889 annual report briefly noted that a man had been arrested for selling pictures in which the faces of "reputable" New York girls were substituted for those of nudes (NYSSV 1889, p. 15), presumably a prosecution the upper class would support. In the years before the turn of the century, Comstock renewed his crusade against gambling, an issue that earlier had garnered considerable support for the anti-vice society because it targeted corrupt immigrant politicians (Beisel 1990).

Discussion: contested meanings and the politics of censorship

I have argued that censorship is a struggle over the meaning of cultural objects. The debate over photographic reproductions of Salon nudes raises the question of what makes claims about the status and meaning of a cultural object compelling. Arguments in the Knoedler debate were compelling because they resonated with cultural schemas underlying relationships between classes, ethnic groups, and genders. A compelling argument, which mobilizes its audience to support or oppose censorship, connects the meaning of an object, like photographic reproductions of art, with these larger social structures and the ideologies that maintain these structures.

Arguments about censorship of Salon art referred to ideologies about the social class of the art's consumers: Claims about the purity or obscenity of paintings of nudes referred not to what was depicted (neither Comstock nor Knoedler gave the titles of the works that had been confiscated), but to the presumed natures of upper-class people versus those of common people. If, as Comstock claimed, the uncultured masses were buying photographs of nude paintings, then the photographs produced lust. Comstock also claimed that children were endangered by the sexual feelings aroused by viewing pictures of nudes, and that these sexual feelings might lead to dissolution, e.g., patronage of prostitutes. Thus, Comstock invoked the need to protect society from the dangerous classes.

Knoedler's defenders also invoked the presumed natures of the people who bought photographic reproductions to claim that the photographs were art, not obscenity. European cultural sophisticates were the consumers of art, rather than dirty-minded denizens of the Bowery, an appeal that resonated with the identities of elite New Yorkers. Knoedler's defenders claimed that Europe's elite would find supporters of censorship ludicrous. This rhetoric implies that the meaning imputed to events or objects invokes the construction of a self and creates claims based on the social order.

My argument contrasts rather sharply with Bourdieu's (1984) argument that actors' social positions determine the meaning imputed to art. Bourdieu's (1984) argument that art objects demarcate class positions and affirm class status has a long history in sociological theory (Goffman 1951; Veblen 1931 [1899]), but his theorizing on the role of cultural markers in processes of social (and class) exclusion was a significant contribution to sociologists' understanding of the reproduction of social inequality.

Bourdieu argued that fields like the arts become sites of symbolic conflict between classes and class fractions seeking to establish the legitimacy (and thus the power) of their cultural symbols (Bourdieu 1984). Clearly the Knoedler case exemplifies such a conflict, but it leads to a reconsideration of Bourdieu's interpretations.

Bourdieu (1989) postulated that cultural knowledge and predispositions are incorporated in a person's habitus, which then defines the meaning and worth of objects at issue in struggles over cultural symbols. The habitus makes actions self-evident to persons engaged in such struggles:

Legitimation of the social world is not, as some believe, the product of a deliberate and purposive action of propaganda or symbolic imposition; it results, rather, from the fact that agents apply to the objective structures of the social world structures of perception and appreciation which are issued out of these very structures and which tend to picture the world as evident. (p. 21.)

Because the habitus is constructed from and reflects the cultural and economic resources that define an individual's place in the social world, the habitus is, in Bourdieu's theory, an internalized means of reproducing classes – it determines the positions taken by classes or class fractions in every social struggle. Through the habitus, individuals see the world in accordance with their positions as defined by their social and economic resources. Their actions, which are based on their vision of the world, unconsciously reproduce the external world that produced their habitus. Thus, according to Bourdieu, ideology and consciousness are structurally determined (Sewell 1992).

The Knoedler case suggests that Bourdieu was mistaken on at least one count: arguments about art are not solely determined by the social positions of persons making them. People in similar social positions (in this case, wealthy New York City men listed in the *Social Register*) held very different opinions about morality and art. Indeed, the different responses to the Muller and Knoedler cases by the press and the elite suggest that individuals can hold contradictory opinions on morality and art – the Knoedler case involved the same photographs that had convicted Muller four years earlier. This seeming aesthetic fickleness raises a central question in the sociology of culture: how do cultural objects acquire meaning? The answer resides in the relationship between social structure, cultural schemas, and the construction of identities.

References

Appleton's Journal. 1879a. "The Nude in Art." No. 32 (Feb.): 183–185.
    1879b. "The Nude in Art Once More." No. 40 (Oct.): 373–376.

Art Amateur. 1888. "My Note Book." 18 (Jan.): 28.

Beisel, Nicola. 1990. "Class, Culture, and Campaigns Against Vice in Three American Cities, 1872–1892." *American Sociological Review* 55: 44–62.

——— 1992. "Constructing a Shifting Moral Boundary: Literature and Obscenity in Nineteenth-Century America." In M. Lamont and M. Fournier (eds.), *Cultivating Differences: Symbolic Boundaries and the Making of Inequality.* Chicago: University of Chicago Press, pp. 104–128.

Binder, Amy. 1992. "Racial Rhetoric and Cultural Frames: The Media Construction of Harm in Heavy Metal Versus Rap Music." Paper presented at the Annual Meeting of the American Sociological Association, Aug. 23, Pittsburgh.

Blau, Judith. 1988. "The Study of the Arts: A Reappraisal." *Annual Review of Sociology* 14: 269–292.

Bourdieu, Pierre. 1984. *Distinction.* Cambridge, MA: Harvard University Press.

——— 1989. "Social Space and Symbolic Power." *Sociological Theory* 7: 14–25.

Calhoun, Craig. 1991. "The Problem of Identity in Collective Action." In J. Huber (ed.), *Macro–Micro Linkages in Sociology.* Newbury Park, CA: Sage Publications, pp. 51–75.

Clapp, Jane. 1972. *Art Censorship: A Chronology of Proscribed and Prescribed Art.* Metuchen, NJ: Scarecrow Press.

Clayson, Hollis. 1991. *Painted Love: Prostitution in French Art of the Impressionist Era.* New Haven: Yale University Press.

Comstock, Anthony. 1887. *Morals Versus Art.* New York: J. S. Ogilvie and Co.

——— 1888. "Indictable Art." *Our Day* 1 (Jan.): 44–48.

Cook, Clarence. 1881a. "Our Mismanaged Museum," pt. 1. *Art Amateur* 5 (July): 24–25.

——— 1881b. "Our Mismanaged Museum," pt. 2. *Art Amateur* 5 (Aug.): 46–47.

Dubin, Steven C. 1992. *Arresting Images. Impolitic Art and Uncivil Actions.* New York: Routledge.

Gamson, William A. 1992. "The Social Psychology of Collective Action." In A. D. Morris and C. M. Mueller (eds.), *Frontiers in Social Movement Theory.* New Haven: Yale University Press, pp. 53–76.

Gans, Herbert J. 1974. *Popular Culture and High Culture.* New York: Basic Books.

Goffman, Erving. 1951. "Symbols of Class Status." *British Journal of Sociology* 2: 294–304.

Gusfield, Joseph. 1963. *Symbolic Crusade.* Urbana: University of Illinois Press.

——— 1981. *The Culture of Public Problems.* Chicago: University of Chicago Press.

Jaher, Frederic Cople. 1982. *The Urban Establishment.* Urbana: University of Illinois Press.

Lamont, Michele. 1992. *Money, Manners, and Morals.* Chicago: University of Chicago Press.

Luker, Kristin. 1984. *Abortion and the Politics of Motherhood.* Berkeley: University of California Press.

Nead, Lynda. 1988. *Myths of Sexuality: Representations of Women in Victorian Britain.* New York: Basil Blackwell.

New York Society for the Suppression of Vice (NYSSV). 1888–1889. *Annual Reports*. New York.

Page, Ann L., and Donald A. Clelland. 1978. "The Kanawa County Textbook Controversy: A Study in the Politics of Lifestyle Concern." *Social Forces* 57: 265–281.

Sewell, William H., Jr. 1992. "A Theory of Structure: Duality, Agency, and Transformation." *American Journal of Sociology* 98: 1–29.

Shively, JoEllen. 1992. "Cowboys and Indians: Perceptions of Western Films Among American Indians and Anglos." *American Sociological Review* 57: 725–734.

Thompson, John B. 1990. *Ideology and Modern Culture*. Stanford: Stanford University Press.

Tompkins, Calvin. 1970. *Merchants and Masterpieces: The Story of the Metropolitan Museum of Art*. New York: E. P. Dutton.

Veblen, Thorstein. 1931 [1899]. *The Theory of the Leisure Class*. New York: Viking Press.

Walkowitz, Judith R. 1992. *City of Dreadful Delight*. Chicago: University of Chicago Press.

Wood, Michael, and Michael Hughes. 1984. "The Moral Basis of Moral Reform: Status Discontent vs. Culture and Socialization as Explanations of Anti-Pornography Social Movement Adherence." *American Sociological Review* 49: 86–99.

Zolberg, Vera. 1990. *Constructing a Sociology of the Arts*. New York: Cambridge University Press.

Zurcher, Louis A., and R. George Kirkpatrick. 1976. *Citizens for Decency: Antipornography Crusades as Status Defense*. Austin: University of Texas Press.

8

The Devil, social change, and Jacobean theatre[*]

Wendy Griswold

Culture orients people. As a shared system of meaning embodied in symbols, culture provides the categories and models human beings use to take their bearings and steer through the exigencies of social and economic life. Where these exigencies themselves are changing rapidly, such bearings take on significant causal force.

The following investigation starts from a cultural puzzle: the rehabilitation of the Devil's techniques. Innovation, calculation, and the seizure of profitable opportunities presented by another person's weakness had long been condemned by the Church as damnable and regarded by the English elite as contemptible. English drama from the medieval through the mid-Renaissance periods portrayed the prevalent theological and social disdain for entrepreneurs bent on the pursuit of money. But these very economic activities, the Devil's techniques, became admirable on the Jacobean London stage. In a remarkable cultural somersault, that which earlier drama had condemned as vicious was now being offered as practical instruction for the ambitious young men who attended the theatres. Culture, in the character of the Gallant, made a social virtue out of an economic necessity.

The genealogy of the Gallant

New cultural forms never simply "arise" from social circumstances. To be comprehended and enjoyed by an audience, they must draw upon a history of recognizable cultural conventions. The City Comedy Gallant was the Jacobean avatar of an old character in Western culture, the Trickster, who

* First published in 1983 as "The Devil's techniques: cultural legitimation and social change," *American Sociological Review* 48(2): 668–680.

had undergone a number of transformations on the English stage while retaining his essential attributes.

The Trickster

The Trickster, a universal figure in folklore (Leach 1950), is the weak character who uses his cunning to triumph over the strong. Tricksters are creatures of their appetites, gastronomic and priapic. They are bundles of contradictions: foolish yet clever; irresponsible yet culture heroes responsible for human existence; greedy, erotic, duplicitous; often unsuccessful yet never wholly defeated; and immensely entertaining. Free, dangerous, and surprising, the Trickster is a rebel against the existing structure of power and an intensely dramatic figure. Playwrights have recognized the usefulness of this archetype and used him in many dramatic contexts, for the Trickster's freedom from determination gives him a universal fascination.

The Devil

The Trickster has assumed many forms in English culture, one being that of the Devil in late medieval religious drama. The conventional role of Satan in English mystery plays was the Trickster archetype adapted for a theatre that was both popular and religious but constrained by traditional Christian theology.

The Satan of the mystery plays was a Trickster, but a dignified one. Performances were sanctioned only for religious festival occasions, and both Church and town authorities saw to it that the guildsmen did not stray far from orthodoxy in their dramatic enthusiasm. This need to adhere to scriptural and traditional accounts of Satan constrained dramatic innovation in his long-established character. The guildsmen did exercise their theatrical fancies in Satan's costuming; he was "monstrously transformed" by elaborate costumes of hair and feathers, horns and blackening. In addition, it was the Devil who ran around the towns prior to the performance of plays, drumming up business (Bakhtin 1968). But the limits of the performed role of the Devil were the limits of the mystery plays themselves. Suitable for occasional, ritual performances by amateurs, their predetermined plots confined the dramatic imagination. The Devil character was, therefore, the not entirely satisfactory solution to a real dramatic problem: how to incorporate the power and appeal of the Trickster into a character whose scope and outcome were absolutely defined, and for whom ultimate victory was theologically precluded.

The Vice

The Trickster was soon to take a more liberated form. By the end of the fourteenth century, dramatic production was no longer limited to religious festivals. Troupes of wandering actors performed morality plays, allegories of a soul torn between the forces of good and evil, in guild halls, noble houses, inns, or wherever an audience might congregate. These players were professionals; they needed to attract an audience from whom they took up a collection, and they did not have to answer to their fellow townsmen in case their productions departed from orthodoxy. Their plays could therefore be far more innovative than the mysteries in having non-Biblical characters personifying virtues and vices, contemporary settings, increasingly topical allusions, and an open concern with stagecraft and entertainment. And the chief entertainer was the Vice.

In early morality plays, there appeared several vices representing some of the deadly sins, such as Covetousness, Lust, or Pride. Later plays, particularly those performed between 1560 and 1575, featured a single, composite character labeled as "the Vice" (Miyajima 1977). The Vice, like the Devil, operated by capitalizing on observed human vulnerability. For example in *Mankind*, Titivillus notices that Mankind is somewhat lazy and weak-willed. He buries a board where Mankind is digging, correctly anticipating that when his shovel hits the unyielding board, Mankind will become discouraged and forsake his labor for jollier pastimes.

The Vice was often presented as apprentice to or son of the Devil, who himself played only a minor role in the morality plays. The Vice tempted men away from virtue, trying to win another soul for Hell. He resembled the Devil in his cunning, his seductive duplicity, and his wickedness. However, the morality play dramatists, familiar with the audience appeal of Satan's Trickster attributes from the mystery cycles, were free to elaborate on these in the Vice's characterization without having to maintain the diabolic dignity of God's chief adversary. Unlike the Devil, the Vice could be first and foremost entertaining. He initiated all of the action. He was bawdy and scurrilous, he sang, danced, and rode on the Devil's back, he distorted language, and he played both buffoon and satirist. He was usually played by the troupe's best actor (Bevington 1962). The Vice appealed directly to the audience during the play, commenting on the action, soliciting their approval as well as their contributions, forcing their participation in the temptation being enacted (Johnson 1970; Jones 1973).

To recapitulate, the Vice and the Devil were both Tricksters in their defiance of authority, their craftiness, and their energy at making mischief. The previously established characterization of the Devil influenced that of the Vice by determining his wickedness, his role as tempter, and his enmity to mankind, none of these moral attributes being necessary to the Trickster archetype. Unconstrained by theology, however, the Vice was less dignified, less powerful, but wittier and more inventive than his dramatic forebearer. He was above all a crowd pleaser. The reasons for this partial transformation were institutional. The morality playwrights were literary intellectuals, generally in the employ of the Church or a wealthy patron. The actors were professionals, depending on the drama for their livings. So the morality plays made unconcealed efforts to win an audience, as the prologue to Fulwell's (1974 [1568]) *Like Will To Like* makes clear:

And because divers men of divers minds be, Some do matters of mirth and pastime require, Other some are delighted with matters of gravity; To please all men is our author's chief desire, Wherefore mirth with measure to sadness is annexed, Desiring that none here at our matter will be perplexed. (Lines 25–30.)

In their desire to please all men, the morality playwrights could go further than their mystery counterparts in emphasizing the Trickster side of the Vice, although some religious constraints still existed.

A change in theatrical production caused the abrupt decline of the morality play. In 1576 the first permanent English playhouse opened in London. Elizabethan statutes against vagabonds had made the status of wandering actors precarious; the permanent theatres, together with the legal fiction of the actors being the servants of a noble household, afforded the companies some security. The consequences of fixed playhouses were immediate. Plays were no longer occasional events, but "buyable pleasures" competing for the consumer's money (Wickham 1981). The repertory of the companies had to consist of a large number of plays appealing to a regular theatre audience. Now, fully professional dramatists, often members of the acting companies themselves or under contract with a single company, were forced to ascertain and cater to the tastes of their audiences (Bentley 1971; Miller 1959; Sheavyn 1967).

These tastes were not confined to religious allegory, no matter how inventive. Social and political themes had been prominent in the late moralities, as the art of dying and *contemptus mundi* had given way to concerns involving a more earthly morality (Spivack 1958). However, this trend towards particularization was ultimately incompatible with allegory. New genres quickly emerged to supply the London audience. One such genre was the City Comedy.

City Comedy Gallants

City Comedies depicted the pursuit of wealth, status, and women in Jacobean London. In a typical plot, a ne'er-do-well young gentleman dupes his older relatives out of money, while lower-class rascals play cruder tricks on respectable citizens. For example, in Thomas Middleton's *A Mad World, My Masters*, Follywit, the Gallant, repeatedly robs his uncle by preying on the old man's hospitality and pride. Meanwhile the wife of a "citizen" (an urban dweller with the city's rights and privileges) and her would-be seducer arrange to put horns on her jealous husband, and a prostitute and her mother (who is also her pimp, a typical manifestation of the genre's cynical attitude towards kinship) contrive to catch Follywit to be the girl's husband. All schemes succeed. Follywit wins both money and forgiveness from his uncle but is himself conned into marrying a bride with a past.

The Gallant is a human offspring of the Vice in City Comedy, one who claims membership among the society of gentlemen. A typical City Comedy Gallant is from an elite background, usually country gentry. He is disinherited or penniless from his own extravagance. Thus he feels dispossessed and outside his accustomed social circle, that of gentlemen. He determines to live off his wits. Usually this means concocting an elaborate scheme to extract money from a tightfisted older man, either a relative or a City usurer. The Gallant is in love, but acquisition dominates eroticism in his motivation: either the woman he loves is wealthy, or he needs money to court her. He succeeds in his schemes, getting the money and the woman. Then, after a half-hearted renunciation of his past follies and deception, supremely unconvincing in that his tricks have been so successful, he is forgiven by his elders. Thus a slightly foolish and more than slightly unscrupulous young man is transformed into a conquering hero of wit and is welcomed back into the community of the elite.

The Gallant was another manifestation of the old archetype, the Trickster. Devils, Vices, and Gallants were homologous in the following respects:

(1) Apparently less powerful than their opponents, they try to overcome resistance and win something from those in a stronger position.
(2) They rely on cunning, devices, tricks.
(3) They have an eye for opportunities, which usually take the form of an observed weakness or vanity of their prey.
(4) They invest time, effort, and often material substance in their enterprises, anticipating a return on the investment.
(5) They are initiators of the action, rather than responders to circumstances. They are typically characterized as restless, active, persistent.

The Gallant completed the Trickster's progressive secularization in English drama, from the theologically controlled Devil, through the semi-religious Vice, to the entirely secular Gallant. More particularly, the Vice, flamboyant entertainer of a previous genre, had a direct influence on the dramatic expression of the Gallant. The Gallant's verbal wit, his delight in his own cleverness, his bravado, his occasional obscenities, his contrived plotting with frequent resorts to disguises and impersonations are all drawn from the pattern set by the Vice. Jacobean dramatists took a proven dramatic convention, the Vice, and modified it for the secular urban theatre.

In one crucial respect, however, the Gallant sharply differed from the Vice: the Gallant was a success and was integrated into elite society. To begin to understand why the playwrights reversed the convention on this outcome, we must consider the theatres in which the Gallant appeared. City Comedies were popular from the late 1590s through the second decade of the seventeenth century. They were written by professional dramatists, men who lacked either patrons or Church offices and who thus depended on their writings for their income. They were usually written for performance in so-called private theatres, although successful plays might migrate to the public theatres (Gibbons 1980). The private theatre audience was of gentler breeding than Shakespeare's audience at the Globe or other public theatres. Dramatists often remarked on the fact that at Paul's, Whitefriars, and Second Blackfriars there was "a good gentle Audience," among whom a visitor would not be "Choakte with the stench of Garlicke" (Harbage 1941, p. 88; cf. Harbage 1952, p. 50). This audience differed from that of the Globe both in social background and in its sense of being a coterie (Harbage 1952). Central to this coterie were the fashionable young men who had come to the city seeking advancement.

The country cadets in London

We have examined the cultural and theatrical background of the Gallant. Now let us turn to his social history. The Gallant was a human, secular Vice, but he was also a dramatic analogue to a large segment of his audience. The real-world counterparts of City Comedy Gallants were cadets, the younger sons of the country elite, who poured into London during the late sixteenth and seventeenth centuries. London grew rapidly in the Elizabethan and early Stuart periods, trebling in population from 70,000 in 1550 to about 200,000 by the turn of the century, and doubling again to 400,000 by 1650 (Finlay 1981, table 3.1). Immigration, not natural increase, accounted for this growth, for the city and suburban death rate generally exceeded its birth rate (Finlay 1981, table A.1). The metropolitan magnet attracted people seeking political, social, and economic opportunities not available in the provinces. Adjacent to the seat of government in Westminster, hub of internal and foreign trade, and legal, financial, professional, and social center of England, London was of a different order of magnitude than even the largest provincial towns (Fisher 1948, 1976). The medieval city had represented freedom (Pirenne 1937), and ambitious youth had long flocked to London to escape feudal bondage and pursue their fortunes. Beginning about 1590, however, a combination of demographic circumstances, customs of inheritance, and a century of inflation made the pressure on the elite cadets especially acute, sending many on the road to London.

The 1570s saw a baby boom in England, and the babies began to come of age by the late 1580s. While historical demographers present a picture of accelerating population increase from the late fifteenth through the early seventeenth centuries (Chambers 1972), at times this increase was stalled. One such period occurred during the 1550s and 1560s, when a series of influenza epidemics plus the plague crisis of 1563 brought the population growth to a temporary halt (Finlay 1981; Fisher 1965). By about 1570, however, the population growth had resumed.

The elite proportion of this cohort was unusually large. The elite had a higher fertility rate than the population at large, due to better health, an earlier age of marriage, and shorter birth intervals (Chambers 1972; Finlay 1981; Hollingsworth 1957; Stone 1966, 1967). In addition, the numbers of families included within the category of gentlemen increased during the late Tudor period. Greater availability of land following the dissolution of the monasteries and the increasing prosperity of landowners during a century of inflation allowed many substantial yeomen and land-purchasing merchants to assert their status as gentlemen during the sixteenth century. Such families were able to solidify their claims with coats of arms, especially from about 1568 onwards when heraldic visitations were taking place (Wagner 1960). Grants of arms were at an all-time high during the 1570s, and almost as high during the following decade (Stone 1967, pp. 38–39; Wagner 1960).

For this swollen cohort of a swollen elite coming of age by the 1590s, customary inheritance practices made the economic position of all but the eldest sons extremely precarious. Primogeniture had been increasingly the practice among the landed groups since the early sixteenth century. In contrast with the custom on the Continent, English primogeniture extended far down on the social scale, through the least of the gentry, and did not necessarily imply some sort of provision for the younger sons (Thirsk 1976). Keeping the estate intact was especially problematic for the lesser and often newer gentry, whose status was less secure in the first place. Thus, as a rule, the eldest son inherited the land. Younger brothers might receive some properties acquired during the lifetime of the father or some small annuity, but often all they got was, as one younger son memorably put it, "that which the catt left on the malt heape" (Wilson 1936 [1600], p. 24).

A German visitor to England in the mid-1580s may have exaggerated the limitations on the younger brothers' options when he noted that "the eldest son inherits all; the others enter into some office or pursue highway robbery" (Von Wedel 1895 [1585], p. 269), but the situation for the cadets was indeed grim. Since the Reformation, there were no longer available monasteries to absorb surplus children. Some made their fortunes in military service, many went to the colonies, but most made their way to London.

What type of economic opportunities awaited the cadets in London? England, it must be remembered, was still a poor country whose economy was heavily dependent on the cloth trade. Certain geographic and social sectors, however, exhibited disproportionate growth during this period. London's burgeoning may have been economically parasitic on the rest of England (Clark and Slack 1976), but nevertheless the city had become by far the largest market for commercial goods. Domestic industries and trading enterprises increasingly concentrated in and around the city, especially in its less regulated liberties and suburbs (Pearl 1961).

There were various ways in which the wealthier members of the elite could take advantage of the city's commercial and industrial growth. They might directly invest in speculative ventures including trading, colonizing, industrial enterprises, or urban development itself (Stone 1957). They could buy a patent or office. By restricting themselves to the roles of directors and risk-takers rather than dirtying their hands with day-to-day management, they could profit while maintaining their aristocratic aloofness from the vulgar aspects of making money. Such enterprises, however, like their rural counterparts of estate development, fens drainage, or mining, required more than "that which the catt left on the malt heape." Younger sons of the elite, without capital, had to enter the world of commercial or industrial opportunity at a level that was both lower and more obvious, giving a greater pointedness to the contradiction between their social backgrounds and their economic activities. Thomas Fuller described the more viable options: the younger brother, "being debarr'd from all hopes of his fathers inheritance, must seek by warre, learning, or merchandize to advance his estate" (1938 [1642], p. 47). The young gallants of London were largely preoccupied with the latter two possibilities.

The cadets' greatest source of opportunity lay in "merchandize." The normal access to commerce or craft was through an apprenticeship. A young man apprenticed himself to a master at about the age of sixteen and served him for seven years or until he was twenty-four, whichever came later, according to the Statute of Artificers (1563). After completing his service, he could join (become "free of") one of London's seventy-odd companies, the most desirable being the twelve Great Companies. Apprentices were numerous, constituting from 13.7 to 17 percent of the city's population in 1600 (Finlay 1981, table 3.7), and they were increasingly from elite backgrounds. In the late fifteenth century, 16 percent of the apprentices of two of the Great Companies (Skinners and Merchant Taylors) came from the gentry (Thrupp 1948, table 21). By the 1630s a comparable Great Company, the Grocers, saw 36 percent of its apprentices coming from elite backgrounds (Smith 1973). The majority of these gentleman apprentices were younger sons.

The second option was learning. In addition to receiving young men down from the universities, London was a major educational center itself. Instruction was to be found at the Merchant Taylors' School, St. Paul's, a wide variety of schools in everything from writing and foreign languages to dancing and astrology, the College of Physicians and Surgeons, the Inns of Chancery, and, most attractive to the elite, the Inns of Court.

Enrollments at the Inns of Court were rising steeply, going from 100 per year around 1550 to 250 by 1600 (Prest 1972). Admissions peaked during the middle years of James I's reign but stayed high until the Civil War. Only 10 percent of the students were Londoners, the rest being part of the metropolitan immigration discussed above. The great majority (89 percent) of the Inns of Court students were gentlemen (Prest 1972, table 4). Some were preparing for a profession in the common law, others were seeking a smattering of education along with an introduction to London society. For the former group, their future professional activities would cover a broader domain than their modern counterparts; lawyers served as accountants, brokers, financiers, entrepreneurs in various projects, and land agents, for much of the growth of the legal profession may be attributed to the active land market of the period. Like the apprentices, the law students were notorious for their rude and occasionally violent behavior, and were criticized for spending so much of their time frequenting the playhouses (Cook 1981; Prest 1972).

At the turn of the century there were 4,000–5,000 apprentices newly bound in London every year (Finlay 1981, p. 67). If roughly 18 percent of them were gentlemen's sons (Smith 1973), then 720–900 elite young men entered the commercial and industrial world at its lowest ranks each year. They, plus some 225 elite entrants at the Inns of Court, constitute most of our young gallants: younger or otherwise financially incapacitated sons forced to come to London and make their fortunes by their wits rather than by their lands.

These law students, apprentices, and a few hopeful hangers-on at Court appear to have had a great deal of leisure time to fill. In addition to promenading around St. Paul's, gambling, frequenting the taverns and ordinaries, patronizing the bear rings and brothels, and listening to sermons, they attended the public and, especially, the private theatres. Contemporary references to the high profile of the young gallants in the theatres abound (Armstrong 1959; Cook 1981). In his sketch of "An Idle Gallant," Earle said that "his business is the street, the Stage, the Court, and those places where a proper man is best shown" (Earle 1933 [1628], p. 46). Thomas Dekker (1952 [1609], pp. 135–136) advised the aspiring gallant on how to display himself advantageously at the theatre: sit right up on the stage; arrive only after the play has begun ("for if you should bestow your person vpon the vulgar, when the belly of the house is but halfe full, your apparell is quite eaten vp, the fashion lost"); "laugh alowd in the middest of the most serious and saddest scene of the terriblest Tragedy"; leave before the play ends while ostentatiously waving to your friends; and above all convey the impression that you have come to the theatre not because of any interest in drama or acting, "but onely as a Gentleman, to spend a foolish houre or two, because you can doe nothing else." Nashe pointed out that it was perfectly reasonable that the gallants should pass their time at the theatres, "whereas the after-noone beeing the idlest time of the day; wherein men that are their owne masters (as Gentlemen of the Court, the Innes of the Courte, and number of Captaines and Souldiers about London), do wholy bestow themselves upon pleasure." After all, attending plays was better than the alternative, "gameing, following of harlots, drinking" (quoted in Cook 1981, pp. 98–99). Even men who were not their own masters slipped off to the theatres, as the constant complaints of merchants and craftsmen about their disappearing apprentices make clear. All this time spent in the theatres was to leave these young gallants with a lasting cultural impression.

Devilish necessities become social virtues

As has been shown, the City Comedy playwrights created the Gallant to solve a professional problem: how to incorporate the dramatic power of the Trickster in a figure that would have the greatest appeal to their particular audience. They took the familiar and successful Vice, made him human, made him a penniless young gentleman in London seeking his fortune, and made him free to enjoy the full economic and social rewards of his cleverness. Note that if the dramatists had simply wanted to entertain the cadets by showing them how to succeed, they might have created a Gallant who overcame economic obstacles through luck, hard work, or innate virtue.

However, because they selected as their model a proven crowd pleaser – the Vice – the Gallant perpetuated the Vice's wit, guile, and economic opportunism. This dramaturgical solution to a cultural problem had unintended consequences, however. It taught the cadets in the audience that economic activism did not do violence to one's social status as a gentleman. In doing so, it provided them with a solution to their very real problem of the conflict between their social status and their economic practices.

Young men from the privileged classes forced to "go into traffic" (i.e., commerce) or otherwise seek their economic advancement encountered social and psychological obstacles. Some of these obstacles had roots in an earlier economic ethos. In the late medieval period, Avarice had challenged Pride as chief among the Deadly Sins. Chasing money distracted one from the only goal worth seeking, the soul's salvation, and engendered an unseemly amount of frantic activity. Seeking profit was still tainted with avarice. Making money was less a worthwhile goal in itself than a pleasant possible side-effect of a certain aristocratic style of life which involved living and investing dangerously.

Going into traffic, however, meant profiting through cunning, calculating another's weakness and seizing the chance to capitalize on it – and these were the Devil's techniques. How were they transformed into respectable entrepreneurial activities? How was a cultural virtue made from this economic necessity?

There were several cultural routes for revaluation of the status of a gentleman engaged in "merchandize." Puritanism was one. Although few sons of the country gentry came from Puritan backgrounds, once in town some may have adopted the urban religion that would have, among other things, dignified their economic activities. We have no indication, however, that any significant number of the young gallants of London adopted Puritanism. It is unlikely that any that did would have been among the coteries at the private theatres, given the Puritan antipathy for the stage.

There was also a gradual change in the definition of what it meant to be a gentleman. During the sixteenth century there had been a de-emphasis on birth in favor of virtue or ability (Kelso 1923), and during the early seventeenth century there was a vigorous, if inconclusive, debate over such things as whether a young man would forfeit his gentle status by undertaking an apprenticeship (Smith 1973). In his much-read guide for *The Compleat Gentleman*, Henry Peacham (1906 [1622], pp. 11–12) demonstrates the new open-mindedness on the question:

the exercise of Merchandize hath beene (I confesse) accounted base, and much derogating from Nobility . . . [and yet] I cannot . . . but account the honest Merchant among the number of Benefactors to his Countrey.

For the cadets, however, the stage was the most immediate cultural arena for the revaluation of economic pursuits. City Comedies legitimated economic acquisition by taking a familiar cultural convention, the Trickster archetype, and giving it a new twist. Instead of remaining outside the social and moral pale, the Trickster-as-Gallant ends up an insider. His devious activities were not presented as ultimately vicious, but acceptable and even heroic. The Gallant mediated between the culture of the country elite and that of the city merchant. He made it possible for the gallants in his audience to see that they might undertake the economic activities of the latter without losing the social status of the former.

How does such cultural legitimation take place? Legitimation, rooted in the Latin word for law, means making something fit a pattern, rule, or order. If the something is not in accordance with a larger, external structure of meaning, it is illegitimate; it represents discord, dirt, danger (Douglas 1966). Human beings seek to reconcile their behavior with some larger pattern in order to give it meaning.

In order for a system of meaning to have the leverage to legitimate action, it must be, or must appear to be, external to the system of action. In Max Weber's classic examples (1958 [1904–05], 1964 [1922]), it is because religious systems are other than everyday economic behavior that the former can legitimate the latter. Religion is not the only source of legitimation. Cultural texts appear in many institutional settings. Societies have basic texts (the Magna Charta, the Constitution) which are primordial, attended by myth, and whose socially celebrated origins are not regarded as simply emanating from interest. Such texts become the sources and criteria of legitimacy. Unwritten texts such as tradition serve the same function. Literary or artistic texts, by their removal from the utilitarian, their otherness, allow for the expression of ideas not conventionally accepted in daily social life. A text – religious, traditional, constitutional, or literary – is a structure according to which homologous behavior in the world of human activity may be viewed. If widely received, such texts legitimate behavior by making it explicable, unsurprising, by fitting it to a recognized pattern of actions and outcomes.

Popular City Comedies legitimated the Devil's techniques for the non-Puritan younger sons of the country elite. They presented texts in which characters readily identifiable with a segment of their audience, the ambitious young men, operated in ways that had previously been regarded as illegitimate, involving hustling, guile, and the single-minded pursuit of profits. However, whereas other representations of such behavior were theologically damned and ultimately reprehensible (the Devil, the Vice), or were pointedly not integrated into the social order (the thieves and usurers of City Comedy), the Gallant is both successful and integrated. Identification, anticipated outcome, and social integration are the mechanisms whereby a cultural text legitimates behavior.

Like all cultural symbols, the Gallant was, to borrow Geertz's (1973) felicitous terms, both gloss and template. He was a product of cultural history and theatrical practice in a society undergoing social change. He displayed to his audience the economic and social rewards that might accrue to enterprising economic behavior, thereby facilitating a change in attitudes towards such behavior. The City Comedy dramatists, themselves entrepreneurs, reconstructed an old, dramatically powerful cultural figure, the Trickster. They legitimated the Devil's techniques for a particular audience having particular concerns. They profited thereby, as innovators often do. In their professional need to write plays having audience appeal, however, they delineated the attractive and cunning, Gallant, always looking out for "number one," who made respectable the acquisitive entrepreneurial activities suitable for early commercial capitalism.

References

Armstrong, William A. 1959. "The Audience of the Elizabethan Private Theaters." *Review of English Studies*, n.s., 10: 234–249.

Bakhtin, Mikhail. 1968. *Rabelais and His World*, trans. Helene Iswolsky. Cambridge, MA: MIT Press.

Bentley, Gerald Eades. 1971. *The Profession of Dramatist in Shakespeare's Time, 1590–1642*. Princeton: Princeton University Press.

Bevington, David M. 1962. *From "Mankind" to Marlowe: Growth of Structure in the Popular Drama in Tudor England*. Cambridge, MA: Harvard University Press.

Chambers, J. D. 1972. *Population, Economy, and Society in Pre-Industrial England*, ed. W. A. Armstrong. London: Oxford University Press.

Clark, Peter, and Paul Slack. 1976. *English Towns in Transition, 1500–1700*. London: Oxford University Press.

Cook, Ann Jennalie. 1981. *The Privileged Playgoers of Shakespeare's London, 1576–1642*. Princeton: Princeton University Press.

Dekker, Thomas. 1952 [1609]. "The Gull's Hornbook." In A. M. Nagler (ed.), *A Source Book in Theatrical History*. New York: Dover, pp. 133–138.

Douglas, Mary. 1966. *Purity and Danger. An Analysis of the Concepts of Pollution and Taboo*. London: Routledge & Kegan Paul.

Earle, John. 1933 [1628]. *Microcosmography*, ed. Harold Osborne. London: University Tutorial Press.

Finlay, Roger. 1981. *Population and Metropolis: The Demography of London, 1580–1650*. Cambridge: Cambridge University Press.

Fisher, F. J. 1948. "The Development of London as a Centre of Conspicuous Consumption." *Transactions of the Royal Historical Society*, 4th ser., 30: 37–50.

1965. "Influenza and Inflation in Tudor England." *Economic History Review* 18: 120–129.

1976. "London as an 'Engine of Economic Growth.'" In Peter Clark (ed.), *The Early Modern Town*. London: Longman, pp. 205–215.

Fuller, Thomas. 1938 [1642]. *The Holy State and the Profane State*, ed. Maxmilian Graf Walten, 2 vols. New York: Columbia University Press.

Fulwell, Ulpian. 1974 [1568]. "Like Will to Like." In J. A. B. Somerset (ed.), *Four Tudor Interludes*. London: Athlone Press, pp. 128–164.

Geertz, Clifford. 1973. *The Interpretation of Cultures*. New York: Basic.

Gibbons, Brian. 1980. *Jacobean City Comedy*, 2nd. edn. London: Methuen.

Harbage, Alfred. 1941. *Shakespeare's Audience*. New York: Columbia University Press.

1952. *Shakespeare and the Rival Traditions*. New York: Macmillan.

Hardison, O. B., Jr. 1965. *Christian Rite and Christian Drama in the Middle Ages*. Baltimore: Johns Hopkins University Press.

Hollingsworth, T. H. 1957. "A Demographic Study of British Ducal Families." *Population Studies* 11: 4–26.

Johnson, Robert Carl. 1970. "Audience Involvement in the Tudor Interlude." *Theatre Notebook* 24: 101–111.

Jones, Robert C. 1973. "Dangerous Sport: The Audience's Engagement with Vice in the Moral Interludes." *Renaissance Drama*, n.s., 6: 45–64.

Kelso, Ruth. 1923. *The Institution of the Gentleman in English Literature of the Sixteenth Century*. Urbana: University of Illinois Press.

Leach, Marian. 1950. *Standard Dictionary of Folklore, Mythology, and Legend*. New York: Funk & Wagnalls.

Miller, Edwin. 1959. *The Professional Writer in Elizabethan England*. Cambridge, MA: Harvard University Press.

Miyajima, Sumiko. 1977. *The Theatre of Man: Dramatic Technique and Stagecraft in the English Mystery Plays*. Clevedon, Avon: Clevedon Printing Co.

Peacham, Henry. 1906 [1622]. *Peacham's Compleat Gentleman* (1634), ed. G. S. Gordon. Oxford: Clarendon Press.

Pearl, Valerie. 1961. *London and the Outbreak of the Puritan Revolution*. London: Oxford University Press.

Pirenne, Henri. 1937. *Economic and Social History of Medieval Europe*. New York: Harcourt, Brace.

Prest, Wilfred R. 1972. *The Inns of Court Under Elizabeth I and the Early Stuarts, 1590–1640*. London: Longmans.

Sheavyn, Phoebe. 1967. *The Literary Profession in the Elizabethan Age*, 2nd. edn., rev. by J. W. Saunders. Manchester: Manchester University Press.

Smith, Steven R. 1973. "The Social and Geographical Origins of the London Apprentices, 1630–1660." *The Guildhall Miscellany* 4: 196–206.

Spivack, Bernard. 1958. *Shakespeare and the Allegory of Evil*. New York: Columbia University Press.

Stone, Lawrence. 1957. "The Nobility in Business, 1540–1640." In M. M. Postan and H. J. Habakkuk (eds.), *The Entrepreneur*. Cambridge, MA: Research Center in Entrepreneurial History, Harvard University, pp. 14–21.

1966. "Social Mobility in England, 1500–1700." *Past and Present* 33: 16–55.

1967. *The Crisis of the Aristocracy, 1558–1641*. London: Oxford University Press.

Thirsk, Joan. 1976. "The European Debate on Customs of Inheritance, 1500–1700." In Jack Goody, Joan Thirsk, E. P. Thompson (eds.), *Family and Inheritance: Rural Society in Western Europe, 1200–1800*. Cambridge: Cambridge University Press, pp. 177–191.

Thrupp, Sylvia L. 1948. *The Merchant Class of Medieval London*. Ann Arbor: University of Michigan Press.

Turner, Victor W. 1968. "Myth and Symbol." *International Encyclopedia of the Social Sciences* 10: 576–582.

Von Wedel, Lupold. 1895 [1585]. "Journey Through England and Scotland Made by Lupold Von Wedel in the Years 1584 and 1585," trans. Gottfried von Bulow. *Transactions of the Royal Historical Society*, n.s., 9: 223–270.

Wagner, Anthony Richard. 1960. *English Genealogy*. Oxford: Clarendon Press.

Weber, Max. 1958 [1904–05]. *The Protestant Ethic and the Spirit of Capitalism*, trans. Talcott Parsons. New York: Scribner's.

1964 [1922]. *The Sociology of Religion*, trans. Ephraim Fischoff. Boston: Beacon.

Wickham, Glynne. 1981. *Plays and Their Makers to 1576. Early English Stages 1300–1660*, vol. III. London: Routledge & Kegan Paul; New York: Columbia University Press.

Wilson, Sir Thomas. 1936 [1600]. "The State of England (1600)," ed. F. J. Fisher. *Camden Miscellany*, 16; Camden 3rd ser. 52: 1–47.

9

Victorian women writers and the prestige of the novel[*]

Gaye Tuchman and Nina Fortin

> To account for the complete lack not only of good women writers but also
> of bad women writers I can conceive no other reason unless it be that there
> was some external restraint upon their powers.   Virginia Woolf

Students of women's participation in the arts have persuasively argued that
the relative dearth of famous women writers and artists results from the historical structure of opportunities – or more accurately, lack of them. For
instance, until recently, women writers, artists, and composers had less
formal education and training than their male counterparts. Except for the
daughters of families in the arts, as well as some of the social elite, women
were frequently excluded from the social networks central to cultural
milieus (Showalter 1977; Tuchman 1975). But the structure of opportunity
is not merely a matter of training and association with others intent on
learning and creating an art. It also results from the esteem or prestige
accorded a genre, which is in turn strongly influenced by socio-economic
developments and institutional configurations.

The purpose of this chapter is to suggest that the growing prestige of the
novel in England in the Victorian period was one of the factors limiting the
opportunities for women to have their work seriously considered and to
achieve fame. Our procedure is to examine the fate of manuscripts that
women and men submitted to one publishing house, Macmillan and
Company in London, between November 1866 and December 1887.

We have analyzed our data, not qualitatively, but statistically. By so
doing, we hope both to reveal patterns that might otherwise remain hidden
and to show some of the possibilities of a sociological approach to literary

[*] First published in 1980 as "Edging women out: some suggestions about the structure of
opportunities and the Victorian novel," *Signs* 6(2): 308–325.

history. We propose that the Victorian novel displays the "empty-field phenomenon." That is, when a field or occupation is not socially valued, women and other minorities will populate it heavily. If the field grows in prestige, (white) men may push women (and other minorities) out. Conversely, as a field loses social value, when "proletarianization" occurs, (white) men may decamp and leave the field to women (and other minorities). The transformation of the once honored title of secretary, in the late nineteenth century, is a case in point (Benet 1973; Rothman 1978).

Although men – Defoe, Richardson, Fielding, Smollett, Sterne – are credited with "inventing" the novel, the genre was frequently and traditionally associated with women. A high proportion of novel readers were women. Anonymous married ladies who wrote novels probably constituted a significant proportion of fiction authors – although publishing practices prevent determination of even the number of books published, let alone the proportion of women authors.

By the 1840s, a commonplace of cultural history now says, the novel was becoming a serious form. By the mid-1880s the novel dominated the publishing industry. As Colby notes, "In the year 1886 more novels were published in England than any other single category of new books, significantly outdistancing even books on religion" (Colby 1970).

The years between 1840 and 1890 also saw the slow transformation of the publishing industry into its modern form. Moreover, these same years marked the professionalization of writing. If Sir Walter Scott had been unwilling to identify himself as a professional, in the 1850s Dickens tried to organize writers into a quasi-professional society. Although his failure suggests that the aim was premature, in 1883 Sir Walter Besant successfully formed the Society of Authors, which monitored copyright laws, encouraged the use of royalties (as opposed to sale of copyright), and tried to devise a retirement plan. This later period also saw the introduction of literary agents to place manuscripts and to protect authors' rights. Our exploration of the gender dynamics of the field of the Victorian novel is set within this wider context of professionalization and improving status.

Data, methods, and results

The Macmillan Archives at the British Museum contain a series of ledgers, beginning in November 1866, and ending in 1935, which record the submission and disposition of manuscripts. A separate series of copybooks contains transcriptions of most of the readers' reports from 1866 to 1887. Particularly rich data, these records allow identification of authors' gender in all but 8 percent of the cases. Readers' comments enable positive determination of genre; and when such comments are not available, the manuscript's title frequently announces that. All in all, we feel confident of over 90 percent of our determinations of genre. For the sake of rigor, discussions are based only on the 1,015 manuscripts about whose classifications we are confident. Determining the disposition of manuscripts was straightforward: we checked both ledgers and copybooks. In addition, the reader's reports facilitated development of a fourth variable – seriousness of consideration. Manuscripts receiving a long report were more likely to have been taken seriously than those receiving a short one. We used the length of the reader's review as an indicator of "seriousness of consideration," and characterized any review of fifteen lines or less as "short," those with sixteen or more lines as "long." Of course, "serious consideration" refers only to those manuscripts sent to a reader, since many were decided upon without the use of readers.

Rather than include every manuscript submitted between November 1866 and 1890 in our analysis, we sampled in roughly ten-year periods. Fearing that Macmillan's over 95 percent rejection rate for fiction would yield too few published novels in years with fewer submissions and so might obfuscate the very patterns we sought to determine, we sampled in temporal "chunks." The three periods selected were: November 1866–December 1868 (a total of 248 manuscripts of which 38 were accepted for publication), 1877–78 (407 manuscripts, 73 accepted), and 1887 (360 manuscripts, 59 accepted).

Despite Macmillan's preference for nonfiction, fiction manuscripts constituted an increasing proportion of the manuscripts submitted between 1867 and 1887. As the novel attains more prestige, more people try their hand at it and it is taken more seriously. Our data on the number of lines devoted by Macmillan's readers to reviews of fiction manuscripts indicate a significant increase in the seriousness with which fiction was considered relative to nonfiction and poetry. In the late 1860s, about 17 percent of the manuscripts receiving a long review were fiction; in 1887 that figure had risen to 51 percent. As the changes captured in tables 1 and 2 occur, the novel also begins to display characteristics of the empty-field phenomenon.

In each of the three periods sampled, the proportion of all manuscripts that were submitted by women remains constant at roughly 30 percent, and the proportion of nonfiction submitted by women holds at roughly 15 percent. However, the picture for fiction is quite different. As writing novels became more prestigious, men increasingly submitted fiction (see table 3). To be sure, women mainly submitted fiction in each decade, and the proportion of their manuscripts that were fiction also steadily grew – from 62 percent in the late 1860s to 72 percent in 1887. But the proportion of men's

Table 1. *Disposition of fiction and nonfiction manuscripts in the initial stage of processing in selected years (percent)*

	Late 1860s		1877–78		1887		All years		
	Fiction (79)	Non-fiction (125)	Fiction (126)	Non-fiction (252)	Fiction (161)	Non-fiction (171)	Fiction (366)	Non-fiction (548)	N (914)
Immediately accepted	0	7.2	0.8	22.6	0.6	16.9	0.6	17.3	97
Immediately rejected	24.1	36.0	37.3	48.0	14.3	21.1	24.3	36.9	291
Sent to reader	75.9	56.8	61.9	29.4	85.1	61.9	75.1	45.8	526

Note: For ease of presentation, manuscripts whose disposition is unknown and poetry manuscripts are excluded from this table; all columns total 100 percent; numbers in parentheses = N.

Table 2. *Distribution of all manuscripts receiving a long review and of all manuscripts submitted by genre in selected years (percent)*

Genre	Late 1860s		1877–78		1887		All years			
	Long review (30)	Sub-mitted (246)	Long review (36)	Sub-mitted (406)	Long review (59)	Sub-mitted (358)	Long review (125)	N (125)	Sub-mitted (125)	N (1,010)
Fiction	16.7	34.1	38.9	31.5	50.8	45.0	39.2	49	36.9	373
Nonfiction	73.3	54.9	61.0	63.5	45.8	49.7	56.8	71	56.6	571
Poetry	10.0	10.9	0.0	4.9	3.4	5.3	4.0	5	6.5	66

Note: Numbers in parentheses = N.

Table 3. *Proportion of manuscripts submitted by men and women that were fiction in selected years (percent)*

	Late 1860s	1877–78	1887
Men	18.4	12.6	30.4
	(152)	(253)	(224)
Women	61.5	64.1	71.7
	(78)	(131)	(106)

Note: The data in both this table and table 4 are arranged in what is called a partial percentage format. The numbers in parentheses represent the bases upon which the percentages are calculated. E.g., in the late 1860s, of the 152 manuscripts submitted by men, twenty-eight or 18.4 percent of them were fiction. This format allows for the comparison of data in both directions (i.e., across the rows and down the columns); $N=944$.

fiction submissions rose even more, by 65 percent. The increase for women, in contrast, was 16 percent. Indeed, as previously noted, the rise in fiction submissions by men was so marked that although women accounted for almost two-thirds (63.2 percent) of the fiction authors in the late 1860s, by 1887 they constituted only slightly more than half (52.8 percent).

As table 4 indicates, the readers' reports strongly suggest that by 1887, fiction manuscripts submitted by men were given more serious consideration than they received in the late 1860s, and in 1887, male authors were considerably more likely than their female counterparts to receive a long report. Taken together, tables 3 and 4 demonstrate that women did not fare as well once the competition from men had grown. Less educated, women may have submitted more dross. Less integrated into cultural milieus, a smaller percentage of aspiring female authors may have had connections to Macmillan and the members of its circle. Most likely, both factors operated simultaneously to produce the patterns in our data (although one or the other factor may have governed the disposition of any individual case).

In both fiction and nonfiction, women fared better in the late 1860s than in 1887. Table 5 traces the rejection of fiction submitted by men and women

Table 4. *Length of reader's report of fiction manuscripts submitted by men and women in selected years (percentage receiving long report)*

	Late 1860s	1877–78	1887
Men	9.5	23.5	42.1
	(21)	(17)	(57)
Women	9.7	20.8	10.5
	(31)	(48)	(57)

Note: See table 3 for an explanation of this format. Also, note that the numbers in parentheses represent the total number of manuscripts receiving at least one line of review. E.g., in the 1860s, twenty-one manuscripts by men received at least one line of review from a reader, and two or 9.5 percent received a review of sixteen or more lines; $N=231$.

through each of the stages of manuscript processing. Although, in the 1866–68 period, a higher proportion of women's fiction was initially rejected and a lower proportion of their novels sent on to readers, the readers favor their work. Ultimately women fare well in this period, even better than men. In 1887, in contrast, women's novels remain less likely to be sent to a reader, and now women and men are roughly equally likely to have their fiction rejected. In sum, the position of men has improved.

Our preliminary analyses of data for 1897, 1907, and 1917 indicated that 1887 may be a benchmark in the process of edging women out: through 1907 women and men have roughly similar final rejection rates, even though the proportion of novels submitted by men decreases in 1907. In 1917, the proportion of fiction submitted by women far outstrips that by men, but Macmillan is more apt to publish men's novels, just as it accepts a higher proportion of nonfiction by men.

The results of this study must be treated with some caution. Our findings refer to the activities of only one publishing house over a twenty-year period. Macmillan's was an atypical firm. Similarly, the story we have told in tables is more suggestive than definitive. However, it meshes with both sociological and historical accounts of the development of the novel, as does our present attempt to continue the story through World War I. Like

Table 5. *Disposition of men's and women's fiction manuscripts: formal stages of the review process in selected years* (*percent*)

	Late 1860s		1877–78		1887		All years		
	Men	Women	Men	Women	Men	Women	Men	Women	N
Disposition at initial stage:									
Accepted	0	0	0	1.2	0	1.3	0	1.0	2
Rejected	14.3	28.3	45.2	35.4	6.1	19.7	17.7	27.9	79
Sent to reader	85.7	71.7	54.8	63.4	93.8	78.9	82.3	71.1	247
Total	100	100	100	100	100	100	100	100	—
	(28)	(46)	(31)	(82)	(65)	(76)	(124)	(204)	(328)
Disposition after review by reader:									
Accepted	4.2	16.7	0	5.8	6.6	5.0	4.9	6.9	15
Rejected	95.8	87.9	100	94.2	93.4	95.0	95.1	93.1	232
Total	100	100	100	100	100	100	100	100	—
	(24)	(33)	(17)	(52)	(61)	(60)	(102)	(145)	(247)
Summary: percentage rejected	96.4	91.3	100	95.1	93.8	94.7	95.9	94.1	94.8
	(28)	(46)	(31)	(82)	(65)	(76)	(124)	(204)	(328)

Note: Numbers in parentheses= N.

non-quantitative accounts, our findings indicate that between 1866 and 1887, the novel was taken increasingly seriously. As it became more prestigious, and as the split between high culture and popular novels became clearer, the work of apparently mediocre men was given greater consideration than that of apparently mediocre women.

These findings have several implications. First, literary historians have tended to assume that as educational opportunities for women increased, women's participation in literature grew. Such statements are based upon contemporaries' sense of increased numbers and statements about published authors. For instance, Gettmann tells us, "In the 'thirties and 'forties approximately 20 percent of the books published by the House of Bentley were by women whereas in the 'seventies and 'eighties the proportion was more than doubled." Bentley's had a varied list, but it was particularly strong in women novelists. If we examine only the novels Macmillan published in 1887, the results are in line: of the nine works we are sure were novels and whose authors we could positively identify, five were by women.

Yet, analysis of patterns in the submission and processing of fiction manuscripts between 1866 and 1887 tells quite a different story about women's participation in literature relative to that of men: women remained a constant proportion of those submitting book-length manuscripts but a decreasing proportion of those sending fiction. Moreover, women's manuscripts were less likely than men's to be sent on to one of the firm's readers, and the likelihood of a woman's fiction manuscript being rejected increased relative to that of a man's. The historians are correct in stating that women's position in literature shifted during the nineteenth century, but, at least between 1866 and 1887, our data document a shift in a direction opposite to that which has been previously maintained.

Second, our data indicate that the Victorian novel displayed the empty-field phenomenon, found in other periods and in other countries in the higher reaches of social work, gynecology, and preventive medicine. Generally, men have "invaded" occupations that have been in the process of developing into professions – and have abandoned positions being proletarianized. Additional work on the relationship between these processes and women's labor force participation is vital. Finally, we have added another dimension to the increasing research on women's opportunities to be writers. The structure of opportunities is not solely determined by the social and class position of individual women but also by the relative prestige of the genre in which women work. We find an inverse relationship between that prestige and the chance for women to participate successfully in it.

Ultimately, one may argue that quality will out. However, crucial social variables, such as reputation and formal and informal connections, may influence the chance that quality will be recognized. Our data do not speak directly to this point, since we can never know the quality of rejected manuscripts, or even whether those ultimately published by another firm had been extensively revised before their eventual acceptance. We can merely conclude that, since women were at least partially edged from a chance at novelistic fame at precisely the time when educational opportunities were opening for them, the prestige of a genre and the organization of a field are much more important than previously assumed. Indeed, they may constitute a kind of "external restraint" upon the powers of women.

References

Benet, Mary. 1973. *The Secretarial Ghetto*. New York: McGraw-Hill.

Colby, Vineta. 1970. *The Singular Anomaly: Women Novelists of the Nineteenth Century*. New York: New York University Press.

Rothman, Sheila. 1978. *Women's Proper Place*. New York: Basic Books.

Showalter, Elaine. 1977. *A Literature of Their Own: British Women Novelists From Bronte to Lessing*. Princeton: Princeton University Press.

Tuchman, Gaye. 1975. "Women and the Creation of Culture." In Marcia Millman and Rosabeth Moss Kanter (eds.), *Another Voice: Feminist Perspectives on Social Life and Social Science*. Garden City, NY: Anchor Doubleday.

10

The ambiguous and contested meanings of the Vietnam Veterans Memorial*

Robin Wagner-Pacifici and Barry Schwartz

In this chapter, we address two problems, one general and one particular, and claim that they are best approached by referring each to the other. The first, general, problem is that of discovering the processes by which culture and cultural meaning are produced. Collective memory, moral and political entrepreneurship, dominant ideologies, and representational genres are all refracted through these processes and must all be sociologically identified and gauged. The second, particular, problem is the Vietnam Veterans Memorial. This unusual monument grew out of a delayed realization that some public symbol was needed to recognize the men and women who died in the Vietnam War. But its makers faced a task for which American history furnished no precedent – the task of commemorating a divisive defeat.

Dedication

On November 11, 1982, seven years after the last American died in Vietnam, the Vietnam Veterans Memorial was dedicated. Immediately before the dedication ceremony, 150,000 spectators watched and applauded as 15,000 veterans passed before them. Elaborate floats and flyovers by fighter planes and helicopters embellished the three-hour parade. The more solemn aspects of this colorful Veterans Day had been established by the reading out of the names of all 57,939 Americans killed in Vietnam in an earlier fifty-six-hour candlelight vigil at the National Cathedral. The President of the United States participated in the observance, lighting a candle for the dead and listening to part of the long roster of names.

From the very beginning of these commemorative rites, the themes of

* First published in 1991 as "The Vietnam Veterans Memorial: commemorating a difficult past," *American Journal of Sociology* 97(2): 376–420.

recovery and solidarity were repeated. The motto of the Veterans Day parade, "Marching Along Together," reflected these themes and prefaced the dedication day invocation: "Let the Memorial begin the healing process and forever stand as a symbol of our national unity." The rhetoric, however, expressed an ideal, not a reality. If official spokesmen defined the Memorial as a way "to unite our beloved America with her bravest and best," the bravest and best were inclined to ask what took so long. As one veteran put it: "They should have had this when we first came back in 1971." Secretary of Defense Casper Weinberger conceded the delay, but added, "We have finally come to appreciate your sacrifice." Likewise, President Reagan announced that everyone was now "beginning to appreciate that they were fighting for a just cause," as he contemplated the list of those who died for it.

Many people disagreed with the President's assessment. The dedication ceremony itself began with words of contrition rather than unequivocal appreciation: "We ask for grace to face our past." And at the solemn wreath-laying ceremony – the emotional highpoint of the dedication – a bitter voice arose from the crowd: "What were we fighting for?" No one can claim that Americans have reached a unified answer to that question.

Dilemmas of commemoration

The memory of the Vietnam War and its epoch takes place within a culture of commemoration. Current analytic approaches to culture define commemorative objects, and cultural objects in general, as "shared significance embodied in form" (Griswold 1987a, p. 13). However, our concern is in formulating an approach to those kinds of commemoration for which significance is not shared.

One of the most influential perspectives on the social functions of commemoration is Emile Durkheim's. Commemorative rites and symbols, Durkheim tells us (1965, p. 420), preserve and celebrate traditional beliefs; they "serve to sustain the vitality of these beliefs, to keep them from being effaced from memory and, in sum, to revivify the most essential elements of the collective consciousness. Through [commemoration] the group periodically renews the sentiment which it has of itself and of its unity." Associated with Durkheim's conception is a rich research tradition that includes works by Maurice Halbwachs (1941, 1980 [1950]), Robert Hertz (1965), Lloyd Warner (1959), Bernard Barber (1972), Edward Shils (1981), and David Lowenthal (1985), among others. These works, like Durkheim's, emphasize the way commemorative monuments integrate the glory of society's past into its present concerns and aspirations. They assume that the events or individuals selected for commemoration are necessarily heroic or, at the very least, untainted. In this view, commemoration is governed by a kind of pleasure principle that produces a unified, positive image of the past. But suppose a society is divided over the very event it selects for commemoration. Suppose that event constitutes a painful moment for society, such as a military defeat or an era of domestic oppression. What kinds of "traditional beliefs" and "essential elements," and what kind of monuments, if any, can crystallize these moments and unify the society around them? How is commemoration without consensus, or without pride, possible?

The Vietnam Veterans Memorial provides a good case to use in thinking about these issues. The succession of events that led to the Memorial's creation and public reception was a culture-producing process. In that process, contrasting moral evaluations of the Vietnam War and its participants were affirmed.

Commemoration as a genre problem

Controversies over the merits of a war are expressed at some point in debates over measures taken to commemorate it. The stages in the Vietnam Memorial's construction reveal, on the one hand, the desire for a design that reflects the uniqueness of the Vietnam War and, on the other, the desire for a design that recognizes the sense in which the Vietnam War was similar to previous wars. The Vietnam War differed from other wars because it was controversial, morally questionable, and unsuccessful. It resembled other wars because it called forth in its participants the traditional virtues of self-sacrifice, courage, loyalty, and honor. Tension between alternative commemorative designs centers on the problem of incorporating these contrasting features into a single monument.

Attitudes and interests are translated into commemorative forms through enterprise. Before any event can be regarded as worth remembering, and before any class of people can be recognized for having participated in that event, some individual, and eventually some group, must deem both event and participants commemorable and must have the influence to get others to agree. Memorial devices are not self-created; they are conceived and built by those who wish to bring to consciousness the events and people that others are more inclined to forget. To understand memorial-making in this way is to understand it as a construction process wherein competing "moral entrepreneurs" seek public arenas and support for their interpretations of the past. These interpretations are embodied in the memorial's symbolic structure.

Efforts to connect cultural objects to a people's social experience rarely attend to this kind of process. Edward Shils and Michael Young's (1953) account of the Coronation, Clifford Geertz's (1973) work on the Balinese cockfight, Lucien Goldmann's (1964) analysis of Racine's plays – these exemplary works, among others, seek to align synchronically the symbolic structure of cultural objects with the mental structures of the society. Without denying the plausibility of these particular investigations, we can recognize two shortcomings in their method. First, the method admits of contestable conclusions because an astute observer can always find something in the society for a given cultural object to reflect. Second, the method draws attention to what the cultural object is and what it represents but not to how the object came to be what it is and how it came to represent what it does. Analysis of the Vietnam Veterans Memorial made these shortcomings apparent to us. Looking at this memorial at a given point of time, we could find no way to "decode" it, no way to articulate its relation to society. Only by accounting for its inception and development over time did we come to know how the Memorial's symbolic structure expresses or emerges from the society's values and remembrance of the war.

A nation's gratitude: search for a genre

The first official recognition of the Vietnam veteran was not bestowed until 1978, three years after the last American was flown out of Saigon. The recognition itself was hesitant and uncertain. A Vietnam War crypt had already been prepared in the Tomb of the Unknown Soldier, but the army determined that neither of its two unidentified bodies (only 30 percent of the remains in both cases) made for a decent corpse. Instead of honoring its Vietnam battle-dead by symbolically joining them, through entombment of unknown soldiers' remains, with men fallen in earlier wars, the army recommended that a plaque and display of medals be set apart behind the tomb, along with the following inscription: "Let all know that the United States of America pays tribute to the members of the Armed Forces who answered their country's call." This strange declaration bears no reference at all to the Vietnam War, and it required an act of the Veterans Affairs Subcommittee to make it more specific: "Let all people know that the United States pays tribute to those members of the Armed Forces who served honorably in Southeast Asia during the Vietnam era" (*The Nation*, April 8, 1978, p. 389). In even this second, stronger statement, three things are noteworthy: (1) although revised in Congress, the statement was initiated by the military; (2) it received little publicity; and (3) it designated the conflict in Vietnam by the word "era" rather than "war." Thus the recognition came from only a small part of the society for whose interests and values the war was fought; it was communicated to that society without conspicuous ceremony; and it betrayed confusion about the meaning of the war by its failure to find a word to describe it. This last point is the most noteworthy of all. Although a war had not been officially declared, many Congressional resolutions during the 1980s referred to the hostilities in Vietnam as "the Vietnam war." Touchiness during the late 1970s about what to call the conflict stemmed from social, not legal, concerns. To name an event is to categorize it morally and to provide an identity for its participants. Anomalous names betray ambiguity about an event's nature and uncertainty about how to react to the men who take part in it.

The first solution to the war's commemorative genre problem was thus halting and uncertain. The fighters were honored but not by an imposing monument. They were honored by a plaque, inconspicuously placed, whose inscription was, itself, indirect and muted. Undeclared wars are usually fought with restraint, however violent they might be. The Vietnam War's first official commemoration mirrored this restraint, marking the cause without really drawing attention to it.

Vision and revision: from pure to mixed genre

Recreating the context and process out of which the Vietnam Veterans Memorial developed, we came to see it not as a monument that ignores political meanings, but as a kind of *coincidentia oppositorum* – an agency that brings these opposed meanings together without resolving them. In this regard, the first and most fundamental point to emphasize is the nation's failure to reach an agreement on the Vietnam War's purposes and consequences. Hence there is a "genre problem": how to create a memorial that celebrates the virtues of the individual veteran without reference to his cause. As this criterion was set beside the attitude of the Congress towards the Vietnam veteran, an attitude that combined anxiety about his moral shortcomings (crime, drugs, and alcohol) with gratitude for his sacrifices, there arose pressures in the government to specify the Memorial's essential contours before it invited artists to submit their own designs. Informed by ambivalence about both the cause and its participants, these specifications pushed the Memorial in the direction of the muted and unobtrusive. Thus, in a formal letter approving the design competition, Department of Interior official Bill Whalen explained to the chairman of the Subcommittee on Parks, Dale Bumpers: "Since the proposed memorial is of great significance, and does not memorialize a single person or event, but rather a 10-year period of our Nation's history and is envisioned as a landscaped solution emphasizing horizontal rather than vertical elements, we concur with the report which indicates that a site in Constitution Gardens is preferable." Whalen clearly views the memorial as significant and noteworthy, yet he understands that a problem inheres in the design of any monument to commemorate this particular "10-year period." As significant as it might be, the memorial cannot be grand, vertical, or heroic. Like any "landscaped solution," it must hug the ground. It must be modest, horizontal, and nonheroic.

The memorial chosen by the Commission of Fine Arts from the more than 1,400 designs submitted was, indeed, the simplest and least imposing: two unadorned black walls, each about 250 feet in length, composed of seventy granite panels increasing in height from several inches at the end of each wall to 10 feet where they come together at a 125 degree angle. Although this angle aligns the two walls with the Lincoln Memorial and the Washington Monument, the walls themselves are placed below ground level, invisible from most vantage points on or near the Mall. The Vietnam War is thus defined as a national event, but in a spatial context that brackets off that event from those commemorated by neighboring monuments. The walls add to this sense of detachment by their internal format, which draws the viewer into a separate warp of time and space. As one moves from the edge of one wall to the point where it joins the other, one experiences a descending movement in space and a circular movement in time, for the 57,939 soldiers' names appear in the chronological order of the dates of their deaths, such that the war's first and last fatalities are joined at the walls' conjunction.

The commission's preference for this design was unanimous. However, for every layman who approved that choice, another seemed to be enraged by it. Those who shared the designer's goals were inclined to believe she had achieved them. Maya Ying Lin declared that her design was not meant to convey a particular political message but to evoke "feelings, thoughts, and emotions" of a variant and private nature: "What people see or don't see is their own projection." Jan Scruggs concurred: "The Memorial says exactly what we wanted to say about Vietnam – absolutely nothing." Indeed, on the original design the word Vietnam did not even appear (a statement indicating that the names on the wall belong to dead soldiers, and identifying the war in which they fought, was added later). This minimalist response to the commemorative task impressed one of the jurors as being "reverential"; another called it "a simple solution for a confused age"; a third saw "no escape from its power." Ellsworth Bunker, former ambassador to South Vietnam, found it to be "a distinguished and fitting mark of respect." Likewise, the *New York Times* applauded the design's "extreme dignity and restraint." It "seems to capture all the feelings of ambiguity and anguish that the Vietnam War evoked [and] conveys the only point about the war on which people may agree: that those who died should be remembered" (Hess 1983, pp. 123–125; Scruggs and Swerdlow 1985, pp. 63, 68, 69, 97; *New York Times*, May 18, 1981).

It is difficult to tell whether Maya Lin's supporters admired her design because it was an appropriately novel war memorial or because it was not a war memorial at all. The detractors, on the other hand, made frequent comparison between Lin's design and traditional war monuments, highlighting the confrontation between two commemorative styles – a heroic style traditionally associated with noble causes fought for and won, and what could be called an aheroic style, newly conceived for the tasteful recognition of those who had died for a useless and less-than-noble cause. Most veterans, however, did see something noble, if not useful, in the Vietnam War, and for them the Commission of Fine Arts had gone too far. One veteran, a member of the Memorial fund, described the design chosen by the commission as "the most insulting and demeaning memorial to our experience that was possible . . . a degrading ditch." As to its color: "Black is the universal color of shame, sorrow and degradation in all races, all societies worldwide." For another dissenting fund member, the sinking of the monument into the earth was an admission that the United States committed crimes in Vietnam. (Here are enlargements of the criminality theme that marked Congressional discussions about the veterans.) The wall was also condemned as "an open urinal," "a wailing wall for anti-draft demonstrators," "a tribute to Jane Fonda," and a "perverse prank" that would baffle the general public. Another critic, who happened to be the Memorial's biggest financial backer, called the art commission's choice a "slap in the face," a "tombstone," "something for New York intellectuals, a kind of 21st-century art that few would appreciate." To make matters worse, the proposed order of names for the wall presents "a random scattering" that can only confound loved ones. Other critics, including the editors of *National Review*, complained about the names themselves. Since the Memorial focuses on individuals, not the war, "it makes death in war a private matter rather than a sacrifice for a collective cause" (Hess 1983, pp. 122–125; Scruggs and Swerdlow 1985, pp. 68, 71, 82–83).

Opposition to the memorial wall was expressed by attacks on details like color, shape, and location, but underlying all specific objections was a disdain for the style itself. Many believed that that style violated the limits of the war-memorial genre. Designed to be apolitical, this memorial struck critics as nonpatriotic and nonheroic. It conveyed a conception of the war and a conception of the soldier that ran counter to those of many

Americans. These Americans, responded Jan Scruggs, "wanted the Memorial to make Vietnam what it had never been in reality: a good, clean, glorious war seen as necessary and supported by the united country." One leading opponent of the design conceded that the nation had not looked back favorably on the Vietnam War; however, he believed that "history can be re-evaluated" and "a piece of art remains, as a testimony to a particular moment in history, and we are under a solemn obligation to get that moment down as correctly as possible" (quoted in Scruggs and Swerdlow 1985, p. 94).

Most critics believed that only a "real" memorial could correctly represent the Vietnam War, but since that was politically impossible, they sought an addition to the present design in order to offset the "national humiliation" it perpetuated. At length, a compromise was conceived. An American flag, and next to that, a realistic statue of three soldiers, identifiable as white, black, and Hispanic, portrayed returning from patrol and gazing towards the names on the wall, would bring the original design closer to the traditional genre – would make it look more like a real war memorial.

Although their reasons may have differed, over 90 percent of the Vietnam veterans and 75 percent of the nonveterans surveyed after attending the Memorial's dedication ceremony were in favor of including the flag as an integral part of the Memorial site. At least 85 percent of every group surveyed (Vietnam veterans, Vietnam veterans' families, Vietnam-era veterans, other veterans, and nonveterans) approved of placing both a flag and statue somewhere on the Memorial grounds. And a majority in every group, ranging from 85 percent of the Vietnam veterans to 56 percent of the nonveterans, wanted the Memorial to include an inscription of the purpose for which the war was fought. It was the Vietnam veterans who felt most strongly about these changes, if strength of feeling can be gauged from reactions to the design of the wall by itself. Only a third of the veterans, compared with three-quarters of the nonveterans, reported a favorable impression of this design. The addition of the flag and the statue, the veterans claimed, would express a belief they could not find represented in the wall alone: that there is a nobility inherent in serving and dying for one's country. Combat, death, the nation – these are the concepts that many people wanted to see emphasized together.

These openly nationalistic ideas met strong resistance in the Commission of Fine Arts, but Interior Secretary James Watt, moved by widespread support elsewhere, demanded their acceptance as a condition of his approving the Memorial site. And so by mid-1983, the flag was set in place. On Veterans Day 1984, two years after the Memorial's dedication, the statue was unveiled.

With this new configuration, the conservative president and his administration seemed to have warmed up to the Memorial. Echoes of the 1960s anti-war protests from the reading of the names of the war-dead may have induced President Reagan to send an obscure official to represent the government at the 1982 unveiling of the Memorial wall. At the 1984 unveiling of the statue, the President himself officiated. A few days later, the army decided that it would be proper after all to add the meager remains of an American killed in Vietnam to the Tomb of the Unknown Soldier. The Vietnam war-dead were thus sanctified and incorporated into the nation's military heritage and their cause correspondingly elevated. The unpopularity and the outcome of the Vietnam War, however, imposed a limit to how far its commemoration could evolve in this traditional direction.

Flags and effigies in the marking of a lost war

The combination of flag, statue, and name-filled wall reflected profound disagreement as to how the Vietnam War should be remembered and conveyed this disagreement by an apparent binary opposition. The wall was believed to elevate the participant and ignore the cause; the flag and statue were believed to elevate the nation and its causes above the participant. However, the qualities and the relationship between these two patterns of meaning turned out to be more complex than anyone anticipated.

A strictly semiotic reading of the wall would highlight its "femininity." It is an opening in nature. It is womblike in its embrace of the visitor. The wall also reflects the visitor in its stone, thus eliciting a form of empathy, a trait traditionally considered more available to women than to men.

Let us take a closer look at the statue of the three soldiers. It is of a greenish-golden hue. The soldiers, seemingly disoriented, and garbed in finely wrought but distressed uniforms, gaze at the wall. Weapons hang uselessly from two of the soldiers' lowered arms and rest across the other soldier's back. Here, then, is the realism that critics of the wall's abstraction desired. Here is life – as opposed to the wall's expression of death – but it is life exhausted and confused. These men are of the war, but not at the moment in it. And since the soldiers are placed on only a modest pedestal, visitors cannot even figuratively look up to them; instead, they confront the soldiers almost at eye level. The mien of this statue is not heroic.

Considering the Memorial complex as a whole, we find an even broader pattern of assertion and qualification. The wall embodied a controversial assertion: that individuals should be remembered and their cause ignored; the qualifications came with the flag and statue. These, in turn, were beset

by their own internal tensions. The statue was conceived as a reactive assertion of pride, heroism, and masculinity, but, through the particular form it
took, it emerged as a tempering of all these things. The flag seems to be
unconditionally assertive because it is the only part of the Memorial site
that draws our eyes upward, but we notice in the peculiar dedication
inscribed on its base a kind of backing off: "This flag affirms the principles
of freedom for which [the Vietnam veterans] fought and their pride in
having served under difficult circumstances." The euphemism is transparent enough. By "difficult circumstances" we are to understand not the
power of our enemy but the feebleness of our cause. In this light, the
similarities among the three parts of the Memorial become more salient
than their differences, despite the realism of the statue's figures and the vertical prominence of the flag. Whether we look down, across, or up, we find
ambivalence about the meaning of this war and its protagonists refracted
throughout.

While the addition of the flag and statue made the Vietnam Memorial
look more like a traditional war monument, it also amplified the tensions
and ambivalence that induced the original departure from a traditional war
monument design. The vehicle for that departure, the wall of names, admits
of its own internal qualifications, but these are more subtle than the ones
built into the Memorial's two other parts and are perhaps more important
as clues to its sociological significance.

Uses of genre: the enshrinement process

The meaning of the Vietnam Veterans Memorial is defined by the way
people behave in reference to it. Some monuments are rarely talked about
or visited and never put to ceremonial use. Other monuments, like the
Tomb of the Unknown Soldier, are used often as formal ceremonial sites
and visited year after year by large numbers of people. Between the
Vietnam Veterans Memorial and its visitors, a very different relationship
obtains. Not only is the Memorial an object of frequent ceremony and frequent visitation (more than 2.5 million visitors and 1,100–1,500 reunions
per year), it is also an object with which visitors enter into active and
affective relationships. These relationships have thwarted all original intentions as to what the Memorial should be and represent.

Conceived as something to be passively looked at and contemplated, the
Vietnam Memorial has become an object of emotion. This is not the case
for the Memorial site as a whole, just the wall and its names. The names on
the wall are touched, their letters traced by the moving finger. The names
are caressed. The names are reproduced on paper by pencil rubbing and

taken home. And something is left from home itself – a material object bearing special significance to the deceased or a written statement by the visitor or mourner.

The dedications of the aggrieved are a spectacle that to many is more moving than the Memorial wall itself. More goes into spectators' reactions, however, than morbid curiosity, for the scenes of mourning are not altogether private affairs. These scenes make palpable a collective loss known to all. Not only, therefore, do friends and family bring their personal grief to the Memorial wall, but society exercises a moral pressure over those not directly affected by loss to add their presence to the situation and to align their sentiments with it.

Uses of genre: the representation of ambivalence

All nonperishable articles left at the Vietnam Veterans Memorial are collected each day and kept at the Museum and Archaeological Regional Storage Facility. Row after row of airtight shelters preserve these "gifts" for the future, thus extending the Memorial in space and in time. This part of the Veterans Memorial complex is the most populist, for its contents, in accordance with Interior Department policy, are determined by the people who visit the Memorial and not by professional curators. It is difficult to tell whether or not the idea for such a museum was part of the Interior Department's struggle against the elitism of the Commission of Fine Arts. That the museum collection negates the complaints of the Memorial's early detractors as well as the praise of its early defenders is more certain. An assessment of the objects themselves shows this to be so.

The most colorful objects left by visitors are flowers, taped to the wall or placed on the ground beneath a loved one's name. Nothing of a political nature is embodied in these floral displays; however, the Park Service's inventory of other (nonperishable) items does convey a coherent political message. This inventory shows that the one object most frequently left by the wall is a small American flag attached to a stick and set in the ground below the name that the visitor desired to mark. Through this offering, visitors uttered a political statement that was not supposed to be made. They asserted their patriotism, their loyalty to a nation. Whether they got the idea themselves or copied it from one another, they could think of no better way to dignify their loved one's memory than to associate his name with his country's emblem.

These assertions are amplified by other objects. The largest category of objects, almost a third of everything that has been deposited by the visitors, consists of military items, mostly patches and insignias marking military-unit membership, as well as parts of uniforms, dog tags, identification bracelets, medals, awards, and certificates. The Memorial site was thus decorated by symbols of the roles through which living veterans once enacted their commitment to the nation. These symbols began to appear in great profusion as soon as the Memorial was dedicated and continued to appear two years later when the statue of the three soldiers was unveiled. Designed to draw attention to the individual and away from the nation and its cause, the Memorial's wall turns out to be a most dramatic locus of patriotic feeling. The wall's use moved it towards that traditional war monument genre that opponents and supporters alike once believed it deviated from.

When profusely decorated with patriotic emblems, the wall alone may enhance our idea of the traditional war monument, but it cannot embody that idea. This is because patriotism is not the only response that the wall excites. The Memorial wall has in fact become a kind of debating forum – a repository of diverse opinions about the very war that occasioned its construction. Traditional war monuments serve no such reflexive function.

From its very inception, the Memorial's sponsors insisted that it would make no statement about the war – a promise predicated on the assumption that political silence could somehow be ensured by the Memorial's design. An ordinance that expressly prohibits political demonstrations on memorial grounds supplemented this assumption. Thus deprived of a traditional public forum, political opinions were, instead, inserted into many of the written statements brought to the wall. Letters, poems, and memos, often accompanied by photographs, can be viewed analytically as publicly accessible private sentiments or as privatized public opinion. Either way, they articulate the public's diverse visions of Vietnam.

Discussion

Effective commemorative tools check ambivalence. The ambivalence attending the Vietnam War, as we have seen, is not suppressed but summarized by the several parts of the Vietnam Memorial's physical makeup. This ambivalence is not necessarily something the individual feels. It is a social fact, an outcome of the incompatible commemorative viewpoints that were held and the measures that were taken by different constituencies. The Memorial is thus a ritual symbol that expresses the contradictions of society. This study of the Vietnam Veterans Memorial highlights the broad range of variation presently possible within the war monument genre. Unlike the kinds of monuments that mark popular wars, the Vietnam Memorial underwent frequent changes that both affirmed and modified the traditional conception of the war monument. Starting as a modest plaque, it became a politically sanitized wall sculpture, then a more differentiated memorial that included a flag and a realistic statue. These changes resulted from a political process involving competing claims on how the Vietnam War should be remembered. The process was itself a reflection of contradictory assessments of the war in American society as a whole.

Our analysis of this process has turned on the way genre enters into the act of commemoration. Although Griswold (1987a, p. 18) is undoubtedly right in her belief that genres admit of no "Aristotelian fixity," we have identified constraints on how far a genre can change before it is no longer itself, as well as how far it must change in order to commemorate its object credibly. A relatively fixed idea about what war monuments should look like and a realization that the Vietnam War was, at best, a controversial one – these two conceptions pushed the Vietnam Veterans Memorial in opposing directions. The traditional conception of war memorials, unopposed by any other consideration, would have led to the creation of a device that celebrated martial heroism in the service of a national cause. From this heroic ideal, no specific design can be inferred; however, those who opposed the first version of the Vietnam Memorial had a clear sense of what they wanted. They designated a cluster of features that all proper war memorials must, in some degree, display: a statement engraved on the monument describing the cause for which it was built, realism of human representation, vertical preeminence, lightness of color, grandness of size, and conspicuous national and military symbolism. No monument needs to incorporate all these features, or even a set combination of them, to qualify as a war memorial; however, at least some items from this cluster seem to be required, and some were indeed used to embellish Maya Lin's minimalist design. The addition of a marker identifying the Memorial wall as a monument to the Vietnam War dead and the addition of a national flag and a realistic statue pulled the initial design in the direction of the traditional war memorial genre.

As we outlined it in our introduction, the development of a thick description of the Vietnam Memorial involved the disclosure of relevant social, political, and cultural processes. These processes were, in their substance, interactive: moral entrepreneurs interacting with their constituencies and with political and cultural authorities; politicians interacting with their colleagues and within a conservative social climate; veterans interacting with their memories and their current situations; artists interacting with politically forged competition guidelines, with denizens of the art world and with lay audiences; visitors interacting with the wall. The key to the

Memorial's multifold meaning lies in this interaction web. The Memorial's ability to bring off commemoration of a dark and controversial part of the past comes to rest on the surrounding society's interaction with the Memorial itself. Whatever processes brought this cultural object into being in the first place, it is the use made of it that brings it into the life of the society. Wendy Griswold, in her outline of a model for analyzing cultural objects, notes that meaning is produced by the interaction between "the symbolic capacities of the object itself and the perceptual apparatus of those who experience the object" (1987b, p. 1079). We have come to understand the complex evolution of the Vietnam Veterans Memorial in the same way: as a succession of interacting producers, sponsors, and audiences.

Given our effort to discover the various meanings of the Vietnam Veterans Memorial, we have come to appreciate the distinctions that Victor Turner (1967, pp. 19–47) made in his own analysis of symbolic devices. Turner, in this connection, identified three levels of meaning. "Exegetical meaning" is expressed in what people say about a given symbol; "positional meaning" is the relation of one symbol to others in a broader semiotic system; and "operational meaning" is expressed in the way the symbol is used. It is the last, the operational, meaning that most strikingly draws our attention at the end of this chapter. For, to a large extent, we read the Vietnam Veterans Memorial through its uses. Ironically, the memorial designed to be least visible has become the most visible because its users have opened up its spaces and extended them outward. They have done this by the depositing of items at the wall, by the creation of a vast facility for their storage and their display, by the addition to the original site of a flag and statue, by the devising of a Moving Wall, and by the establishment in cities across the land of Vietnam War Memorials that resemble the Washington prototype.

The rituals that take place at the Vietnam Memorial are not the kind Durkheim would have understood. These are not rituals that strengthen common sentiments by bringing together those who hold them and putting them into closer and more active relations with one another (1965, p. 241). We are dealing with ritual assemblies that are intense even though, or perhaps because, the volume of common thoughts and sentiments about their object is so sparse. In studying the Vietnam Memorial, we have come to believe that people may need more ritual to face a painful and controversial part of the past than to deal with a painful part of the past about whose cause and meaning there is agreement. Rituals, however, do not resolve historical controversies; they only articulate them, making their memory public and dramatic. Unable to convince one another about what went wrong in Vietnam, therefore, the men and women who assemble at the Vietnam Memorial do so with more gravity than is displayed at shrines commemorating any other war.

In the end, contexts and meanings change. A day will come when the names that appear on the Vietnam Memorial's wall are known to few living persons. On this day, the intensity of feeling evoked by the wall will be less acute; the flags and objects that decorate the wall will be less dense; the solemnity that now grips those who enter the Memorial site will be diluted by an air of casualness; the ritual relation that now links shrine and pilgrim will become a mundane relation that links attraction and tourist. On this day, the Vietnam War will have become a less fitful part of American history. But the Vietnam Veterans Memorial, its several parts continuing to reflect different aspects of and beliefs about the war, will echo the ambivalence with which that war was first commemorated.

References

Barber, Bernard. 1972. "Place, Symbol and the Utilitarian Function in War Memorials." In Robert Gutman (ed.), *People and Buildings*. New York: Basic Books, pp. 327–334.

Durkheim, Emile. 1965. *The Elementary Forms of Religious Life*. New York: Free Press.

Geertz, Clifford. 1973. *The Interpretation of Cultures*. New York: Basic Books.

Goldmann, Lucien. 1964. *The Hidden God: A Study of Tragic Vision in the Pensées of Pascal and the Tragedies of Racine*. London: Routledge & Kegan Paul.

Griswold, Wendy. 1987a. "A Methodological Framework for the Sociology of Culture." In Clifford Clogg (ed.), *Sociological Methodology*, vol. XVII. Washington, DC: American Sociological Association, pp. 1–35.

1987b. "The Fabrication of Literary Meaning." *American Journal of Sociology* 92: 1077–1117.

Halbwachs, Maurice. 1941. *La Topographie légendaire des évangiles*. Paris: Presses Universitaires de France.

1980 (1950). *The Collective Memory*. New York: Harper & Row.

Hertz, Robert. 1965. *Death and the Right Hand*. London: Black.

Hess, Elizabeth. 1983. "A Tale of Two Memorials." *Art in America* (April), pp. 121–126.

Lowenthal, David. 1985. *The Past Is a Foreign Country*. Cambridge: Cambridge University Press.

Scruggs, Jan C., and Joel L. Swerdlow. 1985. *To Heal a Nation: The Vietnam Veterans Memorial*. New York: Harper & Row.

Shils, Edward. 1981. *Tradition*. Chicago: University of Chicago Press.

Shils, Edward, and Michael Young. 1953. "The Meaning of the Coronation." *Sociological Review* 1: 63–81.

Turner, Victor. 1967. *The Forest of Symbols*. Ithaca: Cornell University Press.

US House Committee on Veterans' Affairs. 1981. *Legacies of Vietnam: Comparative Adjustment of Veterans and Their Peers*. Report no. 14. March 9. Washington, DC: Government Printing Office.

Warner, W. Lloyd. 1959. *The Living and the Dead*. New Haven: Yale University Press.

PART III

Culture in action

As Anne Kane remarked in her contribution to this book, a central problem in social theory has been to connect culture (the ideal, intangible, abstract) with the real world (the material, concrete, real). In other words to explain how culture can make a difference. Whilst various proposals can be located in the history of social scientific thought, contemporary American solutions are turning increasingly to theories of social action, locating an efficient cause in the actor (either individual or collective) rather than in the social systems. Remembering the introductory essay to this volume, this is a move that can be understood as reflecting the continuing positive influence of American pragmatism and the continuing negative influence of Parsons's structural functionalism. The central theme of this last selection of essays is the exploration of recent theoretical progress in this area.

Almost every essay contained in the earlier parts of this collection has made some reference to culture's consequences, even if in an implicit way. Legitimacy, power, status, stigma, self- and other-understandings, social conflict, attitudes, and institutional forms have all been invoked as products of cultural forms and meanings and the circumstances of their transmission and reception. Yet these sorts of issues have been somewhat tangential, with the research questions underlying the previous papers directing attention away from either a detailed demonstration of culture's consequences or a targeted exploration of the ways that it exerts a determinate impact on social life. By contrast the contributions to this third part place these matters at the center of their agenda. It begins with two theoretical arguments, one from Ann Swidler and the other from William Sewell, Jr.

Swidler's intention is to develop a model of how culture informs action. Starting from a critique of the Parsonian stance on this puzzle she rejects idealism and moves towards a broadly pragmatist solution. Culture, she suggests, should no longer be seen as providing goals for action. Rather we should see it as providing deeply embedded forms of practical, common-sense know-how. These routinized and taken-for-granted ways of organizing action shape the ways that people go about doing things. Recognizing that such a position runs the danger of leaving little room for human innovation (thus repeating Parsons's error), Swidler then goes about unpacking the relationship between culture and agency in terms of what she calls "unsettled" and "settled" periods. In "unsettled" periods, she argues, new ideologies are often reflexively constructed and deployed by actors. In "settled" periods too there is room for creativity. Using the analogy of culture as a "tool-kit" Swidler suggests that agents can build up lines of action from the repertoire of cultural elements at their disposal. However, in both cases there are cultural limits to innovation. New ideologies determine only some aspects of social action (usually in public arenas) and their ultimate fate often depends upon their ability to mesh with, or construct, nonreflexive forms of conduct and ethos. In the case of tool-kit using humans, the act of imaginative bricolage is constrained by the patterns of thinking and symbolic odds and ends that people have ready to hand.

Although his essay is centered on the structure/agency debate rather than the culture/action issue, William Sewell, Jr. arrives at a similar conclusion to Swidler. According to Sewell an adequate theory of how culture works must encompass issues of both stability and change. That is to say culture's role in both the reproduction of the social order and in generating innovative new practices. In making this point he indicates, like Swidler, the crucial role that cultural schemas play in informing social action by operating as a resource for improvising and transposing lines of conduct. Sewell demonstrates the utility of this position in his exploration of how culture relates to the problematic issues of "agency" and "structure." Sewell's answer is one of which Kane would approve. On the one hand, he points out that cultural forms like language are structures with their own autonomy that provide a resource for concrete actors. On the other, he contends that material structures and historical contingencies mediate the impact of culture on real social life. Culture, then, is just one force among many that informs human action.

The remaining essays in the section are empirical in orientation and demonstrate in detail the kinds of themes given theoretical treatment by Swidler and Sewell. In particular they suggest the various ways in which culture provides a tool-kit or resource for actors in endeavors as varied as managing difficult interactions, justifying fun to oneself and others, getting good school grades, and protesting against nuclear power.

William Gamson's essay seeks to explain public attitudes towards nuclear power. The explanatory variable is discourse. Gamson makes no simple distinction between political and rhetorical or symbolic struggle. His argument here is that collective actions by social movements will be successful only when they are able to impose destabilizing narratives and symbolic codings on previously legitimate events and actors. For this reason cultural factors should be considered as a resource that is as important as social structural factors in determining social movement outcomes. Central to these struggles are pre-existing symbols which (à la Swidler) have to be innovatively packaged in order to address new issues. Particularly noteworthy is Gamson's anti-idealist emphasis on the key role of the institutional media in propagating dominant or oppositional frames and his stress on the role of contingent actions and historical accidents in accelerating or delaying processes of discursive change.

Like Gamson, Gary Alan Fine's work also addresses the way that conflicts over meanings are pivotal to social life. Although he is making a very similar cultural argument, Fine draws heavily upon the traditions of labeling theory, symbolic interactionism and, to a lesser extent, ethnomethodology, and builds a much-needed bridge between these traditions and the traditionally more macro-oriented field of cultural sociology. His major point is that the legitimacy of activities depends upon the ability of actors to furnish adequate accounts and justifications for the moral worth of their pursuits. In other words, there is an active and creative dimension to justifying fun which involves actors attempting to mobilize wider symbolic systems. Although Fine's case study concerns issues of recreation and leisure, the general analytic point about the role of culture in justifications holds in other contexts, as Gamson's essay demonstrates in the case of nuclear power.

Whilst the contributions of Gamson and Fine focus on the question of discourse, legitimacy, and action in civil and public spheres, Calvin Morrill's paper considers how culture does things in the work environment. Morrill's argument could be read in functionalist terms. Namely, the culture of honor is an adaptation that enables conflicts to be regulated in a new environment of matrix management. The result is a corporation that remains more or less integrated. But to make this reading would be to ignore the important ways in which Morrill's work moves beyond traditional functionalist analyses of organizational culture as well as the lineage of Weberian organizational theory. In Morrill's work there is a persistent emphasis on agency and interpersonal negotiation that derives from the American pragmatist tradition, and there are borrowings from cultural anthropology, semiotics, the "new institutionalism," and rhetorical analysis. Cumulatively these suggest that the "iron cage" thesis advanced by Weber is as false. In the modern corporation we find a world characterized by a fusion of creativity, choice, interpretation, symbolism, and strategy rather than routine and meaninglessness.

Paul DiMaggio draws on Bourdieu's concept of cultural capital to explain how culture is mobilized in action. According to DiMaggio, cultural capital that has little to do with the school curriculum provides a resource that students are able to translate into good school performance via tacit knowledge. What is particularly noteworthy is the elegant way in which DiMaggio is able to formulate, operationalize, and test competing theories explaining the link between cultural background and school performance. Whilst this essay makes somewhat difficult reading for those with limited statistical skills, it provides a useful illustration of the way in which quantitative research can address cultural theory. In so doing, this relatively early essay highlights the more general contribution that quantitative work has subsequently made to the field of American cultural sociology.

11

Culture and social action[*]

Ann Swidler

The reigning model used to understand culture's effects on action is fundamentally misleading. It assumes that culture shapes action by supplying
ultimate ends or values towards which action is directed, thus making
values the central causal element of culture. This paper analyzes the conceptual difficulties into which this traditional view of culture leads and
offers an alternative model.

Among sociologists and anthropologists, debate has raged for several
academic generations over defining the term "culture." Since the seminal
work of Clifford Geertz (1973a), the older definition of culture as the entire
way of life of a people, including their technology and material artifacts, or
that (associated with the name of Ward Goodenough) as everything one
would need to know to become a functioning member of a society, have
been displaced in favor of defining culture as the publicly available symbolic forms through which people experience and express meaning (see
Keesing 1974). For purposes of this essay, culture consists of such symbolic
vehicles of meaning, including beliefs, ritual practices, art forms, and ceremonies, as well as informal cultural practices such as language, gossip,
stories, and rituals of daily life. These symbolic forms are the means
through which "social processes of sharing, modes of behavior and
outlook within [a] community" (Hannerz 1969, p. 184) take place.

The recent resurgence of cultural studies has skirted the causal issues of
greatest interest to sociologists. Interpretive approaches drawn from
anthropology (Clifford Geertz, Victor Turner, Mary Douglas, and Claude
Lévi-Strauss) and literary criticism (Kenneth Burke, Roland Barthes) allow
us better to describe the features of cultural products and experiences.

* First published in 1986 as "Culture in action: symbols and strategies," *American
Sociological Review* 51(3): 273–286.

Pierre Bourdieu and Michel Foucault have offered new ways of thinking about culture's relationship to social stratification and power. For those interested in cultural *explanation* (as opposed to "thick description" [Geertz 1973a] or interpretive social science [Rabinow and Sullivan 1979]), however, values remain the major link between culture and action. This is not because sociologists really believe in the values paradigm. Indeed, it has been thoroughly criticized. But without an alternative formulation of culture's causal significance, scholars either avoid causal questions or admit the values paradigm through the back door.

The alternative analysis of culture proposed here consists of three steps. First, it offers an image of culture as a "tool-kit" of symbols, stories, rituals, and world-views, which people may use in varying configurations to solve different kinds of problems. Second, to analyze culture's causal effects, it focuses on "strategies of action," persistent ways of ordering action through time. Third, it sees culture's causal significance not in defining ends of action, but in providing cultural components that are used to construct strategies of action.

This chapter proceeds, first, by outlining the failures of cultural explanation based on values. It then argues for the superior intuitive plausibility and explanatory adequacy of the alternative model. Finally, it suggests research approaches based on seeing culture in this new way.

Culture as values

Our underlying view of culture derives from Max Weber. For Weber, human beings are motivated by ideal and material interests. Ideal interests, such as the desire to be saved from the torments of hell, are also ends-oriented, except that these ends are derived from symbolic realities. In Weber's (1946 [1922–3], p. 280) famous "switchmen" metaphor:

Not ideas, but material and ideal interests, directly govern men's conduct. Yet very frequently the "world images" that have been created by "ideas" have, like switchmen, determined the tracks along which action has been pushed by the dynamic of interest.

Interests are the engine of action, pushing it along, but ideas define the destinations human beings seek to reach (inner-worldly versus other-worldly possibilities of salvation, for example) and the means for getting there (mystical versus ascetic techniques of salvation).

Talcott Parsons adopted Weber's model, but blunted its explanatory thrust. To justify a distinctive role for sociology in face of the economist's model of rational, interest-maximizing actors, Parsons argued that within a means–ends schema only sociology could account for the ends actors pursued. For Weber's interest in the historical role of ideas, Parsons substituted global, ahistorical values. Unlike ideas, which in Weber's sociology are complex historical constructions shaped by institutional interests, political vicissitudes, and pragmatic motives, Parsonian values are abstract, general, and immanent in social systems. Social systems exist to realize their core values, and values explain why different actors make different choices even in similar situations. Indeed, Parsons does not treat values as concrete symbolic elements (like doctrines, rituals, or myths) which have histories and can actually be studied. Rather, values are essences around which societies are constituted. They are the unmoved mover in the theory of action.

Parsons's "voluntaristic theory of action" describes an actor who makes choices in a situation, choices limited by objective conditions and governed by normative regulation of the means and ends of action (Warner 1978, p. 1321). A "cultural tradition," according to Parsons (1951, pp. 11–12), provides "value orientations," a "value" being defined as "an element of a shared symbolic system which serves as a criterion or standard for selection among the alternatives of orientation which are intrinsically open in a situation." Culture thus affects human action through values that direct it to some ends rather than others.

The theory of values survives in part, no doubt, because of the intuitive plausibility in our own culture of the assumption that all action is ultimately governed by some means–ends schema. Culture shapes action by defining what people want.

What people want, however, is of little help in explaining their action. To understand both the pervasiveness and the inadequacy of cultural values as explanations, let us examine one recent debate in which "culture" has been invoked as a major causal variable: the debate over the existence and influence of a "culture of poverty."

The culture of poverty

Why does a member of the "culture of poverty" described by Lewis (1966) or Liebow (1967) (or an Italian street-corner youth of the sort Whyte [1943] described) not take advantage of opportunities to assimilate to the dominant culture in conduct and dress, acquire the appropriate educational credentials, and settle down to a steady job? Much of the argument has revolved around whether the very poor "really" value the same things that more secure middle- and working-class people do.

The irony of this debate is that it cannot be resolved by evidence that the very poor share the values and aspirations of the middle class, as indeed they seem to do. In repeated surveys, lower-class youth say that they value education and intend to go to college, and their parents say they want them to go (Jencks *et al.* 1972, pp. 34–5). Similarly, lower-class people seem to want secure friendships, stable marriages, steady jobs, and high incomes. But class similarities in aspirations in no way resolve the question of whether there are class differences in *culture*. People may share common aspirations, while remaining profoundly different in the way their culture organizes their overall pattern of behavior (see Hannerz 1969).

Culture in this sense is more like a style or a set of skills and habits than a set of preferences or wants. If one asked a slum youth why he did not take steps to pursue a middle-class path to success (or indeed asked oneself why one did not pursue a different life direction), the answer might well be not "I don't want that life," but instead, "Who, me?" One can hardly pursue success in a world where the accepted skills, style, and informal know-how are unfamiliar. One does better to look for a line of action for which one already has the cultural equipment.

Indeed, the skills required for adopting a line of conduct – and for adopting the interests or values that one could maximize in that line of conduct – involve much more than such matters as how to dress, talk in the appropriate style, or take a multiple-choice examination. To adopt a line of conduct, one needs an image of the kind of world in which one is trying to act, a sense that one can read reasonably accurately (through one's own feelings and through the responses of others) how one is doing, and a capacity to choose among alternative lines of action. The lack of this ease is what we experience as "culture shock" when we move from one cultural community to another. Action is not determined by one's values. Rather action *and* values are organized to take advantage of cultural competences.

The Protestant ethic

These causal issues appear again when we turn to the paradigmatic sociological argument for the importance of culture in human action – Max Weber's *The Protestant Ethic and the Spirit of Capitalism* (1958 [1904–5]). Weber sought to explain rational, capitalist economic behavior by arguing that culture, in the shape of Calvinist doctrine, created a distinctive frame of mind which encouraged rationalized, ascetic behavior. The doctrine of predestination channeled the desire to be saved into a quest for proof of salvation in worldly conduct, thus stimulating anxious self-examination and relentless self-discipline. Ends created by ideas (that is, the desire for salvation) powerfully influenced conduct.

If we take seriously the causal model Weber offers (both in *The Protestant Ethic* and in his theoretical writings on religion), however, we cannot understand his larger claim: that the ethos of Protestantism endured even after the spur of the Calvinist quest for proof of salvation had been lost. If ideas shape ethos, why did the ethos of ascetic Protestantism outlast its ideas?

Weber argues for continuity between the desire of early Calvinists to know whether they were saved or damned and the secular ethic of Benjamin Franklin. We recognize other continuities as well: in the Methodist demand for sobriety, humility, and self-control among the working class; and even in the anxious self-scrutiny of contemporary Americans seeking psychological health, material success, or personal authenticity.

How, then, should we understand continuity in the style or ethos of action, even when ideas (and the ends of action they advocate) change? This continuity suggests that what endures is *the way action is organized*, not its ends.

These two cases illustrate the chronic difficulties with traditional efforts to use culture as an explanatory variable and suggest why many have written off the effort altogether.

Cultural explanation

If values have little explanatory power, why expect culture to play any causal role in human action? Why not explain action as the result of interests and structural constraints, with only a rational, interest-maximizing actor to link the two?

The view that action is governed by "interests" is inadequate in the same way as the view that action is governed by nonrational values. Both models have a common explanatory logic, differing only in assuming different ends of action: either individualistic, arbitrary "tastes" or consensual, cultural "values."

Both views are flawed by an excessive emphasis on the "unit act," the notion that people choose their actions one at a time according to their interests or values. But people do not, indeed cannot, build up a sequence of actions piece by piece, striving with each act to maximize a given outcome. Action is necessarily integrated into larger assemblages, called here "strategies of action." Culture has an independent causal role because it shapes the capacities from which such strategies of action are constructed.

The term "strategy" is not used here in the conventional sense of a plan consciously devised to attain a goal. It is, rather, a general way of organizing action (depending upon a network of kin and friends, for example, or relying on selling one's skills in a market) that might allow one to reach several different life goals. Strategies of action incorporate, and thus depend on, habits, moods, sensibilities, and views of the world (Geertz 1973a). People do not build lines of action from scratch, choosing actions one at a time as efficient means to given ends. Instead, they construct chains of action beginning with at least some prefabricated links. Culture influences action through the shape and organization of those links, not by determining the ends to which they are put.

Our alternative model also rests on the fact that all real cultures contain diverse, often conflicting symbols, rituals, stories, and guides to action. The reader of the Bible can find a passage to justify almost any act, and traditional wisdom usually comes in paired adages counseling opposite behaviors. A culture is not a unified system that pushes action in a consistent direction. Rather, it is more like a "tool-kit" or repertoire (Hannerz 1969, pp. 186–188) from which actors select differing pieces for constructing lines of action. Both individuals and groups know how to do different kinds of things in different circumstances (see, for example, Gilbert and Mulkay 1984). People may have in readiness cultural capacities they rarely employ; and all people know more culture than they use (if only in the sense that they ignore much that they hear). A realistic cultural theory should lead us to expect not passive "cultural dopes" (Garfinkel 1967; Wrong 1961), but rather the active, sometimes skilled users of culture whom we actually observe.

If culture influences action through end values, people in changing circumstances should hold on to their preferred ends while altering their strategies for attaining them. But if culture provides the tools with which persons construct lines of action, then styles or strategies of action will be more persistent than the ends people seek to attain. Indeed, people will come to value ends for which their cultural equipment is well suited (cf. Mancini 1980). To return to the "culture of poverty" example, a ghetto youth who can expertly "read" signs of friendship and loyalty (Hannerz 1969), or who can recognize with practiced acuity threats to turf or dignity (Horowitz 1983), may pursue ends that place group loyalty above individual achievement, not because he disdains what individual achievement could bring, but because the cultural meanings and social skills necessary for playing *that* game well would require drastic and costly cultural retooling.

This revised imagery – culture as a "tool kit" for constructing "strategies of action," rather than as a switchman directing an engine propelled by

interests – turns our attention towards different causal issues than do traditional perspectives in the sociology of culture.

Two models of cultural influence

We need differing models to understand two situations in which culture
works very differently. In one case, culture accounts for continuities in
"settled lives." In settled lives, culture is intimately integrated with action;
it is here that we are most tempted to see values as organizing and anchor-
ing patterns of action; and here it is most difficult to disentangle what is
uniquely "cultural," since culture and structural circumstance seem to reinforce each other. This is the situation about which a theorist like Clifford
Geertz (1973b) writes so persuasively: culture is a model of, and a model
for, experience; and cultural symbols reinforce an ethos, making plausible
a world-view which in turn justifies the ethos.

The second case is that of "unsettled lives." The distinction is less
between settled and unsettled lives, however, than between culture's role in
sustaining existing strategies of action and its role in constructing new ones.
This contrast is not, of course, absolute. Even when they lead settled lives,
people do active cultural work to maintain or refine their cultural capacities. Conversely, even the most fanatical ideological movement, which
seeks to remake completely the cultural capacities of its members, will
inevitably draw on many tacit assumptions from the existing culture. There
are, nonetheless, more and less settled lives, and more and less settled cultural periods. Individuals in certain phases of their lives, and groups or
entire societies in certain historical periods, are involved in constructing
new strategies of action. It is for the latter situation that our usual models
of culture's effects are most inadequate.

Unsettled lives

Periods of social transformation seem to provide simultaneously the best
and the worst evidence for culture's influence on social action. Established
cultural ends are jettisoned with apparent ease, and yet explicitly articulated cultural models, such as ideologies, play a powerful role in organizing
social life (see, for example, Eisenstadt 1970; Geertz 1968; Hunt 1984;
Walzer 1974).

In such periods, ideologies – explicit, articulated, highly organized
meaning systems (both political and religious) – *establish* new styles or
strategies of action. When people are learning new ways of organizing indi-

vidual and collective action, practicing unfamiliar habits until they become familiar, then doctrine, symbol, and ritual directly shape action.

Assumed here is a continuum from *ideology* to *tradition* to *common sense*. An "ideology" is a highly articulated, self-conscious belief and ritual system, aspiring to offer a unified answer to problems of social action. Ideology may be thought of as a phase in the development of a system of cultural meaning. "Traditions," on the other hand, are articulated cultural beliefs and practices, but ones taken for granted so that they seem inevitable parts of life. Diverse, rather than unified, partial rather than all-embracing, they do not always inspire enthusiastic assent. (A wedding, in our own culture, may seem odd, forced, or unnatural when we actually attend one, for example. But it will still seem the natural way to get married, so that going to a justice of the peace requires special explanation.) Traditions, whether the routine ones of daily life or the extraordinary ones of communal ceremony, nonetheless seem ordained in the order of things, so that people may rest in the certainty that they exist, without necessarily participating in them. The same belief system – a religion, for example – may be held by some people as an ideology and by others as tradition; and what has been tradition may under certain historical circumstances become ideology. (This is the distinction Geertz [1968, p. 61] makes when he writes about a loss of traditional religious certainty in modern "ideologized" Islam – coming to "hold" rather than be "held by" one's beliefs.) "Common sense," finally, is the set of assumptions so unselfconscious as to seem a natural, transparent, undeniable part of the structure of the world (Geertz 1975).

Bursts of ideological activism occur in periods when competing ways of organizing action are developing or contending for dominance. People formulate, flesh out, and put into practice new habits of action. In such situations, culture may indeed be said to directly shape action. Members of a religious cult wear orange, or share their property, or dissolve their marriages because their beliefs tell them to. Protestants simplify worship, read the Bible, and work in a calling because of their faith. Doctrine and casuistry tell people how to act and provide blueprints for community life.

During such periods, differences in ritual practice or doctrine may become highly charged, so that statuary in churches (Baxandall 1980), the clothing and preaching styles of ministers (Davis 1975; Zaret 1985), or the style and decoration of religious objects are fraught with significance.

Ritual acquires such significance in unsettled lives because ritual changes reorganize taken-for-granted habits and modes of experience. People developing new strategies of action depend on cultural models to learn styles of self, relationship, cooperation, authority, and so forth. Commitment to such an ideology, originating perhaps in conversion, is more conscious than is the embeddedness of individuals in settled cultures, representing a break with some alternative way of life.

These explicit cultures might well be called "systems." While not perfectly consistent, they aspire to offer not multiple answers, but one unified answer to the question of how human beings should live. In conflict with other cultural models, these cultures are coherent because they must battle to dominate the world-views, assumptions, and habits of their members.

Such cultural models are thus causally powerful, but in a restricted sense. Rather than providing the underlying assumptions of an entire way of life, they make explicit demands in a contested cultural arena. Their independent causal influence is limited first because, at least at their origins, such ideological movements are not complete cultures, in the sense that much of their taken-for-granted understanding of the world and many of their daily practices still depend on traditional patterns.

Second, in a period of cultural transformation, ideology forms around ethos, rather than vice versa. To illustrate this we may turn once again to arguments about the Protestant ethic. Remember that for Max Weber the consequences of Calvinism flowed from its doctrine, operating on believers' overwhelming psychological interest in salvation. But even in *The Protestant Ethic* (1958 [1904–5]), Weber is hard pressed to explain why the doctrines of predestination and proof produced the rationalized, ascetic conduct of the saint (as opposed to fatalistic resignation, or even hedonism).

In *The Revolution of the Saints* (1974), Michael Walzer makes a very different argument about the relation between ethos and doctrinal logic in Calvinism. Walzer shows that the ethos of methodical self-control was not an accidental byproduct of Calvinism's doctrine. Rather, Calvin repeatedly adjusted the logic of this theology to stimulate the discipline he saw as necessary for fallen man. He "opportunistically" revised and reworked his doctrine *in order* to achieve a particular psychological effect. Calvin needed potent theological imagery to inscribe within his congregants the rigorous control of thought and action he sought. Indeed, tightly argued doctrine, austere ritual, and potent imagery were the weapons Calvin crafted to teach a new ethos. But doctrine "caused" ethos only in an immediate sense. In a larger explanatory perspective, commitment to a specific ethos, a style of regulating action, shaped the selection and development of doctrine.

Walzer also suggests a new way of thinking about the relationship between ideology and interests. As the ruler of a small theocracy, Calvin certainly had immediate interests in controlling the citizens of Geneva, and he bent his doctrine to those ends. Walzer also argues, however, that the wider appeal of Calvinism was to those displaced clergy and insecure gentry who were looking for new ways to exercise authority and a new ethos to regulate their own conduct as elites. Interests are thus important in shaping ideas, but an ideology serves interests through its potential to construct and regulate patterns of conduct. And indeed, those new capacities for action and for regulating the action of others shape the interests its adherents come to have.

To understand culture's causal role in such high-ideology periods, we need, third, to consider ideologies in a larger explanatory context. Coherent ideologies emerge when new ways of organizing action are being developed. Such ideologies, often carried by social movements, model new ways to organize action and to structure human communities. These ideological movements, however, are in active competition with other cultural frameworks – at the least in competition with common sense and usually with alternative traditions and ideologies as well. Explaining cultural outcomes therefore requires not only understanding the direct influence of an ideology on action. It also requires explaining why one ideology rather than another triumphs (or at least endures). And such explanation depends on analyzing the structural constraints and historical circumstances within which ideological movements struggle for dominance.

Culture has independent causal influence in unsettled cultural periods because it makes possible new strategies of action – constructing entities that can act (selves, families, corporations), shaping the styles and skills with which they act, and modeling forms of authority and cooperation. It is, however, the concrete situations in which these cultural models are enacted that determine which take root and thrive, and which wither and die.

Settled lives

The causal connections between culture and action are very different in settled cultural periods. Culture provides the materials from which individuals and groups construct strategies of action. Such cultural resources are diverse, however, and normally groups and individuals call upon these resources selectively, bringing to bear different styles and habits of action in different situations. Settled cultures thus support varied patterns of action, obscuring culture's independent influence.

Specifying culture's causal role is made more difficult in settled cultural periods by the "loose coupling" between culture and action. People profess ideals they do not follow, utter platitudes without examining their validity, or fall into cynicism or indifference with the assurance that the world will go on just the same. Such gaps between the explicit norms, world-views, and rules of conduct individuals espouse and the ways they habitually act create little difficulty within settled strategies of action. People naturally "know" how to act. Cultural experience may reinforce or refine the skills, habits, and attitudes important for common strategies of action, but established ways of acting do not depend upon such immediate cultural support.

In settled cultural periods, then, culture and social structure are simultaneously too fused and too disconnected for easy analysis. On the one hand, people in settled periods can live with great discontinuity between talk and action. On the other hand, in settled lives it is particularly difficult to disentangle cultural and structural influences on action. That is because ideology has both diversified, by being adapted to varied life circumstances, and gone underground, so pervading ordinary experience as to blend imperceptibly into common-sense assumptions about what is true. Settled cultures are thus more encompassing than are ideologies, in that they are not in open competition with alternative models for organizing experience. Instead, they have the undisputed authority of habit, normality, and common sense. Such culture does not impose a single, unified pattern on action, in the sense of imposing norms, styles, values, or ends on individual actors. Rather, settled cultures constrain action by providing a limited set of resources out of which individuals and groups construct strategies of action.

There is nonetheless a distinctive kind of cultural explanation appropriate to settled cultures. First, while such cultures provide a "tool-kit" of resources from which people can construct diverse strategies of action, to construct such a strategy means selecting certain cultural elements (both such tacit culture as attitudes and styles and, sometimes, such explicit cultural materials as rituals and beliefs) and investing them with particular meanings in concrete life circumstances. An example might be young adults who become more church-going when they marry and have children, and who then, in turn, find themselves with reawakened religious feelings. In such cases culture cannot be said to have "caused" the choices people make, in the sense that both the cultural elements and the life strategy are, in effect, chosen simultaneously. Indeed, the meanings of particular cultural elements depend, in part, on the strategy of action in which they are embedded (so, for example, religious ritual may have special meaning as part of a family's weekly routine). Nonetheless, culture has an effect in that the ability to put together such a strategy depends on the available set of cultural resources. Furthermore, as certain cultural resources become more central in a given life, and become more fully invested with meaning, they anchor the strategies of action people have developed.

Such cultural influence can be observed in "cultural lag." People do not readily take advantage of new structural opportunities which would require them to abandon established ways of life. This is not because they cling to cultural values, but because they are reluctant to abandon familiar strategies of action for which they have the cultural equipment. Because cultural expertise underlies the ability of both individuals and groups to construct effective strategies of action, such matters as the style or ethos of action and related ways of organizing authority and cooperation are enduring aspects of individual, and especially of collective, life.

Second, the influence of culture in settled lives is especially strong in structuring those uninstitutionalized, but recurrent situations in which people act in concert. When Americans try to get something done, they are likely to create voluntarist social movements – from religious revivals, to reform campaigns, to the voluntary local initiatives that created much of American public schooling. Such strategies of action rest on the cultural assumption that social groups – indeed, society itself – are constituted by the voluntary choices of individuals. Yet such voluntarism does *not*, in fact, dominate most of our institutional life. A bureaucratic state, large corporations, and an impersonal market run many spheres of American life without voluntary individual cooperation. American voluntarism persists, nonetheless, as the predominant collective way of dealing with situations that are not taken care of by institutions.

Culture affects action, but in different ways in settled versus unsettled periods. Disentangling these two modes of culture's influence and specifying more clearly how culture works in the two situations, creates new possibilities for cultural explanation. Table 1 summarizes the two models of cultural explanation proposed here. Neither model looks like the Parsonian theory of values, the Weberian model of how ideas influence action, or the Marxian model of the relationship of ideas and interests. However, between them the two models account for much of what has been persuasive about these earlier images of cultural influence while avoiding those expectations that cannot be supported by evidence.

Implications for research

First, these two models of cultural causation identify the limited sense in which values *are* important in shaping action. In unsettled lives, values are unlikely to be good predictors of action, or indeed of future values. Kathleen Gerson (1985), for example, in an insightful study of women's career and family choices, notes what a small role is played by the values and plans young women have, and how much their choices are shaped by their immediate situations – a first job which works out, or a boyfriend who

Table 1. *Two models of culture*

	Characteristics	Short-term effects	Long-term effects
Settled culture (traditions and common sense)	Low coherence, consistency	Weak direct control over action	Provides resources for constructing strategies of action
	Encapsulates	Refines and reinforces skills, habits, modes of experience	Creates continuities in style or ethos, and especially in organization of strategies of action
Unsettled culture (ideology)	High coherence, consistency	Strong control over action	Creates new strategies of action, but long-term influence depends on structural opportunities for survival of competing ideologies
	Competes with other cultural views	Teaches new modes of action	

does not. Young women's choices are not driven by their values, but by what they find they have become good at, or at least accustomed to.

Within an established way of life, however, values – both "terminal" and "instrumental" – may play a significant role. A woman preoccupied with juggling the demands of husband and children against those of her work may well have developed a settled policy about whether "happiness," "an exciting life," "self-respect," or "social recognition" are more important to her. She may even refer to those values in making particular choices. Indeed, values are important pieces of cultural equipment for established strategies of action, since part of what it means to have a strategy of action is to have a way of making the choices that ordinarily confront one within it. We can thus recognize the significance of values if we acknowledge that values do not shape action by defining its ends, but rather fine-tune the regulation of action within established ways of life.

This perspective could reorient research on culture in a second way, by directing attention to a set of historical questions about the interaction of culture and social structure. Distinguishing culture's role in settled and unsettled periods, we can focus on those historical junctures where new cultural complexes make possible new or reorganized strategies of action. We can then ask how concrete structural circumstances affect the relative success of competing cultural systems. We could also ask how the capacity of particular ideas, rituals, and symbols to organize given kinds of action affects the historical opportunities actors are able to seize. Such questions might finally begin to give us a systematic view of the dynamic interactions between culture and social structure.

A third reorientation of cultural research would focus not on cultures as unified wholes, but on chunks of culture, each with its own history. Culture provides resources for constructing organized strategies of action. Particular cultural resources can be integrated, however, into quite different strategies of action. A crucial task for research is to understand how cultural capacities created in one historical context are reappropriated and altered in new circumstances. An example of such research is William Sewell's (1974, 1980) examination of how, faced with the threats of early industrialism, nineteenth-century French artisans drew on traditions of corporate organization to construct a new ideology of radical socialism.

At least since E. P. Thompson's *The Making of the English Working Class* (1963), of course, sociologists have examined how established cultural resources are reappropriated in new contexts. The argument proposed here goes beyond this, however. The significance of specific cultural symbols can be understood only in relation to the strategies of action they sustain. Culture does not influence how groups organize action via enduring psychological proclivities implanted in individuals by their socialization. Instead, publicly available meanings facilitate certain patterns of action, making them readily available, while discouraging others. It is thus not the rearrangement of some free-floating heritage of ideas, myths, or symbols that is significant for sociological analysis. Rather, it is the reappropriation of larger, culturally organized capacities for action that gives culture its enduring effects.

Conclusion

The approach developed here may seem at first to relegate culture to a subordinate, purely instrumental role in social life. The attentive reader will see, though, that what this chapter has suggested is precisely the opposite. Strategies of action are cultural products; the symbolic experiences, mythic lore, and ritual practices of a group or society create moods and motivations, ways of organizing experience and evaluating reality, modes of regulating conduct, and ways of forming social bonds, which provide resources for constructing strategies of action. When we notice cultural differences we recognize that people do not all go about their business in the same ways; how they approach life is shaped by their culture.

The problem, however, is to develop more sophisticated theoretical ways of thinking about how culture shapes or constrains action, and more generally, how culture interacts with social structure. This essay has argued that these relationships vary across time and historical situation. Within established modes of life, culture provides a repertoire of capacities from which varying strategies of action may be constructed. Thus culture appears to shape action only in that the cultural repertoire limits the available range of strategies of action. Such "settled cultures" are nonetheless constraining. Although internally diverse and often contradictory, they provide the ritual traditions that regulate ordinary patterns of authority and cooperation, and they so define common sense that alternative ways of organizing action seem unimaginable, or at least implausible. Settled cultures constrain action over time because of the high costs of cultural retooling to adopt new patterns of action.

In unsettled periods, in contrast, cultural meanings are more highly articulated and explicit, because they model patterns of action that do not "come naturally." Belief and ritual practice directly shape action for the community that adheres to a given ideology. Such ideologies are, however, in competition with other sets of cultural assumptions. Ultimately, structural and historical opportunities determine which strategies, and thus which cultural systems, succeed.

In neither case is it cultural end values that shape action in the long run. Indeed, a culture has enduring effects on those who hold it, not by shaping the ends they pursue, but by providing the characteristic repertoire from which they build lines of action.

A focus on cultural values was attractive for sociology because it suggested that culture, not material circumstances, was determinative "in the last instance." In Parsons's (1966) ingenious "cybernetic model," social structure may have constrained opportunities for action, but cultural ends directed it. The challenge for the contemporary sociology of culture is not, however, to try to estimate how *much* culture shapes action. Instead, sociologists should search for new analytic perspectives that will allow more effective concrete analyses of how culture is used by actors, how cultural elements constrain or facilitate patterns of action, what aspects of a cultural heritage have enduring effects on action, and what specific historical changes undermine the vitality of some cultural patterns and give rise to others. The suggestion that both the influence and the fate of cultural meanings depend on the strategies of action they support is made in an attempt to fill this gap. Such attempts at more systematic, differentiated causal models may help to restore the study of culture to a central place in contemporary social science.

References

Baxandall, Michael. 1980. *The Limewood Sculptors of Renaissance Germany, 1475–1525: Images and Circumstances.* New Haven: Yale University Press.
Davis, Natalie Zemon. 1975. "The Rites of Violence." In Davis (ed.), *Society and Culture in Early Modern France.* Stanford: Stanford University Press, pp. 152–187.
Eisenstadt, S. N. 1970. "The Protestant Ethic Thesis in an Analytical and Comparative Framework." In S. N. Eisenstadt (ed.), *The Protestant Ethic and Modernization.* New York: Basic Books, pp. 3–45.
Garfinkel, Harold. 1967. *Studies in Ethnomethodology.* Englewood Cliffs, NJ: Prentice-Hall.
Geertz, Clifford. 1968. *Islam Observed: Religious Development in Morocco and Indonesia.* New Haven: Yale University Press.
  1973a. *The Interpretation of Cultures.* New York: Basic Books.
  1973b. "Religion as a Cultural System." In Geertz, *The Interpretation of Cultures,* pp. 87–125.
  1975. "Common Sense as a Cultural System." *Antioch Review* 33: 5–26.
Gerson, Kathleen. 1985. *Hard Choices: How Women Decide about Work, Career, and Motherhood.* Berkeley: University of California Press.
Gilbert, G. Nigel, and Michael Mulkay. 1984. *Opening Pandora's Box: A Sociological Analysis of Scientists' Discourse.* Cambridge: Cambridge University Press.
Hannerz, Ulf. 1969. *Soulside: Inquiries into Ghetto Culture and Community.* New York: Columbia University Press.
Horowitz, Ruth. 1983. *Honor and the American Dream: Culture and Identity in a Chicano Community.* New Brunswick, NJ: Rutger's University Press.
Hunt, Lynn. 1984. *Politics, Culture, and Class in the French Revolution.* Berkeley: University of California Press.
Jencks, Christopher, Marshall Smith, Henry Ackland, Mary Jo Bane, David Cohen, Herbert Gintis, Barbara Heyns, and Stephan Michelson. 1972. *Inequality: A Reassessment of the Effects of Family and Schooling in America.* New York: Basic Books.
Keesing, Roger M. 1974. "Theories of Culture." In *Annual Review of Anthropology* 3. Palo Alto: Annual Reviews, Inc., pp. 73–97.
Lewis, Oscar. 1966. *La Vida: A Puerto Rican Family in the Culture of Poverty – San Juan and New York.* New York: Random House.

Liebow, Elliot. 1967. *Tally's Corner: A Study of Negro Streetcorner Men*. Boston: Little, Brown.

Mancini, Janet K. 1980. *Strategic Styles: Coping in the Inner City*. Hanover, NH: University Press of New England.

Parsons, Talcott. 1951. *The Social System*. New York: Free Press.

  1966. *Societies: Evolutionary and Comparative Perspectives*. Englewood Cliffs, NJ: Prentice-Hall.

Rabinow, Paul, and William M. Sullivan (eds.). 1979. *Interpretive Social Science: A Reader*. Berkeley: University of California Press.

Sewell, William, Jr. 1974. "Social Change and the Rise of Working-Class Politics in Nineteenth-Century Marseille." *Past and Present* 65: 75–109.

  1980. *Work and Revolution in France: The Language of Labor from the Old Regime to 1848*. Cambridge: Cambridge University Press.

Thompson, E. P. 1963. *The Making of the English Working Class*. New York: Random House.

Walzer, Michael. 1974. *The Revolution of the Saints*. New York: Atheneum.

Warner, R. Stephen. 1978. "Toward a Redefinition of Action Theory: Paying the Cognitive Element its Due." *American Journal of Sociology* 83: 1317–1349.

Weber, Max. 1946 [1922–3]. "The Social Psychology of the World Religions." In H. H. Gerth and C. Wright Mills (eds.). *From Max Weber*. New York: Oxford University Press, pp. 267–301.

  1958 [1904–5]. *The Protestant Ethic and the Spirit of Capitalism*. New York: Charles Scribner and Sons.

Wrong, Dennis. 1961. "The Oversocialized Conception of Man in Modern Sociology." *American Sociological Review* 26: 183–193.

Whyte, William Foote. 1943. *Street Corner Society: The Social Structure of an Italian Slum*. Chicago: University of Chicago Press.

Zaret, David. 1985. *The Heavenly Contract: Ideology and Organization in Pre-Revolutionary Puritanism*. Chicago: University of Chicago Press.

12

Culture, structure, agency, and transformation*

William H. Sewell, Jr.

"Structure" is one of the most important and most elusive terms in the vocabulary of current social science. The concept is central not only in such eponymous schools as structural functionalism, structuralism, and post-structuralism, but in virtually all tendencies of social scientific thought. But if social scientists find it impossible to do without the term "structure," we also find it nearly impossible to define it adequately. Many of us have surely had the experience of being asked by a "naive" student what we mean by structure, and then finding it embarrassingly difficult to define the term without using the word "structure" or one of its variants in its own definition. Sometimes we find what seems to be an acceptable synonym – for example, "pattern" – but all such synonyms lack the original's rhetorical force. When it comes to indicating that a relation is powerful or important it is certainly more convincing to designate it as "structural" than as "patterning."

Three problems with the concept of structure

There are, nevertheless, three problems in the current use of the term that make self-conscious theorizing about the meanings of structure seem worthwhile. The most fundamental problem is that structural or structuralist arguments tend to assume a far too rigid causal determinism in social life. Those features of social existence denominated as structures tend to be reified and treated as primary, hard, and immutable, like the girders of a building, while the events or social processes they structure tend to be seen as secondary and superficial, like the outer "skin" of a skyscraper, or as mutable within "hard" structural constraints, like the layout of offices on

* First published in 1992 as "A theory of structure: duality, agency, and transformation," *American Journal of Sociology* 98(1): 1–29.

floors defined by a skeleton of girders. What tends to get lost in the language of structure is the efficacy of human action – or "agency," to use the currently favored term. Structures tend to appear in social scientific discourse as impervious to human agency, to exist apart from, but nevertheless to determine the essential shape of, the strivings and motivated transactions that constitute the experienced surface of social life. A social science trapped in an unexamined metaphor of structure tends to reduce actors to cleverly programmed automatons.

A second and closely related problem with the notion of structure is that it makes dealing with change awkward. The metaphor of structure implies stability. For this reason, structural language lends itself readily to explanations of how social life is shaped into consistent patterns, but not to explanations of how these patterns change over time. In structural discourse, change is commonly located outside of structures, either in a telos of history, in notions of breakdown, or in influences exogenous to the system in question. Consequently, moving from questions of stability to questions of change tends to involve awkward epistemological shifts.

The third problem is of a rather different order: the term structure is used in apparently contradictory senses in different social scientific discourses, particularly in sociology and anthropology. Sociologists typically contrast "structure" to "culture." Structure, in normal sociological usage, is thought of as "hard" or "material" and therefore as primary and determining, whereas culture is regarded as "soft" or "mental" and therefore as secondary or derived. By contrast, semiotically inclined social scientists, most particularly anthropologists, regard culture as the preeminent site of structure. In typical anthropological usage, the term structure is assumed to refer to the realm of culture, except when it is modified by the adjective "social." As a consequence, social scientists as different in outlook as Theda Skocpol and Marshall Sahlins can be designated as "structuralists" by their respective disciplines. Sociologists and anthropologists, in short, tend to visualize the nature and location of structure in sharply discrepant, indeed mutually incompatible, ways.

In view of all these problems with the notion of structure, it is tempting to conclude that the term should simply be discarded. But this, I think, is impossible: structure is so rhetorically powerful and pervasive a term that any attempt to legislate its abolition would be futile. Moreover, the notion of structure does denominate, however problematically, something very important about social relations: the tendency of patterns of relations to be reproduced, even when actors engaging in the relations are unaware of the patterns or do not desire their reproduction. In my opinion, the notion of structure neither could nor should be banished from the discourse of social science. But it does need extensive rethinking. This article will attempt to develop a theory of structure that overcomes the three cardinal weaknesses of the concept as it is normally employed in social science. The theory will attempt (1) to recognize the agency of social actors, (2) to build the possibility of change into the concept of structure, and (3) to overcome the divide between semiotic and materialist visions of structure.

Why structural change is possible

It is my conviction that a theory of change cannot be built into a theory of structure unless we adopt a far more multiple, contingent, and fractured conception of society – and of structure. What is needed is a conceptual vocabulary that makes it possible to show how the ordinary operations of structures can generate transformation. To this end, I propose five key axioms: the multiplicity of structures, the transposability of schemas, the unpredictability of resource accumulation, the polysemy of resources, and the intersection of structures.

The multiplicity of structures

Societies are based on practices that derive from many distinct structures, which exist at different levels, operate in different modalities, and are themselves based on widely varying types and quantities of resources. While it is common for a certain range of these structures to be homologous, like those described by Bourdieu in *Outline of a Theory of Practice*, it is never true that all of them are homologous. Structures tend to vary significantly between different institutional spheres, so that kinship structures will have different logics and dynamics than those possessed by religious structures, productive structures, aesthetic structures, educational structures, and so on. There is, moreover, important variation even within a given sphere. For example, the structures that shape and constrain religion in Christian societies include authoritarian, prophetic, ritual, and theoretical modes. These may sometimes operate in harmony, but they can also lead to sharply conflicting claims and empowerments. The multiplicity of structures means that the knowledgeable social actors whose practices constitute a society are far more versatile than Bourdieu's account of a universally homologous habitus would imply.

The transposability of schemas

Social actors are capable of applying a wide range of different and even incompatible schemas and have access to heterogeneous arrays of resources. Moreover, the schemas to which actors have access can be applied across a wide range of circumstances.

Whether we are speaking of rules of grammar, mathematics, law, etiquette, or carpentry, the real test of knowing a rule is to be able to apply it successfully in *unfamiliar* cases. Knowledge of a rule or a schema by definition means the ability to transpose or extend it – that is, to apply it creatively. If this is so, then *agency*, which I would define as entailing the capacity to transpose and extend schemas to new contexts, is inherent in the knowledge of cultural schemas that characterizes all minimally competent members of society.

The unpredictability of resource accumulation

But the very fact that schemas are by definition capable of being transposed or extended means that the resource consequences of the enactment of cultural schemas is never entirely predictable. A joke told to a new audience, an investment made in a new market, an offer of marriage made to a new clan, a cavalry attack made on a new terrain, a crop planted in a newly cleared field or in a familiar field in a new spring – the effect of these actions on the resources of the actors is never quite certain. Investment in a new market may make the entrepreneur a pauper or a millionaire, negotiation of a marriage with a new clan may result in a family's elevation in status or its extinction in a feud, planting a crop in the familiar field may result in subsistence, starvation, or plenty. Moreover, if the enactment of schemas creates unpredictable quantities and qualities of resources, and if the reproduction of schemas depends on their continuing validation by resources, this implies that schemas will in fact be differentially validated when they are put into action and therefore will potentially be subject to modification. A brilliantly successful cavalry attack on a new terrain may change the battle plans of subsequent campaigns or even theories of military tactics; a joke that draws rotten tomatoes rather than laughter may result in the suppression of a category of jokes from the comedian's repertoire; a succession of crop failures may modify routines of planting or plowing.

The polysemy of resources

The term polysemy (or multiplicity of meaning) is normally applied to symbols, language, or texts. Its application to resources sounds like a contradiction in terms. But, given the concept of resources I am advocating here, it is not. Resources, I have insisted, embody cultural schemas. Like texts or ritual performances, however, their meaning is never entirely unambiguous. The form of the factory embodies and therefore teaches capitalist notions of property relations. But, as Marx points out, it can also teach the necessarily social and collective character of production and thereby undermine the capitalist notion of private property. The new prestige, wealth, and territory gained from the brilliant success of a cavalry charge may be attributed to the superior discipline and élan of the cavalry officers and thereby enhance the power of an aristocratic officer corps, or it may be attributed to the commanding general and thereby result in the increasing subordination of officers to a charismatic leader. Any array of resources is capable of being interpreted in varying ways and, therefore, of empowering different actors and teaching different schemas. Again, this seems to me inherent in a definition of agency as the capacity to transpose and extend schemas to new contexts. Agency, to put it differently, is the actor's capacity to reinterpret and mobilize an array of resources in terms of cultural schemas other than those that initially constituted the array.

The intersection of structures

One reason arrays of resources can be interpreted in more than one way is that structures or structural complexes intersect and overlap. The structures of capitalist society include both a mode of production based on private property and profit and a mode of labor organization based on workplace solidarity. The factory figures as a crucial resource in both of these structures, and its meaning and consequences for both workers and managers is therefore open and contested. The intersection of structures, in fact, takes place in both the schema and the resource dimensions. Not only can a given array of resources be claimed by different actors embedded in different structural complexes (or differentially claimed by the same actor embedded in different structural complexes), but schemas can be borrowed or appropriated from one structural complex and applied to another. Not only do workers and factory owners struggle for control of the factory, but Marx appropriates political economy for the advancement of socialism.

Structures, then, are sets of mutually sustaining schemas and resources that empower and constrain social action and that tend to be reproduced by that social action. But their reproduction is never automatic. Structures are at risk, at least to some extent, in all of the social encounters they shape – because structures are multiple and intersecting, because schemas are transposable, and because resources are polysemic and accumulate unpredictably. Placing the relationship between resources and cultural schemas at the center of a concept of structure makes it possible to show how social change, no less than social stasis, can be generated by the enactment of structures in social life.

Agency

Such enactments of structures imply a particular concept of agency – one that sees agency not as opposed to, but as constituent of, structure. To be an agent means to be capable of exerting some degree of control over the social relations in which one is enmeshed, which in turn implies the ability to transform those social relations to some degree. As I see it, agents are empowered to act with and against others by structures: they have knowledge of the schemas that inform social life and have access to some measure of human and nonhuman resources. Agency arises from the actor's knowledge of schemas, which means the ability to apply them to new contexts. Or, to put the same thing the other way around, agency arises from the actor's control of resources, which means the capacity to reinterpret or mobilize an array of resources in terms of schemas other than those that constituted the array. Agency is implied by the existence of structures.

I would argue that a capacity for agency – for desiring, for forming intentions, and for acting creatively – is inherent in all humans. But I would also argue that humans are born with only a highly generalized capacity for agency, analogous to their capacity to use language. Just as linguistic capacity takes the form of becoming a competent speaker of some particular language – French, or Arabic, or Swahili, or Urdu – agency is formed by a specific range of cultural schemas and resources available in a person's particular social milieu. The specific forms that agency will take consequently vary enormously and are culturally and historically determined. But a capacity for agency is as much a given for humans as the capacity for respiration.

That all humans actually exercise agency in practice is demonstrated to my satisfaction by the work of Erving Goffman (1959, 1967). Goffman shows that all members of society employ complex repertoires of interaction skills to control and sustain ongoing social relations. He also shows that small transformative actions – for example, intervening to save the face of an interactant who has misread the situation – turn out to be necessary to sustain even the most ordinary intercourse of daily life (Goffman 1967, pp. 5–46). Once again, knowledge of cultural schemas (in this case of interaction rituals) implies the ability to act creatively. Actors, of course, vary in the extent of their control of social relations and in the scope of their transformative powers, but all members of society exercise some measure of agency in the conduct of their daily lives.

It is equally important, however, to insist that the agency exercised by different persons is far from uniform, that agency differs enormously in both kind and extent. What kinds of desires people can have, what intentions they can form, and what sorts of creative transpositions they can carry out vary dramatically from one social world to another depending on the nature of the particular structures that inform those social worlds. Without a notion of heaven and hell a person cannot strive for admission into paradise; only in a modern capitalist economy can one attempt to make a killing on the futures market; if they are denied access to the public sphere, women's ambitions will be focused on private life. Agency also differs in extent, both between and within societies. Occupancy of different social positions – as defined, for example, by gender, wealth, social prestige, class, ethnicity, occupation, generation, sexual preference, or education – gives people knowledge of different schemas and access to different kinds and amounts of resources and hence different possibilities for transformative action. And the scope or extent of agency also varies enormously between different social systems, even for occupants of analogous positions. The owner of the biggest art gallery in St. Louis has far less influence on American artistic taste than the owner of the biggest gallery in Los Angeles; the president of Chad has far less power over global environmental policy than the president of Russia. Structures, in short, empower agents differentially, which also implies that they embody the desires, intentions, and knowledge of agents differentially as well. Structures, and the human agencies they endow, are laden with differences in power.

Finally, I would insist that agency is collective as well as individual. The transpositions of schemas and remobilizations of resources that constitute agency are always acts of communication with others. Agency entails an ability to coordinate one's actions with others and against others, to form collective projects, to persuade, to coerce, and to monitor the simultaneous effects of one's own and others' activities. Moreover, the extent of the agency exercised by individual persons depends profoundly on their positions in collective organizations. To take the extreme case, a monarch's personal whims or quarrels may affect the lives of thousands (see, e.g., Sahlins 1991). But it is also true that the agency of fathers, executives, or professors is greatly expanded by the places they occupy in patriarchal families, corporations, or universities and by their consequent authority to bind the collectivity by their actions. Agency, then, characterizes all persons. But the agency exercised by persons is collective in both its sources and its mode of exercise. Personal agency is, therefore, laden with collectively produced differences of power and implicated in collective struggles and resistances.

Varieties of structures

The concept of structure I elaborate in this chapter is very general and therefore could be applied to structures of widely differing character – ranging in import from structures that shape and constrain the development of world military power to those that shape and constrain the joking practices of a group of Sunday fishing buddies or the erotic practices of a single couple. This immense range in the scope and character of the structures to which this essay's concepts can be applied is appropriate, given the premise that all social action is shaped by structures. But it suggests a need for some means of distinguishing the character and dynamics of different sorts of structures. I will offer no detailed typology – both because space is short and because I feel that typologies should arise out of concrete analyses of social change and reproduction. Instead, I shall simply indicate two important dimensions along which structures vary: depth, which refers to the schema dimension of structure, and power, which refers to the resource dimension. I shall try to demonstrate that thinking in terms of depth and power can help to illuminate the very different dynamics and durabilities of three important types of structures: those of language, states, and capitalism.

Depth has long been a key metaphor of linguistic and structuralist discourse. To designate a structure as "deep" implies that it lies beneath and generates a certain range of "surface" structures, just as structures underlie and generate practices. In structuralist discourse, deep structures are those schemas that can be shown to underlie ordinary or "surface" structures, in the sense that the surface structures are a set of transformations of the deep structures. Thus the structural schemas for the performance of a fertility ritual may be shown to be particular transformations of a deeper set of oppositions between wet and dry or male and female that also underlie structures informing other institutionally distinct practices – from housebuilding, to personal adornment, to oratory. Consequently, deep structural schemas are also pervasive, in the sense that they are present in a relatively wide range of institutional spheres, practices, and discourses. They also tend to be relatively unconscious, in the sense that they are taken-for-granted mental assumptions or modes of procedure that actors normally apply without being aware that they are applying them.

Different structures also vary enormously in the resources, and hence the power, that they mobilize. Military structures or structures shaping state finance create massive concentrations of power, whereas the grammatical structures of a language or the structures shaping school-children's play create much more modest power concentrations. Structures also differ in the kinds of power they mobilize. For example, the power created by apostolic succession is based primarily (although far from exclusively) on persuasion, while that created by the military government of a conquering army is based primarily on coercion.

Language

I believe that thinking about structures in terms of their depth and power can lead to insights about the structures' durability and dynamics. Consider, for example, linguistic structures, which scholars in many disciplines have used as the prime example of structure in general. Linguistic structures, which of course tend to be remarkably durable, actually fall at extremes on the dimensions of both power and depth. Linguistic structures are unusually deep. Intricate phonological, morphological, syntactical, and semantic structures underlie every sentence. Sentences, in turn, are aggregated into meaningful utterances or texts in accord with the discursive structures of rhetoric, narrative, metaphor, and logic. And all of these layered linguistic structures underlie the multitude of structures that rely at least in part on speech and writing – which is to say the immense preponderance of all structures.

Yet the *power* of linguistic structures is unusually slight. The enactment of phonological, morphological, syntactical, and semantic structures in speech or writing in itself has relatively modest resource effects. It confirms the speaker's membership in a linguistic community and reinforces the schemas that make the generation of grammatical sentences possible. Assuming that an utterance is made to other competent speakers of the language, the speaking of a grammatical sentence in itself creates no significant power disparities but rather establishes an equality among the conversants. Language, of course, serves as a medium for all kinds of enactments of power relations, but at the level of phonology, morphology, syntax, and semantics, it is as close as we are likely to get to a neutral medium of exchange. This relative neutrality with respect to power helps to account for the other peculiarity of linguistic structures: their extraordinary durability. If the enactment of linguistic schemas serves only to sustain the linguistic empowerment of speakers without sharply shifting resources towards some speakers and away from others, then no one has much incentive to engage in innovations that would transform linguistic structures.

If it is true that linguistic structures are much less implicated in power relations and much deeper and more durable than most structures, it follows that we should be wary of the widespread tendency to use linguistic structures as a paradigm for structures in general. Although the elegance of the linguistic model may set an enviable standard, structures that operate nearer the surface of social life and that are more directly implicated in power relations may have very different principles and dynamics. One danger that arises from accepting the linguistic model uncritically is a tendency to think of structures as composed purely of schemas, while ignoring the resource dimension. In studying the syntactic structure of languages, where the enactment of schemas has minor power consequences, it does not matter much if the resource aspect of structure is neglected. But when we try to make sense of the arenas of life more permeated by power relations, it may be downright crippling to apply the linguistic analogy and conceptualize structures purely as schemas.

States

Particularly poor candidates for the linguistic analogy would be state or political structures, which commonly generate and utilize large concentrations of power and which are usually relatively near the surface of social life. State and political structures are consciously established, maintained, fought over, and argued about rather than taken for granted as if they were unchangeable features of the world. Although one might initially imagine that large power concentrations would tend to assure a structure's durability, this may not actually be true. Although centralized states with immense coercive power impose high costs on those who would challenge them, it is far from clear that centralized and coercive states have generally proved more durable than relatively decentralized or uncoercive states. Compare, for example, Britain and France between 1750 and 1850, the United States and Germany from 1870 to 1950, Costa Rica and Nicaragua, El Salvador, or Guatemala since World War II, or India and China over the same time span. Even the relatively stable states are subject to periodic structural transformations. Although the United States has had a single constitution since 1789, it has experienced a succession of fundamental political crises that produced at least five sharply distinct party systems over the past two centuries (Burnham 1967). One might argue that state structures are relatively mutable precisely because the massiveness (power) and obviousness (lack of depth) of their resource effects make them natural targets for open struggles.

But if most political structures are characterized by both high power and low depth, an inverse relationship between power and depth is by no means necessary. There are some political structures with immense power implications that are nevertheless relatively deep, that have become "second nature" and are accepted by all (or nearly all) political actors as essentially power-neutral, taken-for-granted means to political ends. Such structures also appear to be unusually durable. This would appear to be true of political structures as diverse as the American constitutional system, the French public bureaucracy, or the English community legal structures whose persistence Margaret Somers (1986) has traced from the fourteenth to the mid-nineteenth century. Durability, then, would appear to be determined more by a structure's depth than by its power.

Capitalism

How do structures with huge power effects become or remain deep? One would normally expect the massiveness of the effects to make social actors aware of and willing to contest the schemas and resource accumulations of those structures. I will approach this question by examining the case of capitalism, a spectacular case of a power-laden yet long-enduring structure. Capitalism is, of course, highly dynamic. Yet it is commonly maintained that the past 250–300 years (if not the entire period since the sixteenth century, according to Wallerstein [1974]) constitutes a unified capitalist era with a continuous dynamic of capital accumulation guided by an enduring core structure, or what in Marxian parlance is called the capitalist mode of production.

Marx himself noted the extraordinarily dynamic and changeable character of capitalist development, but he saw the change converging on a single form: the large-scale, mechanized factory staffed by an increasingly homogeneous proletariat. Recent developments have tended to make the changeability of capitalism seem more radical and permanent. Far from registering the onrush of the classic factory, the current era of world economic growth has been characterized by an increasing use of subcontracting, sweatshops, outsourcing, and "cottage industry," and by the burgeoning of services at the expense of manufacturing. At the same time, scholars are increasingly pointing out the unevenness, contingency, and openness of development patterns under capitalism, whether in the past (Sabel and Zeitlin 1985; Samuel 1977; Sewell 1988) or in the present and future (Piore and Sabel 1984). Sabel (1988) has even suggested that forms of economic change in the so-called capitalist era are so indeterminate that the very concept of capitalism, with its implication of underlying regularity, is misleading and should be abandoned. I think Sabel is right as far as he goes: a wide variety of institutional arrangements and property relations are compatible with "capitalism," and never in its history has capitalism obeyed uniform "laws of motion." Capitalist development has always been a messy and uneven affair. But I think that the messiness has been at the level of secondary or surface structures and that beneath the surface mutability lies a far more stable deep structure of schemas that are continually reinforced by flows of resources – even on occasions when the surface structures are revolutionized.

Unlike most Marxians, I see the core schemas not as those defining the wage-labor relationship but as those governing the conversion of use value into exchange value. The core procedure of capitalism – the conversion of use value into exchange value or the commodification of things – is exceptionally transposable. It knows no natural limits; it can be applied not only to cloth, tobacco, or cooking pans, but to land, housework, bread, sex, advertising, emotions, or knowledge, each of which can be converted into any other by means of money. The surface instability of capitalism arises precisely from this interconvertibility, which encourages holders of resources to trade them for other resources as relative values change and which always makes it possible for resources not previously treated as commodities to enter the circuit of monetized exchanges. To put it otherwise, the commodity form, by making almost all resources readable as exchangeable commodities, organizes a virtually universal intersection of structures, which means that changes in any one structure – an increased or decreased accumulation of resources or a new procedure – can affect an indefinitely vast number of other structures that intersect through the medium of money. Changes at any point in the circuit of exchange will give rise to resource effects and innovations elsewhere. And these changes are not necessarily constrained to follow any particular institutional form, so long as they are profitable. Thus the rise of the automobile industry stimulated the simultaneous development of rubber plantations based on indentured or forced labor, automobile assembly operations based on immense factories manned by wage-earning proletarians, and a proliferation of repair shops run by self-employed petty capitalists.

But this chronic instability or unpredictability of capitalism's surface structures actually reinforces its deeper structures. An alteration anywhere along the vast chain of commodity exchanges is a new incitement to invest; the logic inherent in the commodity form makes any new array of resources or new procedure a potential opportunity for profit. And of course any new investment results in further changes. Even investments that fail create new opportunities that can be seized by following the normal procedures of capitalist investment and exchange – when a firm goes under there is plant and equipment to be bought up at bargain prices, a residual market for the firm's former competitors to exploit, and so on. Consequently, the procedures themselves are remarkably impervious to – indeed, paradoxically,

are reinforced by – the failures of particular capitalist enterprises or industries. The displacement of handweavers by the power loom or of coal by
petroleum may have destroyed skills, wrecked businesses, or blighted the
economies of certain localities: but it simultaneously proved that following
the logic of the commodity form creates wealth for those who do so, and
even – over the long run and in spite of important local exceptions – for the
capitalist economy as a whole. In some cases, structures can combine depth
with great power and, consequently, can shape the experiences of entire
societies over many generations.

Conclusion

Beginning from the premise that structure is an unavoidable epistemic
metaphor in the social sciences, I have tried to specify how that metaphor
should be understood. Structures, I have argued, are constituted by mutually sustaining cultural schemas and sets of resources that empower and
constrain social action and tend to be reproduced by that action. Agents
are empowered by structures, both by the knowledge of cultural schemas
that enables them to mobilize resources and by the access to resources that
enables them to enact schemas. This differs from ordinary sociological
usage of the term because it insists that structure is a profoundly cultural
phenomenon and from ordinary anthropological usage because it insists
that structure always derives from the character and distribution of
resources in the everyday world. Structure is dynamic, not static; it is the
continually evolving outcome and matrix of a process of social interaction.
Even the more or less perfect reproduction of structures is a profoundly
temporal process that requires resourceful and innovative human conduct.
But the same resourceful agency that sustains the reproduction of structures also makes possible their transformation – by means of transpositions
of schemas and remobilizations of resources that make the new structures
recognizable as transformations of the old. Structures, I suggest, are not
reified categories we can invoke to explain the inevitable shape of social life.
To invoke structures as I have defined them here is to call for a critical analysis of the dialectical interactions through which humans shape their history.

References

Burnham, Walter Dean. 1967. "Party Systems and the Political Process." In William
     Nisbet Chambers and Walter Dean Burnham (eds.), *The American Party
     Systems*. New York: Oxford University Press, pp. 277–307.
Goffman, Erving. 1959. *The Presentation of Self in Everyday Life*. New York:
     Doubleday.

1967. *Interaction Ritual: Essays on Face to Face Behavior*. New York: Pantheon.

Piore, Michael J., and Charles H. Sabel. 1984. *The Second Industrial Divide: Possibilities for Prosperity*. New York: Basic.

Sabel, Charles H. 1988. "Protoindustry and the Problem of Capitalism as a Concept: Response to Jean H. Quataert." *International Labor and Working-Class History* 33: 30–37.

Sabel, Charles H., and Jonathan Zeitlin. 1985. "Historical Alternatives to Mass Production: Politics, Markets, and Technology in Nineteenth-Century Industrialization." *Past and Present*, no. 108, pp. 133–176.

Sahlins, Marshall. 1991. "The Return of the Event, Again; With Reflections on the Beginnings of the Great Fijian War of 1843 to 1855 Between the Kingdoms of Bau and Rewa." In A. Biersack (ed.), *Clio in Oceanta: Toward a Historical Anthropology*. Washington, DC: Smithsonian, pp. 37–100.

Samuel, Raphael. 1977. "The Workshop of the World: Steam Power and Hand Technology in Mid-Victorian Britain." *History Workshop* 3: 6–72.

Sewell, William H., Jr. 1988. "Uneven Development, the Autonomy of Politics, and the Dockworkers of Nineteenth-Century Marseille." *American Historical Review* 93: 604–637.

Somers, Margaret Ramsay. 1986. "The People and the Law: The Place of the Public Sphere in the Formation of English Popular Identity." Ph.D. dissertation, Department of Sociology, Harvard University.

Wallerstein, Immanuel. 1974. *The Modern World System*, vol. I: *Capitalist Agriculture and the Origins of the European World*. New York: Academic.

13

Discourse, nuclear power, and collective action*

William A. Gamson

Introduction

Sustained collective action involves a symbolic struggle. In the broadest sense, it is a struggle over the legitimacy of a regime and trust in the incumbent political authorities. Every regime has a legitimating frame that provides the citizenry with a reason to be quiescent. It is a constant, uphill struggle for those who would sustain collective action in the face of official myths and metaphors.

At a more contextual level, collective action focuses on particular historical conditions and policies. It has a substantive content. It takes place in some issue arena, however broadly or narrowly defined. People act on the basis of some meaning system, and the definition of issues, actors, and events is a matter of constant contention. A central part of the symbolic struggle, then, is about the process of constructing specific meanings.

As theories about ideological hegemony and false consciousness have emphasized, challengers face a formidable task. But the difficulty varies over time for all challengers and, at any single moment, among them. For some, the official meanings with which they must contend are deeply embedded and well-defended; for others, official meanings are in crisis and disarray or perhaps even discredited. Such moments offer opportunities for challengers that may not last.

Mobilization potential has, then, a strong cultural component. To understand it, we need to assess not only structural conduciveness but also cultural conduciveness. Not all symbols are equally potent. Certain packages have a natural advantage because their ideas and language resonate with larger cultural themes. Resonances increase the appeal of a package; they

* First published in 1988 as "Political discourse and collective action," *International Social Movement Research* 1(2): 219–244.

make it appear natural and familiar. Those who respond to the larger cultural theme will find it easier to respond to a package with the same sonorities. Snow and Benford (1988) make a similar point in discussing the "narrative fidelity" of a frame. Some framings "resonate with cultural narrations, that is with the stories, myths, and folk tales that are part and parcel of one's cultural heritage."

The case of American nuclear power

Consider the case of the movement against nuclear power in the United States.

The culture of nuclear power has been indelibly marked by Hiroshima and Nagasaki. Public awareness begins with these images of sudden, enormous destruction, symbolized in the rising mushroom cloud of a nuclear bomb blast. Even when discourse focuses on the use of nuclear reactors to produce electricity, the afterimage of the Bomb is always in the back of one's mind.

Boyer's rich analysis of American nuclear discourse from 1945 to 1950 shows how rapidly these images of unlimited destruction became central. H. V. Kaltenborn, in his NBC evening news broadcast reporting on the first atomic bomb, told his radio audience that "For all we know, we have created a Frankenstein! We must assume that with the passage of only a little time, an improved form of the new weapon we use today can be turned against us" (Boyer 1985, p. 5). *Life* magazine, with a circulation of over five million, devoted much of its August 20, 1945 issue to the Bomb, presenting full-page photographs of the towering mushroom clouds over Hiroshima and Nagasaki. The language that accompanied these frightening images was equally ferocious. Today, fears of extinction seem, as Boyer points out, "so familiar as to be almost trite, but it is important to recognize how *quickly* Americans began to articulate them" (1985, p. 15).

The "Faith in Progress" package on nuclear energy was just as quick off the mark. A dualism about nuclear energy is part of its core. Boyer points to the "either/or" structure of so many post-Hiroshima pronouncements. "The official platitude about Atomic Fission is that it can be a Force for Good (production) or a Force for Evil (war), and that the problem is simply how to use its Good rather than its Bad potentialities" (Macdonald 1945, p. 258)

Boyer argues that the faith expressed in the atom's peacetime promise was "part of the process by which the nation muted its awareness of Hiroshima and Nagasaki and of even more frightening future prospects" (1985, p. 127). Not only was it an "anodyne to terror" but it also helped to assuage any lingering discomfort over the destruction that America had already wrought with the fearful atom. A peace-loving America should embrace the challenge of making the atom "a benevolent servant" to produce for humankind "more comforts, more leisure, better health, more of real freedom [and] a much happier life" (Waymack 1947, p. 214).

Not all the discourse that Boyer reviews was equally optimistic. There were certainly cautious skeptics challenging the utopian claims. But this disagreement is a debate within a frame, a disagreement over how fast and how easily the promise of nuclear energy will be realized. As long as the issue is framed as a choice between atoms for war and atoms for peace, it is hard to see who could be against nuclear power development.

Over the next four decades, the discourse on nuclear power underwent dramatic changes. In reviewing different periods, I will consider the role of collective action in adding value to the production of its characteristic discourse.

The age of dualism (the 1950s)

Nuclear dualism remained essentially unchallenged for the first quarter century of the nuclear age. On December 8, 1953, President Eisenhower addressed the United Nations on nuclear power, presenting what media discourse labeled his "Atoms for Peace" speech. In it, he proposed to make American nuclear technology available to an international agency that would attempt to develop peaceful uses of nuclear energy.

The discourse on Eisenhower's speech further entrenched the dualism between atoms for peace and atoms for war. The Faith in Progress package remained unchallenged throughout. Atomic Energy Commission (AEC) chairman Lewis Strauss set the tone for the decade with a phrase that became a permanent part of the issue culture when he told the National Association of Science Writers in 1954 that "It is not too much to expect that our children will enjoy in their homes electrical energy *too cheap to meter.*"

The either/or structure of nuclear dualism continued to be strongly represented. The dominant metaphor was a road that branches into two alternative paths – one leading to the development of weapons of destruction, the other to the eradication of human misery. Again, there were optimists and cautious skeptics who warned that the technological problems in tapping this energy source for human betterment were formidable and far from solved. But no opposition to nuclear power development was presented, and no alternative package was ever offered.

The role of collective action

The first opposition to nuclear power did surface during this period, but its source was, to quote Mitchell (1981), an "elite quarrel" rather than a mass movement. The Joint Congressional Committee on Atomic Energy and the AEC fell out over the latter's construction permit for the Enrico Fermi breeder reactor, thirty miles south of Detroit. In August 1956, Joint Committee leaders encouraged the United Auto Workers (UAW) to oppose the reactor at public hearings and in court. But there was no movement effort during this period to mobilize even a local constituency to take some form of collective action.

The dog that didn't bark (the 1960s)

The UAW, later joined by two other unions, was unsuccessful in blocking the construction of the Fermi reactor. By October 1966, it was going through its final tests prior to going on-line. There were only four other reactors in the United States then operating, but, unlike the others, Fermi was scheduled to be the first breeder reactor. It would not only generate electricity but, in the process, produce plutonium-239, a highly radioactive material with an enormous half-life. To add to the dangers, the Fermi reactor was cooled by liquid sodium, a dangerous and volatile substance in the event of an accident.

On October 5, the cooling system failed and the fuel core experienced a partial meltdown. The automatic shutdown or "scram" system failed to operate and, alerted by alarms signaling the leak of radiation into the containment building, operators shut the plant down manually. The containment building was sealed off.

As far as we know, there was no radiation leak into the atmosphere, but the shutdown did not remove the major threat of a disastrous secondary accident during the following six months as officials tried to figure out what had happened and the damaged fuel was removed. Fuller (1975) likens the process to "look[ing] inside a gasoline tank with a lighted match." During the danger period, plans for the evacuation of a million or more people were discussed by officials but deemed impractical and unnecessary. By almost any reckoning, the Fermi accident was extremely serious. The mystery of Fermi, then, is why it didn't become the center of media discourse and the symbol that Three Mile Island (TMI) became.

Were these events so hidden that extensive media coverage was impossible? A plant official called the sheriff of the county in which the plant was located as well as officials in the state capital to alert them that something was amiss at Fermi. The plant official played down the danger and promised to keep them informed of further developments, asking them not to alert the public for fear of causing undue alarm and panic – a judgment the public officials apparently shared. Furthermore, another plant official called the local newspaper with a brief, somewhat ambiguous statement informing them that something was wrong at the plant.

There the story sat, unreported. More than five weeks after the accident, the *New York Times* carried a story on what it labeled a "mishap" at the Fermi reactor. There was nothing in the least alarming in the *Times* account. Walker Cisler, the president of Detroit Edison and the leading force behind the construction of the Fermi reactor, was quoted as saying "If all goes well ... we could start again shortly after the first of the year." A General Electric official classified what happened as "a minor perturbation," and a reassuring report from the Atomic Industrial Forum was duly noted.

No critic of nuclear power was quoted in the belated *Times* report on the Fermi accident. Indeed, it would have taken great enterprise to have found such a critic in 1966. In effect, there was no significant anti-nuclear-power discourse during this era. Nuclear power was, in general a nonissue. Faith in Progress remained the dominant package, so taken-for-granted in the little discourse that existed that it required no explicit defense.

The role of collective action

In the late 1950s and early 1960s, a movement against the atmosphere testing of nuclear weapons called public attention to the long-range dangers of radiation. Milk, "nature's most nearly perfect food" as the dairy industry advertised it, was found to contain strontium-90. A famous advertisement warned the public that "Dr. Spock is worried."

Some of this increased awareness about radiation dangers spilled over into concern about nuclear reactors. Local controversies developed over the licensing of a few reactors. Perhaps the most striking evidence for the impact of the movement against atmospheric testing can be found in the disappearance of any controversy about the licensing of nuclear power plants after the Limited Test Ban Treaty of 1963. With it, radiation concerns receded from media discourse. By the mid-1960s, the nuclear energy industry was enjoying a wave of new orders and no public opposition.

The rise of an anti-nuclear discourse (the 1970s to TMI)

By the time of the Three Mile Island accident in 1979, media discourse on nuclear power reflected an issue culture in flux. Faith in Progress was still the most prominent package but its earlier hegemony had been destroyed.

Nuclear power advocates were finding themselves increasingly on the defensive in spite of events that might appear to have strengthened support for it. The much publicized "energy crisis" of the 1970s stimulated the articulation of a second major pro-nuclear package, "Energy Independence." This package drew a pro-nuclear meaning from the Arab oil embargo of 1973. The following paragraph reproduces the Energy Independence package in an ideal typical form, drawing its language, imagery, and reasoning from real pamphlets and writings. Subsequent displayed paragraphs in this chapter do the same thing for other packages in the nuclear debate.

The lesson is how dependence on foreign sources for vitally needed energy can make the U.S. vulnerable to political blackmail. Nuclear energy must be understood in the context of this larger problem of energy independence. To achieve independence, we must develop and use every practical alternative energy source to imported oil, including nuclear energy. Nuclear energy, plus domestic oil, natural gas, and coal remain the only practical alternatives to a dangerous and humiliating dependence on foreign and, particularly, Middle Eastern sources. These foreign sources are unstable and unreliable and are likely to make unacceptable political demands. Do we want to be dependent on the whims of Arab sheiks? Ultimately, independence is the cornerstone of our freedom.

This addition to the pro-nuclear arsenal was more than offset by other developments that stimulated the rise of an anti-nuclear discourse. By the 1970s, nuclear dualism had been seriously eroded even among many keepers of the faith. With the advent of the Carter administration, proliferation of nuclear weapons became a presidential priority issue. To deal with the proliferation problem, Carter tried to promote stronger international control of the spread of nuclear technology, including reactor technology. Although a strong supporter of nuclear power generally, Carter turned against the breeder reactor lest the plutonium it produced be diverted to weapons use. Atoms for peace and atoms for war no longer appeared to be such separate paths. Subliminal mushroom clouds had begun to gather over even official discourse on the issue.

More importantly, the dualism was being undermined because of the safety issue. If a serious accident that releases large amounts of radiation into the atmosphere is possible at a nuclear reactor, then the destructive potential of this awesome energy is not confined to bombs.

A broad coalition of anti-nuclear-power groups raised the safety issue but as part of a number of different packages. The environmental wing, epitomized by Friends of the Earth, offered a "Soft Path" package:

Split wood, not atoms. Nuclear energy presents us with a fundamental choice about what kind of society we wish to be. Do we wish to continue a way of life that is wasteful of energy, relies on highly centralized technologies, and is insensitive to ecological consequences? Or do we want to become a society more in harmony with its natural environment? Nuclear energy relies on the wrong kind of technology – centralized and dangerous to the earth's long run ecology. We need to pursue alternative, soft paths. We should change our way of life to conserve energy as much as possible and to develop sources of energy that are ecologically safe, renewable and that lend themselves to decentralized production – for example, sun, wind, and water. Small is beautiful.

Other groups, epitomized by the Ralph Nader organization, Critical Mass, offered a more political, anti-corporate package, "Public Accountability";

If Exxon owned the sun, would we have solar energy? The root of the problem is the organization of nuclear production by profit making corporations, which minimizes accountability and control by the public. Spokesmen for the nuclear industry are motivated to protect their own economic interests, not the public interest. One cannot rely on what they say. Company officials are frequently dishonest, greedy, and arrogant. Who killed Karen Silkwood? The nuclear industry has used its political and economic power to undermine the serious exploration of energy alternatives. Public officials, who are supposed to monitor the activities of the industry, are all too often captives of it. They function more to protect the industry, than to protect the public.

Finally, the anti-nuclear movement, through organizations such as the Union of Concerned Scientists, offered a more pragmatic, cost-benefit package, "Not Cost-Effective." A litany of unsolved problems and delays are cited, leading to the conclusion that:

When one compares the costs and benefits of nuclear energy with the alternatives, it makes a poor showing. Nuclear power, through nobody's fault in particular, has turned out to be a lemon and it is foolish to keep pouring good money after bad by supporting the continued development of nuclear energy.

Media coverage of nuclear power accelerated rapidly in the mid-1970s. The Media Institute study (1979) of network television news reveals a burst of coverage at the time of Earth Day in 1970, followed by very little through 1974. Coverage then tripled in 1975 and doubled again the following year. Except for a temporary decrease in 1978, it continued to increase up to the time of Three Mile Island. In the first three months of 1979, before TMI, the networks ran twenty-six stories related to nuclear power.

A review of media discourse prior to TMI provides a mixed picture. With the exception of cartoons, there is little display of any anti-nuclear package, but the confident dualism of an earlier era has become uneasy at best. Faith in Progress is represented in the acceptance of nuclear power development as necessary and inevitable. But the discourse clearly recognizes it as controversial, even if one can gain only a vague awareness of how nuclear opponents think about the issue.

The apogee of anti-nuclear discourse in terms of impact on popular consciousness came with the release, a few weeks before TMI, of a major Hollywood film, *The China Syndrome*. The film numbered among its stars Jane Fonda, an actress so closely identified with the anti-nuclear movement that pro-nuclear groups used her as a symbol of that movement. The film's most important achievement was to provide a concrete, vivid image of how a disastrous nuclear accident could happen. But, of course, it was just a movie.

The role of collective action

How important was the anti-nuclear movement in opening the discourse on nuclear power to a range of packages and preparing the ground for a critical interpretation of the TMI accident? The process was sometimes subtle and indirect but, I will argue, collective action through noninstitutional channels was a crucial catalytic ingredient in the change.

The single most significant direct action was the site occupation of the Seabrook, New Hampshire nuclear reactor site by a group of over 1,400 demonstrators under the banner of the Clamshell Alliance. New Hampshire Governor Meldrim Thomson blessed the Clam with a major social control error. The 1,414 demonstrators who were arrested were not, as expected, released on their own recognizance. Instead, they were charged with criminal trespass and asked to post bail, ranging from $100 to $500, which they refused to do. They were then held in five National Guard armories for twelve days, and their situation became a continuing national story. Each of the three major television networks ran segments on five different days, although sometimes merely a short update.

The direct coverage of Seabrook in itself contains little discourse about nuclear power. Most media coverage treated the incident as a story about a dyadic conflict between Governor Thomson and the Clam over whether or not the Seabrook reactor would be completed. The central question in this frame was "who will win?" and not "what about nuclear power?" But the action succeeded in gaining broad media recognition that there was a serious controversy about nuclear power, thereby requiring the application of the balance norm.

The Clamshell Alliance did not succeed through its action in becoming the media-designated "other side" called for by the balance norm. This honor fell to the Union of Concerned Scientists (UCS), which presented all the proper cues for media credibility. A Media Institute study (1979) examined the use of "outside sources" (excluding government officials) in ten years of network coverage of nuclear power and found UCS in front by a large margin, almost doubling its nearest competitor. Part of this finding is testimony to the skill and enterprise of UCS in its sponsor activities and media strategies. But the actions of the Clam plus other anti-nuclear demonstrations and site occupations across the country helped to create the conditions for media-initiated contacts. When demonstrators were arrested at Seabrook, phones rang at UCS.

In February 1975, some 30,000 farmers, students, and assorted environmentalists occupied the site of a nuclear plant site in Wyhl, a rural area near the Rhine in the Kaiserstuhl area of southwestern Germany. For the next eight months, they continued, in varying numbers, to occupy the site, in effect creating a local village with a "friendship house" and a "People's High School." Local farmers supported the occupiers with food and in other ways. After eight months, the group agreed to end its occupation, pending a hearing and decision before a panel of judges. The panel ruled against the plant a few months before the Seabrook occupation, providing the anti-nuclear movement with a clear-cut victory. Wyhl became a potent symbol of successful, nonviolent direct action for American anti-nuclear activists.

The Wyhl occupation was a nonstory for American national television, never making it into network news coverage. Nevertheless, through movement enterprise, it became an important and inspiring example for the future Seabrook demonstrators. Descriptions and photographs circulated in movement forums, and a movement film company, Green Mountain Post Films put together a fifteen-minute documentary from footage originally shot by participants.

A second action that influenced the Seabrook demonstrators might, at first blush, seem a lonely act of defiance unworthy of the term "collective." In February 1974, a young man, acting alone, toppled a 500-foot weather tower on a planned nuclear site in Montague, Massachusetts. He then turned himself in to police and conducted his own defense at the subsequent trial.

All the symbols surrounding the act resonated with Yankee independence in the spirit of 1776 and the Boston Tea Party: the man's very name, Samuel Holden Lovejoy; the fact that he chose George Washington's birthday to perform his act; his home in the seedbed of the American Revolution; his occupation as a farmer. Lovejoy evoked this symbolism in a statement that he released, explaining his act by quoting from the Declaration of Independence and the Massachusetts Bill of Rights.

Lovejoy's act was neither planned nor carried out collectively, but it was collective in a broader sense. He was generally described in the coverage of the event as "a farmer" or "an organic farmer," and indeed he did earn his living at farming and as a child had spent his summers working on a farm. But Lovejoy was also a social movement activist. In the late 1960s, he had graduated from Amherst, an elite liberal arts college, where he participated in the anti-Vietnam war movement on campus. He had visited Cuba with the Venceremos Brigade and had joined an organic farm collective as part of the "back to the land" movement of the early 1970s. The collective farm where he lived and worked had earlier been associated with the Liberation News Service, part of the movement infrastructure.

After the trial, he worked with some of his movement friends to make a prize-winning documentary film, *Lovejoy's Nuclear War*. Green Mountain Post Films, the same filmmaker that distributed the Wyhl film, produced and distributed it. One of its writers, Harvey Wasserman, later became a leader and spokesman for the Clamshell Alliance. Lovejoy himself traveled around New England speaking at local anti-nuclear organizing meetings where, in the years leading up to Seabrook, the film was frequently shown.

Lovejoy's original act required individual courage and imagination, but it took place in a movement context. And it was not the act itself but the subsequent collective enterprise based on the act, that influenced the internal discourse of the anti-nuclear movement.

Events such as the "No Nuke" rock concerts, featuring popular singers Jackson Browne and Bonnie Raitt, helped to create a greater sense of solidarity and collective efficacy on the part of movement participants. By fostering an anti-nuclear culture, such events helped to create an appropriate climate and national audience for a film such as *The China Syndrome* and helped prepare media discourse for the accident at Three Mile Island. Had the Fermi accident occurred in the culture of 1979 instead of 1966, it would have become as familiar a symbol in media discourse as TMI.

Life imitates art (from TMI to Chernobyl)

As events unfold, each package must offer an interpretation that is consistent with its story line. Although it is always possible to do this, the task is sometimes labored, particularly if the event is, from the standpoint of the package, unexpected.

Consider the problem of the Faith in Progress package in the face of TMI and Chernobyl:

TMI showed that the safety systems worked even in the face of a string of improbable errors. A total core meltdown was prevented and most of the radiation released never breached the containment building. Furthermore, we learned from the experience and have improved safety even more. Chernobyl has equally sanguine lessons.

It shows the wisdom of the American nuclear industry in building large fortified containment structures as a safety precaution. U.S. nuclear reactors have multiple protective barriers, called "defense in depth." American nuclear reactors cannot be compared with their Soviet counterparts any more than their political systems are comparable. Furthermore, even in this most serious of accidents, it turns out that initial claims of thousands killed reflected mere hysteria, egged on by antinuclear activists.

Events, as the Fermi accident illustrates, do not speak for themselves. By 1979, a Faith in Progress interpretation was forced to compete with others that were saying that a serious nuclear accident could and probably will happen. No complicated interpretation is necessary for a prophecy fulfilled.

In media discourse after TMI, Faith in Progress had shrunk to a minority position, displayed in less than 25 percent of media commentary on nuclear power. Furthermore, its displays were often ironical or mocking ones, quoting the utopian vision of electricity that would be "too cheap to meter" to contrast it with the reality of present costs. Even when expressed more positively, the tone is frequently grudging and defensive. For example, NBC quotes Secretary of Energy James Schlesinger conceding that TMI was an "unfortunate occurrence and the reaction to it will not be beneficial, save that it may permit us to better understand some of the plant operations and that the Nuclear Regulatory Commission will be able to institute measures that will reduce risks."

The most striking fact about post-TMI discourse is the emergence into leading prominence of an unsponsored package, "Devil's Bargain." This package, emphasizing a dilemma, is fundamentally ambivalent about nuclear power, resonating with both the technological progress theme and the soft path countertheme.

So nuclear power turns out to be a bargain with the Devil. We didn't understand what we were getting into. We thought we could harness it to maintain our standard of living. Now we are committed to it and will sooner or later have to pay a price of unknown dimension. We have unleashed it, but we no longer can control it. Nuclear power is a powerful genie that we have summoned and are now unable to force back into its bottle; a Frankenstein monster that might turn on its creator. Nuclear power is a time bomb, waiting to explode. Nuclear energy is not simply one among several alternative energy sources but something more elemental. It defies a cost-benefit analysis. Radiation is invisible and one may be exposed without knowing it; its harmful effects may not show up right away but may strike suddenly and lethally at some later point. Radiation can create grotesque mutants. In a religious version, humans have dared to play God in tampering with the fundamental forces of nature and the universe. He who sows the wind, reaps the whirlwind.

Although the statement above has a negative ring, many expressions of Devil's Bargain do not fit comfortably into the category "against." Some who take this position resolve their ambivalence by becoming NIMBYs (Not In My Back Yard). For those embarrassed by such a stance, resignation rather than opposition is the characteristic position. But resignation and nimbyness seem to need no sponsors and, not surprisingly, neither officials nor challengers help this resignation along. Editorial cartoonists are especially likely to feature it, frequently with gallows humor about nasty nuclear surprises. Gallows humor, as Hodge and Mansfield suggest (1985, p. 210), is a way of "distancing the unthinkable so that it can be turned on its head, and subjected to a sense of control."

Among the anti-nuclear packages, Public Accountability is clearly the leader in media discourse. Soft Paths, in particular, is rarely displayed, except as general environmental concern. Faith in Progress has slipped to a beleaguered and defensive third, a far cry from the 1950s version. Most important, the most prominent package in media discourse has become an ambivalent one, Devil's Bargain. Any overall characterization of media discourse by percentage pro and con necessarily obscures this central fact.

TMI provided a legacy of new symbols as a permanent part of the discourse. Three events seem particularly significant in understanding the further evolution of discourse between the events at TMI and Chernobyl.

(1)   In 1981, Israel bombed an Iraqi nuclear reactor for fear that the highly enriched uranium it would have used as fuel would be diverted to bomb production – a further reminder of the close connection between nuclear power and nuclear weapons.
(2)   *Silkwood*, a second major Hollywood movie with a strong anti-corporate theme, was released in 1982, greatly broadening the recognition of this symbol of Public Accountability.
(3)   The collapse of OPEC and the decline in oil prices undercut fears about exploitation and blackmail through dependence on imported energy, lessening the potential salience of Energy Independence.

All these developments were bad news for supporters of nuclear energy but nothing compared to Chernobyl, framed in the media as a nuclear nightmare come true. Whither dualism in the images of an exploding reactor spewing a cloud of radioactivity over half a continent? The best a Faith in Progress advocate can hope for in media discourse after Chernobyl is a little benign neglect of the issue.

The role of collective action

The nuclear power industry in America is in a defensive position, engaged in damage control. There have been no new orders for nuclear power plants since TMI. Those already under construction but not yet operating are frequently subjected to continuing opposition. An anti-power position has become increasingly attractive to politicians, especially in New England.

Demonstrations against nuclear plants at Diablo Canyon in California and a number of other sites continued after TMI but had become an old story to journalists and stimulated very little new media discourse on nuclear power. But little influence on the discourse is needed at this point, as the existing issue culture is already quite conducive to further collective action. Mobilization against the licensing of new plants is a relatively easy task, as both anti-nuclear and ambivalent constituents can be mobilized around concerns about proximity and safety. Broader anti-nuclear packages are hardly necessary. And anyone who proposes constructing additional nuclear plants is likely to be deterred by the prospects of a long and bitter struggle.

Mobilization against the operation of plants under construction, or the closing of the hundred or so already operating, is, of course, a considerably more difficult task. Here, ambivalence is more likely to lead to paralysis and inaction as doubters face a Hobson's choice. In this case, the advantages of inertia lie with the supporters of nuclear power.

The discourse after Chernobyl boosted trends already under way and added a new exemplar to the anti-nuclear arsenal. Anti-nuclear demonstrators in West Germany added a potent new catchphrase that caught the ears of American journalists: "Chernobyl is everywhere." One can anticipate its further appearance at future demonstrations in the United States or Europe.

Conclusion

This analysis of nuclear power discourse is intended to make broader points about political discourse and collective action. Collective action by challengers can significantly alter issue cultures and thereby contribute to future mobilization efforts. In the case of nuclear power, the struggle over meaning continues, and the anti-nuclear movement is an important actor in that ongoing symbolic contest.

When official packages are in crisis and disarray, opportunities are created for challengers. An analysis of media discourse on nuclear power in America suggests that such a crisis condition exists today. The once dominant Faith in Progress package retains official sponsorship, but it is overwhelmed in media discourse by ambivalent and anti-nuclear alternatives.

Mobilization potential is also affected by the presence of certain themes and counterthemes in the political culture. Packages on a given issue resonate in varying degrees with these larger themes, thereby providing constraints and opportunities. Themes, I have argued, are paired with counterthemes in a dialectic relationship. Two pairs in particular have special relevance for the nuclear power issue – one dealing with the relationship of society and nature, centering on technology; the other dealing with the role of the state in the international order and centering on issues of national autonomy and global interdependence. On other issues, different themes and counterthemes will be relevant.

Issue cultures are the battleground for converting potential into action and challengers can affect them in significant ways. Unloosening the hold of officially sponsored packages in mass media discourse is a necessary first step in any long-term mobilization strategy. The powerful cultural resonances of packages such as Faith in Progress and Energy Independence must be understood and neutralized to accomplish this task.

But weakening official packages is only half the task. Collective action also depends on furthering the careers of mobilizing packages. There are different forums for an issue but general-audience mass media are especially important for consensus mobilization. Media discourse is itself influenced by the enterprise of package sponsors, including the activities of social movement organizations.

On many issues, media practices tend to give advantages to officials while creating handicaps and dilemmas for challengers. But these handicaps were successfully overcome in the case of the anti-nuclear-power movement in America, and media discourse changed dramatically and favorably. This is not the only issue on which officials, regardless of initial advantage, have lost control of the resulting media discourse. Challengers, then, can develop sophisticated strategies that take into account the organization and practices of journalists and can exploit the available opportunities. The synergy between demonstrators occupying nuclear plant sites and concerned scientists is an excellent example.

In emphasizing the role of collective action in altering political discourse, I run the danger of exaggerating it. The anti-nuclear movement did not create the mushroom clouds of Hiroshima and Nagasaki nor the accidents at TMI and Chernobyl that have left such an indelible imprint on the culture of the issue. But events take their meaning from the discourse in which they are embedded, and collective action helps to shape these meanings for both movement constituents and a larger audience.

References

Boyer, Paul. 1985. *By the Bomb's Early Light*. New York: Pantheon.
Fuller, John G. 1975. *We Almost Lost Detroit*. New York: Thomas Y. Crowell.

Hodge, Bob, and Alan Mansfield. 1985. "'Nothing Left to Laugh At': Humor as a Tactic of Resistance." In Paul Chilton (ed.), *Language and the Nuclear Arms Debate: Nukespeak Today*. London: Frances Pinter, pp. 197–211.

Macdonald, Dwight. 1945. "The Bomb." *Politics* 2 (Sept.): 257–260.

Media Institute. 1979. *Television Evening News Covers Nuclear Energy: A Ten-Year Perspective*. Washington, DC: Media Institute.

Mitchell, Robert C. 1981. "From Elite Quarrel to Mass Movement." *Society* 18: 76–84.

Snow, David A., and Robert D. Benford. 1988. "Ideology, Frame Resonance and Participant Mobilization." *International Social Movement Research* 1: 197–217.

Waymack, W. W. 1947. "A Letter to Judith and Dickie." *National Education Association Journal* 36: 214.

14

Moral boundaries, leisure activities, and justifying fun[*]

Gary Alan Fine

Some activities receive social approval; others are sneered at or even punished. Within a community, parties may battle over the meaning of an activity, with competing groups having strikingly different definitions and justifications.

This labeling argument is well recognized in sociological studies of deviance, stigma, and criminal behavior. Behaviors such as gambling, prostitution, or smoking are not automatically rejected but can be made so through public debate and legislative action. This labeling approach has been less discussed in examinations of expressive culture.

Olmsted (1988) spoke of a class of voluntary activities he termed "morally controversial leisure." He recognized that some activities – gun collecting, motorcycling, pool, or pinball – have a moral stigma attached to them. Dungeons and Dragons (Fine 1983; Martin and Fine 1991) is a recent example of a game that has been transformed into a controversial activity: a game that some suggest promotes suicide or Satanism. Moral entrepreneurs attempt to attach a label to a form of play that, for many players, is without a clear moral valuation. The controversy about war toys (Carlsson-Paige and Levin 1990; Sutton-Smith 1988) is another instance in which ideological politics influences the determination of children's play. Play and leisure matter in the organizing of society.

My underlying argument is that play and leisure ultimately are not separate from the values of the society but are a reflection of them and that they are often introjected into the political debate. Olmsted's (1988) emphasis on the class-based dynamics of labeling is compelling. He noted the change in valuation when upper-class billiard parlors were transformed to working-

* First published in 1991 as "Justifying fun: why we do not teach exotic dance in high school," *Play and Culture* 4(1): 87–99.

class pool halls. Class is not the only force that transforms the meaning of play. The increasing numbers of younger children who participated in fantasy role-playing games in the 1980s is probably partially responsible for this activity's controversy with parents. Children are seen as more vulnerable and easily manipulated by evil forces. Gender may also contribute to labeling, as when youth sports and scouting were attacked because of their decision to maintain gender segregation (see Fine 1981).

Play and leisure are vulnerable to cultural and political attacks and labeling because they fly in the face of social beliefs that emphasize the importance of instrumental activity. Play may seem troublingly irrational in a society that values rationality – a perspective that helps to explain why so few elementary school systems now permit recess for their charges. Participants in play and leisure find it difficult to explain their activities in discourse that is acceptable and rational to those outside of the activity. This reflects the emphasis in American culture on the Protestant ethic – a cultural perspective emphasizing that hard work, not play, is a sign of virtue (Olmsted 1988, p. 278).

In this chapter I address the moral valuation of expressive activities and the importance for participants of justifying their participation in light of instrumental concerns. My concern is with the internal and external definitions of these behaviors. To understand external valuation I rely upon my consideration of the social worlds of dance; for internal valuation I present portions of my ethnographic analysis of mushroom collectors. These examples could easily be duplicated and, in fact, one might study mushroom collectors to examine external stigma and dance to exemplify the pride of participants. In each case I argue that expressive behavior has no inherent meaning but is structured by social forces that direct the understandings of interested parties. In this claim I contribute to Brian Sutton-Smith's (1981) argument that play and leisure are not marginal but central cultural activities.

Dance labels

What is dance? Like any definitional question, the real answer is that it is many things, with a large gray boundary around its edges. This, of course, does not prevent scholars from attempting to delineate these boundaries. One useful definition is that of Judith Hanna (1988):

Dance can usefully be conceptualized as human behavior that is purposeful, from the dancer's perspective (usually shared by the society to which he or she belongs), is intentionally rhythmical, and has culturally patterned sequences of nonverbal body movements other than ordinary motor activities, the motion having inherent and aesthetic value. (p. 46)

An incomplete list of dance genres that would fit within this definition might include the following: ballet, interpretive dance, "movement," ballroom dance (and modern rock equivalents such as slam dance and break dance), tap dance, soft shoe, dance lines, folk dance, and exotic dance (including burlesque and striptease). Each of these genres could reasonably be found under the definitional umbrella that Hanna (1988) provided. Yet, not all have equal legitimacy as expressive culture. Dance instructors, if they wish to keep their jobs, cannot teach all of these styles. Certain forms have privileged status denied others – a recognition that is equally true of sports, games, and even imaginative play. For instance, consider the current political incorrectness of playing Cowboys and Indians. Or worse, recognize that fifty years ago children played concentration camp guard (Eitzen 1987).

Ballet, interpretive dance, and "movement" skills are typically taught through formal classes often housed in schools. Training children how to waltz has a respected place in certain prep and finishing schools; folk dances have a legitimate role in ethnically conscious schools and clubs. Attempts are occasionally made to recognize soft shoe and tap dance as high-status artistic endeavors. Even dance lines might be acceptable when placed within the context of cheer-leading and pep rallies.

Yet we do not instruct our daughters in exotic dance in high school. We honor Martha Graham but not Sally Rand. Why? One obvious but inadequate answer is that exotic dance is sexual. Yet, as Judith Hanna (1988) argued compellingly, all dance is sexual. The aesthetic manipulation of the body could hardly be otherwise. Hanna noted:

Sexuality and dance share the same instrument – the human body. Using the signature key of sexuality, essential for human survival and desirable, dance resonates universal behavior needs and particular concerns. With the medium as part of the message, dance evokes, reinforces, and clarifies desires and fantasies, some of which would otherwise be incoherent . . . Feelings and ideas about sexuality . . . take shape in dance. (p. xiii)

Presumably it is not sexuality *per se* that is objectionable in dance. Perhaps it is nudity. However, this cannot be the whole answer. Surely it is possible to teach young women (or young men, as there are calls for Chippendales) to remove their clothing while stopping at a discreet stage – a point as revealing as a ballerina's outfit. Yet, a modest striptease routine would entice few school boards or few dance educators. Further, some artistic dance is performed in the nude with distinctly sexual themes. Exotic dance is not the only form of dance that moves audiences in ways that some feel they should not be moved.

Neither sexuality nor nudity are adequate answers to explain the labeling of this form of dance. My answer – an answer that can be extended to other outlaw forms of play and culture – has to do with the organization of that social world. Certain forms of dance are privileged by both the dance community and the general public. Classical ballet is privileged. It has established critics, expansive venues, charitable events to support it, well-funded companies, international links, textbooks and theories, schools, professional organizations, and so on. Through its historical development, it has been certified as part of elite culture. Exotic dance has no such infrastructure; its performers do not have powerful networks of support, or cultural capital, that they can draw upon to obtain resources or status. Exotic dance is constrained by its grubby and nasty history just as ballet is ennobled by its ethereal one. Those who work in vineyards of exotic dance are typically seen as lower class, and worse, they lack the pretensions that come with Art. And yet, for their audience, they achieve an emotional and meaningful reaction which the producers of ballet can only envy. No one sleeps during burlesque. The label of the activity is analytically distinct from the content within.

The philosopher Arthur Danto (1964) once remarked that what separates an Andy Warhol-created box of Brillo from an actual box of Brillo is a theory of art. Warhol's theory – or the theory of those who stand behind him – permits us to welcome his Brillo box into the precincts of high art and display it in our museums. The sponsors of exotic dance have felt little need to create an intellectual theory behind what they do, and so they perform in disreputable locales. Performance artists, such as postmodern sex professional Annie Sprinkle (MM, 1990) or the NEA Four (four performance artists whose uncovering of their bodies led to their being denied funding by the NEA: Karen Finlay, who pours jello in her bra; Tim Miller; Holly Hughes; and John Fleck), are collectively developing an artistic theory that transforms revealing one's body into a meaningful act. Karen Finlay remarked about her "striptease," "I go through a ceremony, the woman being degraded. . . . It's about social issues that they [opponents of her federal funding] don't want to hear about" (Span and Hall 1990, p. 17). So, even undressing on stage can be backed by a theory.

Traditionally, and still today, the sponsors of exotic dance have felt little urge to create an intellectual theory to undergird their acts, and so they perform in disreputable locales. I do not mean to suggest that creating a justification by itself is enough to legitimate stripping, but, as Karen Finlay

(Span and Hall 1990) has suggested, it is a start. For a theory to be accepted, its sponsors must have adequate cultural capital and social status to make it credible and sufficient power to make it stick. Further, these entrepreneurs must find allies in the elite art world to legitimate their style. In fact, those entrepreneurs who specialize in the world of exotic dance are little concerned with the possibility of being part of an art world. For various historical, cultural, and religious reasons, exotic dance is outside the art world: panels of artists at granting agencies would not recognize this as deserving funding, much less the administrators who are more suscept-ible to political pressures. Exotic dance practitioners are skilled, controlled, and precise in their bodily movements and produce intense reactions in their audiences. Still, their social world is set apart from the world of ballet. The sexuality of the dance or the proportion of exposed flesh is not as crit-ical as who proposes to act that way and with what rationale.

George Dickie (1974) described the institution of art as being critical to aesthetic evaluation. He meant that the criterion for whether an object or performance is art is whether it is accepted by those who have the authority to make such decisions. Extend this to the institution of play, in which moral authorities, often parents, have similar rights. Implicit is the belief that there is no inherent worth in any activity; its definition is a socio-political act by those with power.

In comparing exotic dance and ballet I have deliberately made an extreme distinction. Little movement might be expected in the valuation given to these two dance forms. However, cultural forms change in their public value. The continuing controversy over sport shooting is a dramatic example of status decline in a leisure activity. In contrast, ceramicists and photographers have found that their activities have risen in value. These leisure crafts have become more serious arts – often removed from the world of play and leisure.

In dance, changes have occurred as well: creative movement would have been considered strange a few decades ago; much contemporary dance was impossible or obscene a century ago; and the idea that folk dances should be seriously taught in universities once seemed ludicrous. Such styles were not privileged, but they are becoming so today.

Tap dance seems to be a particularly dramatic case revealing the possibil-ity of change. This form, long associated with black vaudeville performers, has become increasingly accepted by dance critics as a legitimate art form. I doubt whether tap has become sufficiently accepted that it is being taught in high school, but it has probably reached the point where it could be. The images that we give dance, or any expressive activity, need not be static.

Speechless sentiment

These images are connected to public stereotypes. Dance is filled with public stereotypes, in some measure based on a lack of knowledge and familiarity. When many people watch dance, they cannot tell what is happening (striptease is, of course, a notable exception). Particularly in those corners of culture that are not transparently meaningful (e.g., those without spoken language), sophisticated training is needed for appreciation. As a result, musical forms as diverse as modern jazz and classical music appeal to a small audience, an audience educated in the music. In contrast, rock, show tunes, and country and western, being verbal and more accessible, reach a larger audience. The examples of jazz and various forms of ethnic instrumental music suggest that social class is not a prerequisite for musical appreciation. The critical factor is adequate socialization to the idiom. Could the reason that few like Muzak be that we have not been trained to appreciate it?

Dance is similarly situated. Doris Humphrey (1959) argued in *The Art of Making Dances*, "Dance is the only one of the theatre arts which has been divorced from words, whereas opera, musical comedy, drama, and choral music live and thrive entirely or extensively because of their wedding to words" (p. 125). Apparently Humphrey believed that this weakened dance; whether it did or not, it certainly made dance less accessible to a wide public. This has led to attempts to incorporate words with movement, at least in the world of professional dance. The question is how can dance be perceived as the sort of thing with which large numbers feel comfortable?

Population control

A second challenge affects the public image of dance: the image of dancers. When most people think of a dancer, the image is likely to be a woman – a thin, trim, small-breasted woman, perhaps an anorexic woman. To the extent that this image is widely shared, it channels which girls are likely to choose dance and may affect who wishes to see them. Fat girls could dance, but they don't. The point is even more dramatic with regard to men. The public image of the male dancer is of a male who has not fulfilled his sex role expectations. Such a dancer is seen as effeminate and, often, gay. A boy who takes up dance is doing something that, it is felt, should properly be left for girls. I have not seen figures on the proportion of homosexual male dancers, but (a) art worlds tend to have a relatively high proportion of gay participants, (b) whatever the actual proportion, the public perception is of a gay dance world, and (c) a boy who decides to dance will confront the stigma of those who label him in this way. As a consequence, sexual display becomes problematic.

These sexual images affect all aspects of the male dance world: recruitment of dancers, decisions to choose a dance career, and decisions to learn about dance and attend dance performances. If potential dancers and audiences feel uncomfortable watching these dancers because of their perceived gender role deviations or presumed sexual orientations, dance will be the poorer. These issues are often not considered consciously. Rather, an unspoken sense is that "dance is not for people like us." Given the emotionally loaded content of these issues, even a single claim that a boy who likes dance might be a "fag" may be enough to change that boy's leisure. Matters of public sexual persona may take precedence over the niceties of objectively deciding how to have fun.

Two factors limit the acceptance of dance: one is the inaccessibility of dance, arising out of an absence of intensive socialization to a cultural world of opaque significance because the language of dance (the meaning of movement) has not been taught and is not backed by a sub-culture that supports dance as a cultural medium. Second, the dance world's image is of a deviant sexual world and a world in which traditional gender role orientations are ignored. Dance on both counts seems peculiar to many Americans.

This argument must be generalized beyond the dance world to all leisure, culture, and play. All activities can be variously interpreted, and these interpretations have different moral, social, and political evaluations. Each form of expression has cultural meanings, and some of these meanings are known more widely than others. Cultural activities are socially situated; as with dance, this means that some activities have more *gravitas* than others. In addition, the meaning of the activity tends to rub off on the performers. These meanings may be complex: for example, although ballet may be valued, dancers are stigmatized. The question is now: how can a leisure world respond?

Accounts of worlds

Justifying organization

John Irwin (1977), in his research on urban lifestyles, pointed to the truly bewildering array of behavioral options "swirling in and around every large city" (p. 27). These activity systems, or scenes, range from bocce ball to parachuting, from capturing snakes to swinging. Contemporary citizens have more time than ever to meet their lust for leisure. Modernity provides both options and opportunities for engaging in leisure activity (e.g., Toffler 1970).

Many leisure scenes are organized through voluntary associations of like-minded individuals. As Banfield (1958) noted in *The Moral Basis of a Backward Society*, not only do Americans engage in a wide range of activities, they organize themselves into groups to do so. This realization is key to understanding the so-called "Great Change" in American community life (Warren 1972) – the claim that community is increasingly based on differentiated interests and associations and on the voluntary grounding of each. Whether we choose to accept the corollary that the traditional bases of community are in decline, there is little doubt that informal, voluntary groupings have become critical in shaping the sense of self and belonging in many individuals. Sociability is key to expressive satisfaction.

The Minnesota Mycological Society (MMS), which I observed, is but one of many organizations providing opportunities to share leisure, and more specifically to engage nature. For instance, organizations exist devoted to snakes and reptiles, bugs and butterflies, minerals and gems, walking, hunting, fishing, birding, snowmobiling, and cross-country skiing. Although all of these groups encourage their members to spend time away from "humanity" in "nature," paradoxically, this is often a social activity. Organized nature lovers are, for the most part, gregarious. It is as if they bring their community (family, friends) into the woods. Obviously some individuals go into the woods alone, and others do not join clubs, but often nature activity is combined with social interaction. Even when people do enter the woods alone, it is with the backdrop of a formal or informal group with which they can share their experiences. In this sense, being in nature is notable (Garfinkel 1967, pp. 38–41) – an appropriate backdrop for the narration of stories, accounts, and anecdotes.

Justifying participation

We must transcend the recognition that people join groups. It is sociologically equally important to realize that they feel a need to justify their belonging. They rely upon rhetorical strategies to convince themselves and others that their activity is morally and socially proper, that their community has a *raison d'être*. For adults, at least, fun is an insufficient justification for leisure. Indeed, a repeated finding from studies of leisure activity (e.g., Fine 1983; Irwin 1977; Lyng and Snow 1986; Mitchell 1983; Stebbins 1979) is that people provide elaborate and well-constructed rationales for what they choose to do.

Why should this be? We are dealing with the distinction between culturally expressive activity and instrumental activity, with expressive activity traditionally given a lower status. We incorporate experiencing fun into the Protestant ethic. One mushroom collector is explicit that the desire to collect specimens is connected to this attitude:

I suspect this attitude ultimately emanates not from a sense of selfishness, but from the Protestant ethic; it is somehow wrong not to work to gain something. Relaxation needs to be justified by purpose. In this light, mushroom hunting counts as a marvelous excuse to waste a summer's day among the trees, grasses and shafts of soft sunlight. (Strung 1983, p. 17)

It is not that people believe life should be all work – far from it; rather, they attempt to give value to their playful desires. People simultaneously attempt to humanize work and to legitimize leisure. The attempt to justify and magnify the realm of play is evident in the stream of writing following from the Dutch philosopher Johan Huizinga (1938) in *Homo Ludens*. This influential work attempted to justify play in a manner that would be quite unnecessary for work. Huizinga succinctly states his position when he speaks of "the supreme importance to civilization of the play-factor" (p. x). Thus, although seeming to transcend the Marxian equation of man with work, Huizinga and his admirers have accepted the basic proposition that what is important is that which is functional to civilization. Not only do theorists accept this notion, but it is part of our assumption about what work and leisure should be. Even playful activities should be productive and meaningful. As Paul Starr (1988, p. 32) noted:

If happiness lies only in "justified satisfaction," . . . the pursuit of happiness can easily turn into a pursuit of justification. A pig seems happy when merely satisfied, but the happiness of a human being, or an entire society, uniquely requires that its satisfaction be justified. Fortunately, justifications are not difficult to find.

Players have been socialized to believe that leisure is not to be justified for its own sake (Pieper 1963) but is to be awarded the moral trappings of work. Much literature on leisure attempts to describe not just its particular delights, but "the virtues that it breeds in men" (Bourjaily 1963, p. 10). Stebbins (1981), in examining amateurs, listed eight core justifications of leisure: self-actualization, self-expression, enhanced self-conception, self-gratification, self-enrichment, re-creation, sociable interaction, and group accomplishment (pp. 291–292).

It is a regular and expected practice for individuals and groups to invest moral significance in their leisure. For example, consider a quotation from Little League Baseball, Inc.'s (1977) book of rules and regulations that details the goals of the adult organizers:

Little League baseball is a program of service to youth. It is geared to provide an outlet of healthful activity and training under good leadership in the atmosphere of wholesome community participation. The movement is dedicated to helping children become good and decent citizens. It strives to inspire them with a goal and to enrich their lives toward the day when they must take their places in the world. It establishes for them rudiments of teamwork and fair play. (p. 2)

Or consider a disquisition by columnist George Will (1985) on the joys of angling:

Fishing, properly approached, is like the political philosophy of a civilized society: it is less a creed than a climate of opinion. Fishing is a way of life resembling what the incomparable Aristotle considered the best regime. That is, it combines democratic and aristocratic elements . . . Fishing, like the classics, teaches patience, humility, and the joy of life . . . A fisherman soon comes to terms with the fact that there are many forces and mysteries beyond his ken or control. (p. 72)

The same sentiments, though not as elaborately proclaimed, are evident in the comments of mushroomers (Fine 1987). Simply having fun is not reason enough to justify the establishment of a leisure world. The examples can be extended at length: character-building through climbing mountains (Mitchell 1983; Robbins 1987), fair play and ethics in hunting (Rieger 1986, pp. 16, 29), egalitarianism and patriotism in square dancing (Mattson 1987), internationalism from stamp collecting (Olmsted 1987), or increased sociability through being involved in science fiction sub-worlds (Bainbridge 1976; Fine 1983). As one mushroom collector claimed to me, one of the justifications of mushroom collecting is that "people think they're getting something out of it," no matter what cynical jibes outsiders may make.

These elaborated rationales for voluntary activity lead us to question Goffman's (1961) comment that "Games can be fun to play, and fun alone is the approved reason for playing them" (p. 17). When people make a considerable investment of time, money, and self in a leisure world, they need a justification (to themselves and to others) for their participation. They need to specify the rewards that come with the costs of playing. Participation is justified through instrumental rationales. Although recruitment to a play world may be based largely on circumstance (Fine 1983, pp. 50–52), the commitment to the activity must become principled if involvement is to continue.

Every shared leisure world has these elaborated rationales, although each differs in content – thus, explanations are simultaneously normative and idiographic in terms of the particular activity. Mushroomers emphasize the relationship between people and nature and the fact that they are able, through their hobby, to mediate the two. Through mushrooming they claim to learn respect for the beauty and proportion of nature. Mushrooming helps to overcome the dichotomy between these two spheres of experience, as exemplified in the following:

Early in the season, hunting in the cool, magnificent giant redwood forests . . . can produce both many choice edible mushrooms . . . and an exquisite sense of beauty, tranquility and exultation from the deep silence and sheer size of the trees. Right next to a thousand-year-old, 300-foot tall giant, you can find tiny, fragile, elegant Lepiotas and Mycenas, which can set your senses of proportion and perspective atingle. (Stickney 1983–4, pp. 27–28)

We learned that lawns can be like mycological jewel boxes with resplendent rough stones awaiting the motivated seeker capable of transforming each into a brilliant discovery. (Ristich 1984, p. 35)

Mushroomers argue that the moral worth of their hobby is that they do not take nature for granted but respect, appreciate, and understand it. They work at and learn from nature, and their hobby is not only moral but educational as well. Of course, not only mushrooms are at the heart of nature studies; other amateurs attend to birds, snakes, rocks, butterflies, flowers, trout, insects, deer, moss, or ferns. Yet, for each group there is something that is crucial about nature that provokes special feelings of a highly moral and almost religious intensity and provides the justification for engaging in this leisure activity. To the extent that these nature activities connect to political activism in the environmental sphere, such a concern with nature can be said to have a public-policy component to it, such as a deep belief in environmentalism (although the meaning of this slippery term is variable). It is common for hobbyists to connect their interest in mycology with interests that they have in other political movements. Mushrooming becomes a base people could draw on to justify their political involvements, just as their political involvements may lead them to this hobby.

Conclusions

In this essay, I focused on two domains of playful leisure. I argued that the moral character of leisure is open to interpretation. Specifically, the meaning of an activity (e.g., dance) is not inherent in the act itself but in the interpretation. What constitutes morality is not based in the formal characteristics of the activities but in their historical and class-based grounding. Interpretation is a dialogue between external definers and the participants who wish to justify what they do as moral and proper. In my case study of mushroomers, participants believed that this activity, which might seem bizarre to outsiders, was really a moral enterprise, one connected to learning about and appreciating the natural environment.

Ultimately, we choose to elaborate parts of the world, often through organized social interaction. Any group that focuses on and elaborates a core of specialized knowledge is making a value transformation – a claim that this particular corpus of knowledge is worth knowing. Mushrooms or dance in this interpretation can stand for any topic of segmental importance. The world is trivial until some make it less so, frequently through a social organization. That this requires a finely spun rhetoric of justification is evident. Leisure in a world dominated by the Protestant ethic must disguise itself in the garb of a calling.

References

Bainbridge, W. 1976. *The Spaceflight Revolution*. New York: Wiley.

Banfield, E. 1958. *The Moral Basis of a Backward Society*. Glencoe, IL: Free Press.

Bourjaily, V. 1963. *The Unnatural Enemy*. New York: Dial.

Carlsson-Paige, N., and Levin, D. E. 1990. *Who's Calling the Shots? How to Respond Effectively to Children's Fascination with War Play and War Toys*. Philadelphia: New Society.

Danto, A. 1964. "The Artworld." *Journal of Philosophy*, 61: 571–584.

Dickie, G. 1974. *Art and the Aesthetic: An Institutional Analysis*. Ithaca: Cornell University Press.

Eitzen, G. 1987. *Children and Play in the Holocaust*. Amherst: University of Massachusetts Press.

Fine, G. A. 1981. "Little League Baseball and the Development of the Male Sex Role." In R. A. Lewis (ed.), *Men in Difficult Times*. Englewood Cliffs, NJ: Prentice-Hall, pp. 62–74.

    1983. *Shared Fantasy: Role-Playing Games as Social Worlds*. Chicago: University of Chicago Press.

    1987. *With the Boys: Little League Baseball and Preadolescent Culture*. Chicago: University of Chicago Press.

Garfinkel, H. 1967. *Studies in Ethnomethodology*. Englewood Cliffs, NJ: Prentice-Hall.

Goffman, E. 1961. *Encounters*. Indianapolis: Bobbs-Merrill.

Hanna, J. 1988. *Dance, Sex and Gender*. Chicago: University of Chicago Press.

Huizinga, J. 1938. *Homo Ludens*. Boston: Beacon Press.

Humphrey, D. 1959. *The Art of Making Dances*. New York: Grove Press.

Irwin, J. 1977. *Scenes*. Beverly Hills, CA: Sage.

Little League Baseball, Inc. 1977. *Official Regulations and Playing Rules*. Williamsport, PA: Author.

Lyng, S. G., and Snow, D. 1986. "Vocabularies of Motive and High-Risk Behavior: The Case of Skydiving." In E. Lawler (ed.), *Advances in Group Process* (vol. 3, pp. 157–179). Greenwich, CT: JAI Press.

Martin, D. D., and G. A. Fine. 1991. "Satanic Cults, Satanic Play: Is Dungeons and Dragons a Breeding Ground for the Devil?" In J. Richardson, D. Bromley, and J. Best (eds.), *The Satanism Scare*. New York: Aldine de Gruyter, pp. 107–123.

Mattson, P. H. 1987. "Square Dancing: Modern Version of an Old Dance." Paper presented to the Association for the Study of Play, Montreal (March).

Mitchell, R. 1983. *Mountain Experience*. Chicago: University of Chicago Press.

MM. 1990. "Inside Annie Sprinkle." *Monk* 9: 42–50.

Olmsted, A. D. 1987. "Stamp Collectors and Stamp Collecting." Paper presented to the Popular Culture Association, Montreal (March).

  1988. "Morally Controversial Leisure: The Social World of Gun Collectors." *Symbolic Interaction* 11: 277–287.

Pieper, J. 1963. *Leisure: The Basis of Culture*. New York: Random House.

Rieger, J. 1986. *American Sportsmen and the Origins of Conservation* (rev. edn.). Norman: University of Oklahoma Press.

Ristich, S. 1984. "Phenology." *Mushroom* 2(3): 32–35.

Robbins, D. 1987. "Sport, Hegemony and the Middle Class: The Victorian Mountaineers." *Theory, Culture & Society* 4: 579–601.

Span, P., and C. Hall. 1990. "At Home with the NEA4." *American Theatre* 7(6): 14–19.

Starr, P. 1988. "Losing more ground." *The New Republic*, Dec. 5, pp. 32–36.

Stebbins, R. 1979. *Amateurs*. Beverly Hills, CA: Sage.

  1981. "Science Amators?: Rewards and Costs in Amateur Astronomy and Archaeology." *Journal of Leisure Research* 13: 289–304.

Stickney, L. 1983–4. "Mushroom Vagabonding." *Mushroom* 2(1): 27–28.

Strung, N. 1983. "The Greening." *Mushroom* 1(1): 17–18.

Sutton-Smith, B. 1981. *A History of Children's Play*. Philadelphia: University of Pennsylvania Press.

  1988. "War Toys and Childhood Aggression." *Play & Culture* 1: 57–69.

Toffler, A. 1970. *Future Shock*. New York: Random House.

Warren, R. 1972. *The Community in America*, 2nd edn. Chicago: Rand McNally.

Will, G. F. 1985. "The Democracy of Angling." *Newsweek*, August 19, p. 72.

15

Honor and conflict management in corporate life*

Calvin Morrill

The grey-suited managers directing large corporations seem unlikely practitioners of elaborate honor ceremonies. A top manager from Kanter's (1977, p. 48) study of a large corporation, for example, portrayed his executive offices as a "brain center, but there is no activity. It's like an old folks' home. You can see the cobwebs growing. A secretary every quarter of a mile. It's very sterile." Moore's (1962, p. 127) observations on executive conflict echo these sentiments: "Let us understand, this is a discussion among gentlemen, not a barroom brawl. The decor and the demeanor require restraint. This is civilized combat, not the law of the jungle." The images evoked by Kanter, Moore, and studies by Dalton (1959) and Macaulay (1963) suggest a buttoned-down culture in American corporate suites.

Such an expectation might accurately characterize corporate executive suites prior to the 1980s. Since that time two significant developments have disrupted the traditional social structures and "rules of the game" among top management: (1) widespread restructuring of corporate management, particularly experimentation with "matrix" management; and (2) the diffusion of hostile takeovers and their symbolic imagery. In this chapter I explore the impacts of these developments on top managers through the symbolic reframing of their conflict management in a large corporation.

Conflict management refers to any social process by which people or groups handle grievances about each other's behaviors (see generally, Black 1984, 1990; Nader and Todd 1978). At a theoretical level, the essay illustrates the utility of cross-cultural theories of conflict management for understanding behavior in organizational contexts. The study also suggests the *concurrent* importance of both social structural and symbolic factors

---

* First published in 1991 as "Conflict management, honor, and organizational change," *American Journal of Sociology* 97(3): 585–621.

enacted either purposively or conjuncturally in explaining organizational change. In this sense, "structure" and "symbolic systems" interact with each other and exist as overlapping social phenomena: social structure cannot exist without symbolic systems, which individuals use to make sense of, maintain, and change social structure, while symbolic systems cannot exist for long without "plausibility structures," which root symbols in behavioral patterns (Berger and Luckman 1966). Central to this process is what Thompson (1967, p. 148) views as a crucial paradox in complex organizations: the desire for flexibility and certainty to occur simultaneously in administration. In the corporation under study, ideas and practices related to matrix management appeared as a way to achieve administrative flexibility by loosening authority relations. The adoption of the matrix, however, led to great internal uncertainty within a wider environment of uncertainty caused by the advent of hostile takeovers. At the same time, the matrix created the structural conditions conducive to highly ritualized conflict management framed in a code of honor inspired by imagery associated with the rise of hostile takeovers and local imagery associated with the corporation's products. It is this code of honor that allowed executives to make sense of the turbulent American business world born of the 1980s.

Executive social organization, 1984–7

The corporation

Playco manufactures computers, electronic learning aids, and electronic toys and games for children as well as owning publishing houses, movie studios, computer manufacturers, small chemical companies, and numerous other subsidiaries. Forty-three executives (holding titles of vice-president or above) and some 3,000 other employees work at its headquarters. The company is publicly owned.

The majority of Playco top managers are white males between the ages of 35 and 65; they hold college and graduate degrees and are married with children. Women make up nearly one-fifth of its executives (cf. Kanter 1977, pp. 29–68). About one-third of the executives in the company have 15 years of service or more, one-third have 10–15 years of service, and the rest have worked for the company less than 10 years. Executives based at the company's headquarters are rarely transferred to other Playco facilities. Executives at headquarters, however, are transferred between duties.

Executives estimate that Playco replaces between 40 percent and 60 percent of its products every year (slightly lower than the firm's replacement rate in the 1970s). On any of their regular ten-hour work days, top managers from the same departments can be observed talking with one another in hallways, elevators, parking lots, over the phone, and in the lobbies at headquarters. Most of these conversations last less than three minutes. Colleagues who do not share the same department tend to confine their communication to frequent (three or four per week) meetings, or, in the absence of meetings, had sparse interaction.

The executive matrix

Playco has eight departments – operations, research and development (hereafter R&D), marketing, sales, finance, administration, engineering, and product planning – crosscut by seven product teams. This arrangement forms a product × function matrix (Davis and Lawrence 1977) in which product teams and functions are formally equal in decision-making in the organization. The "office of the president" represents the highest reach of the executive ranks and has four offices: the presidents of domestic and international affairs, the chief executive officer (CEO), and the chairman of the board, who is infrequently involved with the daily affairs of the company. Departments contain two executive ranks: vice-president and senior vice-president.

Product teams are responsible for the company's products from conception to distribution. Some teams are responsible for a single product, such as a best-selling learning aid; other teams are responsible for an entire product line, such as games for children six to nine years old. Vice-presidents of marketing are typically product team leaders, and one representative from each of the company's departments (except administration and finance) sits on each of the product teams. In most instances, executives fill out the membership of a product team, although "managers," the rank just below vice-president, may also be included. Several factors determine the membership of product teams: an executive's reputation, task expertise, friendships with product team members and leaders, and individual interest in becoming a member of a particular team.

Playco vice-presidents typically report to a senior vice-president and a team leader. Senior vice-presidents report to one of the presidents or to both a president and the chief executive officer, and they may sit on a product team in which they are also a "follower." An example of such a situation would be when a marketing vice-president leads a team composed, among other executives, of a senior vice-president of engineering or sales. Both of these situations create extremely uncertain lines of authority and can lead to conflict (see the next section for more information).

Similar ambiguities exist in executive evaluation. Although most top managers in business settings appear immune to close, standardized evaluation (Kanter 1977, p. 53), executives in the Playco matrix especially benefit in this regard. Their responsibilities often place them in formal structures with different standards and goals, a situation that creates differential allegiances in terms of authority and time commitments. Department heads, officially charged with the evaluation of their direct subordinates, find it difficult to apply meaningful evaluative criteria.

As Playco executives struggled inside the corporation to manage the uncertainty of their jobs, the American economy came to grips with significant changes in corporate acquisition practices. Hostile takeovers occur when "more than 50% of the shares of a large, publicly held corporation are purchased by another over the loud, public protestations of the target company's management, board of directors, and/or minority shareholders" (Hirsch 1986, p. 801). Playco engaged in several "friendly" takeovers (with the full knowledge and consent of shareholders and management of the target firms) and a few unsuccessful mergers; it also warded off two hostile takeovers and two friendly offers between 1975 and 1987. Executives at the firm considered friendly takeovers a legitimate business strategy, especially the way they "play the game." As the Playco chief executive officer put it, "We've worn white hats [as the good guys would in an Old West movie] in the takeover game. We're not [Carl] Ichan or Texas boys [in reference to particularly ruthless takeover entrepreneurs]. The firm has always been up front when going after [a takeover candidate]." Amid Playco's organizational and environmental changes, the ways executives framed their executive conflict management and the issues surrounding it also changed, as the next section demonstrates.

Executive conflict management patterns, 1984–7

Conflict issues

Like managers in other organizations with matrix management (Butler 1973; Stinchcombe 1985), much of the conflict among top managers at Playco centers around issues of executive coordination and responsibility, or, in the words of the executives themselves, "who's supposed to do what, how soon, and where." Such conflicts typically involve differences in what executives term "vision" between product team leaders and department heads – the heads manage the demands of many product teams while product team leaders, in the words of a department head, "only worry about their products." In one situation, for example, a senior vice-president leading a product team proposed a set of marketing goals that would eventually require significant modification of several of the company's manufacturing facilities. Several operations executives balked at the plan,

claiming that the senior vice-president had failed to take into consideration, as one vice-president put it, "the real constraints of manufacturing
and the time it takes to retool large assembly plants."

The allocation of resources within the company, such as budgetary
increases or decreases, office space, and personnel reductions or additions,
also fuels interpersonal tensions at the executive level. Most departments
at headquarters, for example, share office space in the crowded, multistorey
"main tower." To consolidate their departments, many executives attempt
to place subordinates with whom they most often work in offices near them.
This practice prompts conflict, as executives, trying to build similar spatial
"empires," find themselves outflanked by their colleagues. Still other executives fume at personnel reductions, especially if they face increasingly
difficult group goals but have fewer employees or smaller budgets to meet
them.

The simple scheduling of meetings can cause executive conflict as well.
Top managers often remarked during interviews about how "insulted" they
felt when colleagues canceled meetings without reasonable notice or simply
did not attend scheduled meetings. One executive commented, "We waste
more time around here trying to find meeting times. It takes a bozo to miss
a meeting without calling."

Conflict sometimes occurs over what top managers term "ethical issues":
the acceptance of gifts from supplies or vendors, the fabrication of travel
receipts, or pilfering from the company stores for private use. Conflicts also
arise over executive style. One example concerned a president who frequently delivers "barbed quips" to his opponents at executive meetings.
According to one top manager, "He has to learn to express his opinions,
strongly, even if they are opposed to whatever is on the floor, and not be so
sarcastic. He should treat his people [subordinates] more openly. But I guess
it's just a defense mechanism. It's hard to be shot at when all there is to shoot
is some quip you've thrown out." Some executives are also accused of "risk
aversion," such as when a president criticized a senior vice-president for his
unwillingness to take the lead in a quality control program that might initially generate cost overruns for a new product, but could save the company
millions of dollars in the long run.

Executives also regard the mixture of aggressiveness and excessive "emotional involvement" highly inappropriate. An executive nicknamed "the
Princess of Power" illustrates this tendency. An informant explained that
the Princess of Power sometimes violates executive etiquette: "Sometimes
in meetings, she hammers at you, and gets real emotional about it; lets
things get to a personal level. Most of the time she keeps it together. But
you never know when she's going to red line, when things will get out of

hand. It's one thing to be direct, to defend yourself in a strong manner, and quite another to be so emotional."

It is interesting as well to note what topics rarely cause executive conflict: gender issues related to fair treatment or hiring practices, legal consequences of company practices, idea-stealing from colleagues for new products, and the quality or social value of new products. When these issues do become the bases for conflict, executives are especially prone to focus on *how* the principals pursue their grievances, rather than the substantive content of the disputes themselves.

Honor among executives

Whatever the issues involved, Playco executives place great importance on personal reputation and public esteem in handling conflict with their colleagues – what they call an executive's "honor." At Playco, honor constitutes the core of managerial culture. Playco executives often speak of an executive's honor by reference to his or her "style," characterized as either "weak" or "strong," or whether they wear "white hats" or are "white knights," denoting their hero-like status. Less honorable executives are often referred to as "black hats" or "black knights," denoting a more deviant (in some cases, villainous) status. The origins of executive honor at Playco can be dated to the firm's first corporate acquisition in the mid-1970s. A senior vice-president recounted, "Everyone [executives] seemed to be talking about [hostile] takeovers; white knights this and black knights that; how some takeover players played the game dirty [were not 'up front' in their takeover bids]. The art of the takeover became big conversation at parties and at the office . . . We began talking about the 'art' [using his hands to make quotation marks in the air] of the meeting, getting promoted, dealing with each other; especially fighting with each other. Now it consumes us." A top manager depicts the honorable Playco executive: "What is a strong executive, a guy who wears a white hat? A tough son of a bitch, a guy who's not afraid to shoot it out with someone he doesn't agree with; who knows how to play the game; to win and lose with honor and dignity."

And the "game" at Playco, like many codes of honor (Bourdieu 1965, p. 211; Hoebel 1967 [1940], p. 188; Rieder 1984, p. 138; Wyatt-Brown 1984, p. 372), demands that challenges to one's decisions or behavior by worthy opponents be aggressively answered in a calculated fashion, and that one's colleagues recognize this concern for riposte. In this way, honor is, as Pitt-Rivers generally notes, the "value of a person in his own eyes, but also in the eyes of his society" (1965, p. 21). To be "honorable," then, means to follow a particular code of conduct and to have claim to the esteem of others and superiority over those who deviate from the code. At Playco, honorable individuals and groups often translate their status into decision-making power and greater opportunities for gaining resources and building trust. The informal status conferred by executive honor thus displays less ambiguity than formal titles in the matrix. Highly honorable executives' statements at executive meetings (regardless of content) receive more respect and outward consideration by their colleagues than those of less honorable executives. Formally low-ranking but highly honorable executives are, as the executives say, "brought into" important decision-making processes by members of the office of the president. The company trusts those of great honor with the most sensitive executive tasks (such as negotiating with foreign governments about building manufacturing or distribution facilities). Honorable executives usually receive requested product team assignments. Executives even ask their highly honorable colleagues to facilitate executive conflict management. A thirty-year veteran at the company commented on this aspect of honor among Playco executives: "Unless people [executives] see you have some notches on your gun, you're not going anywhere in this company. You can't back down here. You can't ambush people or shoot 'em in the back. Everyone knows real fast what color hat a manager wears in this organization."

Yet, task performance does not always translate into honor. A product team known as "the Wild Bunch" typifies this tendency as described by Playco's chief executive officer: "That team has been successful with our home computer lines, but they're a bunch of outlaws . . . In what way? They don't understand how we do business at [Playco]. There are appropriate ways and inappropriate ways of fighting. The members of [the Wild Bunch] never learned that."

The subsections that follow analyze how Playco executives handle conflict. First, I examine conflict among honorable executives, then conflict among executives of lesser repute.

Conflict management among honorable executives

The transformation of what Playco executives called conflict management "behind closed doors" during the 1970s into public contests of honor parallels the transformation of corporate acquisitions through symbolic imagery into a "high-stakes drama and spectator sport with a full panoply of characters cast as heroes and villains" (Hirsch 1986, p. 814). Playco executives generally use the imagery of "valiant efforts" and "failed gambits" to frame what they call "honorable" or "strong" conflict management. The Playco imagery used to describe honorable conflict also draws from the more respectful aspects of chivalry, the Old West, sports, and warfare genres, which are used in popular language to describe hostile takeovers and are also used at Playco in reference to the company's entertainment product lines. (Appendix B provides a detailed glossary of these terms.)

Behaviorally, Playco top managers pursue conflict with each other within the framework of a moralistic "tit for tat" (Rieder 1984, p. 133) or "reciprocal aggression" (Black 1990, p. 44) characteristic of vengeful conflict management among honorable disputants everywhere. As argued earlier, codes of honor generally specify the rules of challenge and riposte, including when, where, and with whom vengeance should occur. The social identity of an aggrieved party and the respective foe is particularly salient. Only weak subordinates, as several executives noted, back down from defending their decisions even when challenged by their superiors, and only weak superiors fail to press their claims against recalcitrant subordinates – at least until compromising with them. To protect or advance one's honor, only worthy opponents can be challenged or responded to in a dispute. This prerequisite assumes that the principals recognize each other as honorable (and are aware of their overall reputations in the company), and that with the exception of intradepartmental conflict (discussed below), top managers wait until a strategic public occasion to issue their challenges or responses. Worthy opponents therefore know and follow the rules of the game, generally play well (even if they lose), and abide and accept the consequences of their outcomes. Those who do not play the game well are to be avoided lest they contaminate the reputation of honorable and higher status executives. Table 1 presents the processual character of honorable conflict management and the quantitative distribution of these forms across three important contexts in which they occur at Playco: within departments, within product teams but between principals of different departments, and between principals of neither the same department nor the same product team.

Although reputations are mutable at Playco, early labeling as a "black hat" tends to follow an executive throughout his or her career at the firm. In this sense, one's initial reputation can act as a self-fulfilling prophecy. Behaviors one would find unusual in honorable executives, such as emotional outbursts or covert action, come to be expected from dishonorable Playco executives. Even behavior identical in both honorable and less honorable disputes – for example, arguing – carries with it different labels reflecting the status of the disputants. Arguments are "skirmishes" among honorable executives and "cat fights" among less honorable top managers. At the same time, honorable executives enjoy a certain leeway in explaining and having their behavior explained should they deviate from the code of honor.

Table 1. *Conflict management among honorable executives*

Work-unit membership of principals	Initial exchanges	Secondary exchanges	Probable outcomes
Same department (case 1)	Skirmish	Sit down	Patch up
Same product team (case 2)	Call out	Duel/shoot-out	Withdrawal Patch up Rescue by a white knight
Neither product team nor department (case 3)	Call out Hand grenades	War	War Rescue by a white knight Peace talks Jumping ship

If honor provides the overarching rules of the game for Playco executive disputes, the social distance between honorable disputants determines how those rules are applied in particular cases. Social distance generally increases the aggression between principals (defined here as the degree to which a disputant attempts to achieve a desired outcome at the expense of an adversary), the length of disputes, and their scope in terms of the number of individuals involved (on this general effect, see Koch 1974, pp. 91–158; Rieder 1984, pp. 146–148). Where the principals are more socially intimate, such as in the situation of departmental colleagues, the reciprocity of their actions is less exact, less controlled, but also less aggressive and more likely to end in a mutually agreeable outcome. Conflicts among departmental colleagues not only weaken departmental solidarity, which may be crucial in interdepartmental feuds, but also threaten the department's collective honor, so important in maintaining its status relative to other departments. For these reasons, departmental colleagues (especially department heads) always attempt to prevent a dispute from escalating beyond the private confines of their department. Because of the ambiguities in command created by the matrix, departmental colleagues' influence remains limited to persuasion. Such persuasion is most effective when departmental colleagues have offices near one another, where they can use their intimacy as a resource with one or the other principal. Social distance also affects the imagery used by principals in framing conflict management. More intimate principals tend to use less imagery in describing their own and their opponent's actions, and what imagery they use is less aggressive than that used for interdepartmental conflict. The narrative below offers a representative illustration of the intradepartmental conflict management pattern in table 1. It begins with an argument between the principals. Rather than escalating into a more aggressive pattern, the principals negotiated a compromise to their conflict.

Case 1: The gifted vice-presidents

Representing Playco in dealings with foreign companies is always tricky business. In one instance, two highly regarded operations vice-presidents, Spelling and Roberts, received gifts from a supplier during a trip to the supplier's Southeast Asian country. The gifts, intended to strengthen the relationship between Playco and the supplier, included expensive jade jewelry for the VPs' wives and Rolex watches for themselves. Spelling and Roberts knew they would have an argument with their senior vice-president, Turner, over accepting the gifts. Yet, as Roberts pointed out, "We took a greater risk not taking them and losing face with [the supplier]." The vice-presidents also knew Turner would take a strong stance in handling the matter because he wears one of the "whitest hats" in the firm. An argument did erupt between Spelling and Roberts and Turner when they told him of accepting the gifts. Turner demanded they return them, claiming they had put the company at legal risk. The principals in this case were quite confident that their colleagues recognized the ambiguities of doing business abroad and at the very least the information would not escape the organization in any traceable way to legal authorities. They were more concerned that the department not be viewed, in their words, as weak and torn by indecision. After talking with departmental colleagues about the importance of resolving their dispute, the principals had a "sit down" to "patch things up." Turner agreed to visit the country and meet with Playco's suppliers. Until then, Spelling and Roberts would refrain from accepting any more gifts from suppliers.

Interdepartmental cases exhibit the ritualistic nature of Playco executive conflict management more clearly. Case 2, for example, illustrates what Playco managers refer to as "meeting duels" before which the principals punctuate their challenges and ripostes with more patience and what Rieder (1984, p. 145) observes in general for honorable conflict management as "a quality of calculation . . . the wily sizing up of a rival's mettle" during which the disputants argue until their proposals or ideas are, as the executives say, "killed" and the bearer of the vanquished idea "withdraws." The case recounted below illustrates interdepartmental/product team conflict and also underscores an important principle among Playco executives: The *way* an executive *wins* is as important as the *way* he or she *loses*. Victors rarely claim complete defeat of an opponent. To do so would be to insult the honor of the vanquished and, in the process, do dishonor to themselves. Even executives who do not win, but who play by the rules, maintain a part of their reputations and can more easily restore their honor in a future context. At the same time, the imagery used by executives to frame interdepartmental disputes is more aggressive than that used in intradepartmental conflicts. Such variation conforms to the aggressive imagery used to describe socially distant actors relative to the business mainstream in highly publicized hostile takeovers (Hirsch 1986) and generally by international disputants to describe socially distant opponents (White 1965).

Case 2: The target date duel

Executives on the same product team often split into smaller groups to decide issues relevant to the team as a whole. Three executives (the marketing team leader, Harris, and the executive representatives from R&D,

West, and sales, Holmes) decided to meet separately from their team to devise a set of target dates for the development of a new set of products. West agreed to arrange meetings with Harris and Holmes and attempted to do so over a three-week period. Each time he scheduled a meeting, either Harris or Holmes canceled at the last minute. In the meantime, West quietly gathered the data necessary to organize the plan by himself because he knew he "was dealing with a couple of the strongest people on the product team and he had to be ready if they proposed their own plan." He announced at a regular team meeting he would not be caught by surprise by his colleagues and would put together a plan of his own. Facing Harris in the meeting, West announced that he would have nothing to do with a plan proposed by her or Holmes if, as he phrased it, "they had the balls to talk." Harris and Holmes decided that they might be able to "put some notches in their own guns if they shot [West's] proposal down." Harris responded to West's challenge by walking to his office the day after the meeting and, in the middle of a meeting between him and three other managers, telling West "that they [Harris and Holmes] were insulted that he had gone ahead without their participation, and would present a plan of their own." These challenges and counterchallenges indicated a "duel" would occur at the next team meeting. Besides carefully preparing their presentations, each of the principals prepared themselves through rituals common in such situations. All of the principals wore their lucky ties and "flack vests" (uncommonly worn on a day-to-day basis) to fend off "bullets" from the opposition. They all spent extra time at their respective health clubs: taking more time in the sauna, and each having a massage. They also spent considerable time talking to their departmental colleagues about how they would comport themselves during the presentation. The rest of the team knew of the "duel" via an agenda circulated three days prior to the meeting. As was customary, an uninvolved team member spun a gold ballpoint pen flat on the meeting table; the principal to whom the ink end pointed being allowed to chose the order of presentation. The pen pointed towards West, who elected to present last. Holmes acted as Harris's "second" by handing out copies of the plan to team members and handling all of the visual aids. West used an R&D middle manager as his second. At the conclusion of each presentation, West and Harris began a give and take of questions, criticisms, and rebuttals, each careful not to interrupt the other. During this part of the duel, Harris's rebuttals and criticisms grew weaker until she sat mute in response to two lengthy questions by West. West, on the other hand, grew stronger; his criticisms and rebuttals to Harris became more authoritative each time he spoke. The other team members remained silent until, as the operations representative put it, "the jousting concluded." In the aftermath of her two-minute silence to West's final points, Harris tore up her copy of her's and Holmes's plan signaling her acceptance of West's plan. Holmes then collected their copies of the plans from the rest of the team, and instructed a secretary to feed them into a paper shredder. After the meeting, the combatants ritualistically shook hands. During this duel, none of the other team members spoke until after it concluded, at which time, the meeting moved on to other agenda items. Later, West said to the observer that, although the team had not accepted his colleagues' plan, Harris and Holmes answered his challenge "strongly." "After all," he concluded, "they're strong players. They couldn't just sit there and do nothing after I called them out."

In disputes between principals who do not work in the same product team but reside in "strong" departments, matters that might seem trivial to an outsider – the remodeling of one wing of corporate headquarters, whether the company should fly the flags of representatives of foreign governments when they visit a company installation, and the location of assigned parking places for executive secretaries – may escalate into a collective feud between departments and their allies. In all of these cases, the lack of social links between the disputing departments means there is little social pressure to end hostilities and great social pressure to attack in honorable ways. Executives therefore find it nearly impossible to end interdepartmental conflicts without the aid of third parties who intervene to bring about some sort of settlement (white knights who "rescue" executives "in distress"). Here again the matrix weakens the ability of third parties to constrain or resolve hostilities because of ambiguous and overlapping chains of formal authority. As in intradepartmental conflict, such intervention is limited to persuasion.

Third-party supporters, however, may have the opposite effect on interdepartmental disputes, spreading them to many departments and product teams. The solidarity among marketing and operations executives, for example, engenders the expectation of automatic partisanship in interdepartmental conflict involving one of their own. In less cohesive units, such as sales, partisanship is highly tenuous, and defections to the opposition are not uncommon. Case 3 illustrates the modal patterns of conflict management among executives who do not work in the same unit and who work in departments with staunch allies.

Case 3: The marketing plan feud

Executives at Playco earn colorful nicknames, such as the aforementioned Princess of Power in marketing, as well as "Iron Man" in operations, and "the Wizard" in R&D. Early one calendar year, the Princess of Power became the head of marketing and introduced a new general marketing plan for the company. Playco traditionally concentrates its production in a five-month period. With several months of marketing surveys showing Playco's home computer products leading the way, the Princess of Power wanted to extend production to nine months per year to capitalize on expanding markets in Australia, Southeast Asia, and Europe. As head of operations, Iron Man believed this plan would jeopardize the quality control systems he had personally championed in the company's manufacturing facilities, systems that had become industry standards. The Princess of Power and Iron Man had never sat on a product team together, so when they met twice with members of the office of the president to discuss the nine-month plan, they spent most of their time, as Iron Man observed, "simply trying to understand each other." At some point in these meetings, Iron Man became annoyed with what he called the Princess of Power's "small bursts of fire" about operations' lack of support for the marketing plan. He felt that she treated him like a "horse put out to pasture who didn't know a demand function from a hole in the ground," while "she did not understand, nor want to understand what the hard constraints on manufacturing related to quality were." The Princess of Power believed Iron Man was "inflexible" and "out of touch with the direction the company had to go." At two subsequent meetings, the principals exchanged very direct complaints along the lines described above. By the fourth meeting, the Princess had grown tired of Iron Man's "roadblocks" and, in her words, "carefully questioned whether [Iron Man's] questions were in the company's own interests or his own." Iron Man waited several minutes until the Princess had finished her complaints about his reactions to the plan. He then stood up and, in his words, "threw her a couple of hand grenades by looking her in the eye and saying that [he] would not allow her to kill every idea he brought up in public." The Princess then stood up and said, "If you want a war, fine." The ensuing months witnessed the outbreak of war between operations and marketing and their supporters: several presentation shoot-outs and duels between marketing and operations executives and managers as well as the mobilization of members of other departments on behalf of the principal departments. During the dispute, the vice-president of administration, Johnson, known as a white knight who rescued executives in distress, intervened with two other white knights – the president of international affairs, Sims, and the Wizard – to reduce the "wounded list." These attempts proved initially unsuccessful, but eventually resulted in a two-day off-site set of "peace talks" which nearly thirty executives and managers attended. The meetings produced a truce between the factions and a private

Table 2. *Conflict management among less honorable executives*

Work-unit membership of principals	Initial exchanges	Secondary exchanges	Probable outcomes
Same department (case 4)	Flying low Cat fight	Flying low Hiding Red lining	Amnesia Jumping ship Vaporized
Same product team (case 5)	Waltzing around	Temporary amnesia Gas Crying Hiding Meltdown	Amnesia Jumping ship
Neither product team nor department (case 6)	Call out	Temporary amnesia Crying Bushwhack/ambush/raid	Amnesia Jumping ship

dinner between Iron Man and the Princess at which, according to Johnson, "they agreed they disagreed on a variety of matters."

While these analyses and illustrative cases portray the modal realities of conflict management among Playco executives, there is, as the Playco managers say, a "seamier side" to political life at the top of the corporation that involves only those executives labeled as weak.

Conflict management among less honorable executives

Less honorable executives most clearly indicate their lower status by not responding at all or responding in inappropriate ways to grievances by colleagues. They allow colleagues to verbally "rape" them, simply tolerate their opponents by "flying low," participate in covert action to inconvenience opposition departments through "raids," or avoid inflamed conflicts by "parachuting out of burning fighters" (when they should see them to their end and "ride them down"). Table 2 contains the patterns of conflict that are labeled "less honorable" by Playco executives.

The imagery of conflict used by executives to describe the conflict management among less honorable executives also highlights that group's violations of the code of honor at Playco. Whereas honorable colleagues portray their opponents in worthy lights by referring to them as white hats or serious players, less honorable executives talk about their adversaries as "dicks" or "sleeping beauties." Moreover, honorable executives commonly label their less honorable departmental colleagues as "pigeons" or "bozos" and their arguments as "cat fights" rather than the more value-neutral "skirmish."

The intradepartmental patterns of executives labeled as less honorable are illustrated in case 4 below. It should be noted that Playco executives do not deplore fighting between executives. Rather, they deplore it when it is outside the boundaries of the code of honor. During fieldwork, for example, two boxing matches were arranged between executives at a local gym in order that they might, as one executive observed, "work out their differences." Case 4 involves executives whose long-standing, unexpressed grievances unpredictably escalated from a public argument to scuffling, and eventually to the resignation of one principal.

Case 4: Red lining in the parking lot

A vice-president of sales liked to think of himself as, and liked others to call him, "the Terminator" because, as he put it, "[he] hunts big game anyway he can [looks for honorable opponents whom he can best in conflict]." According to several Playco executives, the Terminator's track record was not as good as he liked to think, and he frequently allowed the strongest executives to rape him in meetings. When he did retaliate, he did so by attacking pigeons. The Terminator and his senior vice-president, Greer, each believed the other to be a dick but flew low in not expressing his grievances. One morning, while employees streamed into Playco's main parking lot, the Terminator was unloading briefcases from the trunk of his car when Greer eased past in his car and asked to see the Terminator in his office later that day. After Greer had parked, the Terminator walked over to his car and said, "Hey, I'm not your dog. What the hell do you want to see me for now?" As the two men argued, other issues surfaced, including the Terminator's open "womanizing" with company secretaries and with married women at a local health club to which many Playco executives belonged. The cat fight quickly "red lined" whereupon Greer shoved the Terminator against the trunk of his Lotus sports car. The Terminator then grabbed Greer and pushed him to the pavement. A crowd of employees gathered to watch the mêlée, and as company security officers arrived on the scene, Greer threatened to "vaporize" the Terminator. Although outward pressure from Greer was not evident, the Terminator "jumped ship" several weeks later.

Social distance has the same general effects on conflict management among less honorable top managers as it does on their honorable colleagues. Intradepartmenal conflict among less honorable executives is less aggressive, is shorter, and has a narrower scope than that which occurs interdepartmentally. The imagery used by less honorable disputants to describe socially distant opponents is also more aggressive (in the sense that the principals attempt to garner zero-sum wins with their opponents). Case 5 illustrates interdepartmental conflict between less honorable executives. Note that this case begins in a similar fashion as one might between two honorable executives. However, it quickly evolves into several nonverbal grievance exchanges, including "temporary amnesia" by one principal of the other's complaints, "crying" about the conflict by both principals to confidants, "hiding" by one principal to avoid the other, and finally a "meltdown."

Case 5: The Wild Bunch

The Wild Bunch is a product team responsible for computer learning aids for children. In one situation, planning vice-president Pound believed operations vice-president Ingle to be unsuitable to present their team's new products at what Playco managers termed a product send-off (presentations attended by hundreds of Playco employees to preview new products before they go into production). At two weekly team meetings, Pound and Ingle "waltzed around" about the latter's suitability to present. At a third meeting the following week, Ingle turned away from his colleague and noticeably frowned as though he had a "gas attack" to a team member sitting on his other side. He then interrupted Pound in mid-sentence with a loud, lengthy comment. Subsequently, both Pound and Ingle went crying to friends, but never confronted each other. Pound hid from team meetings for two weeks because, as he put it, "he couldn't stand to be in the same room as that dick [Ingle]." Rumors began in the company that Pound feared confronting Ingle. Two weeks after the initial incident, at another team meeting, Ingle interrupted Pound loudly again and Pound responded by raking his hand across the burgundy teak meeting table, pushing his and two other colleagues' materials to the carpet. Pound and Ingle then had a meltdown by pushing each other and swinging their fists. The meltdown lasted several minutes, spilling out into the hallway where a security guard watched for two or three minutes before breaking it up. Inside the meeting room, two colleagues continued talking about another issue, and two others were laughing. The principals suffered several bruises and clothing tears. Word of the fight quickly spread through the company. Pound commented in the aftermath that he "couldn't let that dick [Ingle] get away with pretending not to listen to me again."

Whereas honorable disputants can mobilize departmental and cross-departmental allies to attack enemies through meeting duels, less honorable executives command neither the loyalty nor the trust to do the same. The scope of less honorable executive conflict management enlarges in unpredictable ways as executives become allies ("sucked in") because, for example, they happen to work in the physical proximity of a feud. Respectable third parties do not generally intervene to settle such disputes either, because of the same trepidation one would have, an executive noted, in intervening in a fight between rabid dogs: "You never know what's going to happen, even if it's your own dog. You could get bit yourself." The narrative below illustrates this process. Note that it begins with a "call out" (as in interdepartmental conflicts between honorable executives). Yet its path deviates from the honorable way when the principals engage in numerous covert actions ("raids," "ambushes," and "bushwhacks") against each other and allow their grievances to peter out as they tire of the conflict without a public and ritualistic resolution.

Case 6: The finance raid

Two of the executives known for their covert conflict management (who wear the black hats in the firm), Bell, the chief financial officer, and

Tweedle, the president of domestic affairs, became embittered over Tweedle's attempt to transfer Hicks, a finance vice-president, to engineering to create a new position, vice-president of engineering cost control. Financial executives do not meet regularly with product teams but are ultimately responsible for all cost control. Tweedle viewed the transfer as an experimental attempt to integrate finance with the product teams. Hicks would remain a member of finance, have an office in engineering, and meet, when appropriate, with one or two product teams. Bell believed Tweedle had ulterior motives: "This is a chicken shit ambush on my decision power in corporate financial affairs. [Tweedle] tried to do this last year by taking more formal control for the domestic budget. Now this. [Hicks] would end up reporting to [Tweedle]." Bell called out Tweedle at a meeting of the office of the presidents to "lay out his whole strategy for integrating finance into the product teams." Tweedle did not respond at the meeting or subsequently, suffering temporary amnesia in denying to close colleagues that there was any problem between him and Bell. Hicks's reassignment occurred as Tweedle planned. In the ensuing months, Tweedle ignored Bell's many memos questioning the transfer and spread rumors that he and Bell had worked out an agreement for Hicks's transfer and that Bell's word was worth as much as an "Itanian lira money order" and perhaps he "did not have all his dogs on one leash." The dispute escalated during remodeling at headquarters when Tweedle approved plans for temporarily moving finance executives to a building adjacent to the executive "flight deck." Without notifying finance, the move occurred on a weekend. When finance executives arrived the following Monday, they discovered the move and that several important computer tapes and data printouts from an internal audit they had just completed had been thrown away. Tweedle knew that Bell had personally championed the now-disrupted audit. Speculation ran high in the company that Tweedle had involved himself directly in throwing away the data when he had stopped by headquarters for two hours during the move. Tweedle expressed his temporary amnesia by maintaining that he had nothing against finance, although he admitted to some that the move would upset the "sleeping beauties in finance" who were believed to be enamored with their own abilities but ignorant of their negative reputation among other top managers. Bell stopped his memo-writing for two weeks following this incident as his staff attempted to reconstruct the data from older, backup tapes. In the meantime, Bell suspended all financial data reports to teams developing domestic products. Bushwhacks such as these continued for nearly two years until Tweedle and Bell tired of the battle. Tweedle and Bell eventually jumped ship. Hicks now occupies the chief financial officer's position.

Discussion and implications

One could argue that Playco's growth into a multinational corporation during the 1970s, and its high product replacement rate (which decreased in the 1980s), could also have led to the observed conflict patterns. One could also argue that the imagery Playco executives use to frame their conflicts derives solely from their product lines: games and learning aids that encompass the themes of chivalrous duels, Old West shoot-outs, and science fiction warfare. Indeed, only thirty of seventy-two Playco conflict images derive directly from hostile takeover imagery (see Appendix B). Yet, the very same themes in these product lines – the "bread and butter" of the firm, as one executive put it, for over thirty years – existed prior to the firm's restructuring with the matrix and the advent of the hostile takeover. Despite all of these factors, the culture of honor among Playco executives did not exist until the 1980s. Conflict management prior to the 1980s resembled the placid scenes offered by Kanter (1977) and Moore (1962). Thus, many of the local symbols that Playco executives draw on to frame their conflict linguistically into contests of honor existed, but they did not have a plausibility structure associated with them until the transformations brought about by the matrix. By the same token, the imagery of the hostile takeover would not have had the impact on executives if it did not coexist with the particular plausibility structure at Playco. If the language of the hostile takeover represents the institutionalization of a *symbolic* dimension of a macro social change in *intercorporate* American business (Hirsch 1986, p. 821), the experience of executives at Playco illustrates the impact of symbolic *and* structural dimensions of matrix structures and hostile takeovers *inside* corporations.

Small wins and individual uncertainty

In a world where the corporation could be "taken over at any minute," as one Playco top manager put it, in which corporations are increasingly restructuring their operations, executives realize their substantive decisions can become instantly meaningless because of the actions of unknown investors or shareholders. One of Playco's presidents commented that "to worry about a single decision and how it's going to affect the firm is foolish. We can't really control what the market does, what the shareholders do, or what some yahoo investor with big money wants to do [in the case of a hostile takeover]. So you might as well try to affect the things closest to you."

In social psychological terms such behavior tacitly adopts the strategy of "small wins . . . controllable opportunities that produce visible results" (Weick 1984, p. 43). Actual restructuring and its threat in companies that have experienced takeovers has eroded organizational loyalty to the point where small-win strategies often manifest themselves as "managerial free agency" (Hirsch 1987, pp. 107–118): a lack of focus on corporate goals and the continual consideration of viable employment with organizations other than one's own. Playco executives breathe the air of takeovers, have witnessed their effects on companies that have been so acquired, but have successfully fended off takeover attempts themselves. Although Playco executives have not experienced high turnover rates, as indicated by their generally lengthy tenures with the firm, they have adapted to this increasing nihilism towards corporate loyalty by focusing on their own fates as expressed ritualistically through small-win strategies in their culture of honor.

Social similarity and organizational uncertainty

Honor not only allows individuals to maintain a sense of balance and efficacy within the volatility of American business, it also operates as an organizational culture control in terms of social similarity. Social similarity subtly functions to reduce the uncertainty inherent in the discretionary nature of executive jobs (Kanter 1977). Executives tend to hire people who are socially similar to themselves in terms of ethnicity, education, class background, and gender to fill top managerial posts in order to assure some predictability and trust in their behavior (Kanter 1977, p. 53).

The functions of social similarity persist among Playco executives through executive honor. Playco's code of honor defines a particular "masculine" standard to which viable members of its relevant community must adhere. Like codes of honor everywhere, it is the key link between self and community, defining appropriate institutional roles (Berger, Berger, and Kellner 1973, p. 86). Honor at Playco defines who is to be trusted; it helps executives predict what their colleagues will do in a setting that might otherwise seem like a maelstrom of ambiguous authority and continual confrontation. The unnerving experience of conflict is framed as a contest of honor with the roles of the principals and their supporters carefully defined. Honor therefore provides an evaluative criterion for executives that operates outside of the official criteria but one that executives can more easily use in dealing with colleagues. In this way, the fetishism of honor among Playco executives orders their goal-directed behavior.

This is why less honorable executives are avoided by their honorable colleagues. Playco executives fear the unpredictability of their less honorable colleagues far more than the familiar challenges of their honorable colleagues. In one way, less honorable executives possess a more valuable form of capital than their honorable colleagues: unpredictability. Yet, in imperfectly imitating the routine conflict management of their honorable colleagues, less honorable executives ironically become impotent in transforming this capital into power by framing their behavior in relatively predictable patterns.

To be sure, Playco executives do think about substantive organizational productivity, but these concerns are mixed with their framing of their intracorporate conflict as the accumulation of honor through participation in vengeance games. It is not simply a matter of whether structure *or* culture takes precedence in explaining conflict management and organizational change, but how they intertwine to affect social settings and the people that constitute them. The challenge, then, for scholars is to construct theory that simultaneously recognizes the realities and rationalities of formal and informal structures while not ignoring the impact of symbols in conflict management and organizational life.

Appendix A: Fieldwork methods

I secured access to Playco through a personal tie to a highly respected consultant who had previously worked with the firm. Three months of negotiation followed this initial contact, during which I established an independent identity from the consultant. Fieldwork commenced at Playco's world headquarters in summer 1984 and lasted through fall 1985. Data collection derived from: (1) informal, conversational interviewing (Dalton 1959, p. 280) with every Playco executive ($n=43$) and many of their support personnel ($n=12$); (2) formal, semistructured interviews of executives ($n=27$); (3) direct observation of formal meetings and casual interaction on a regular basis with Playco personnel throughout the 15-month fieldwork period; and (4) the collection of company documents. Interviews averaged 90 minutes in length and observations averaged 5 hours in length.

During fieldwork, I was seen as a young, bright, naive observer who needed to be educated, as the executives put it, in the ways of the business world. I also found executives extremely lonely in that they had few confidants (except psychiatrists and other counselors they paid) whom they trusted with the delicate insider information of the corporation. Thus I provided a safe haven to talk about the most intimate matters, which could be politically disastrous for informants and damaging to the corporation as a whole. Recent details about the firm have been learned from informants who work in various capacities in Playco.

These methods were specifically used to gather information on the contemporary setting of the organization and in the service of a "trouble case" strategy that consists of "search[es] for instances of hitch, dispute, grievance, trouble [between people] and inquiry into what the trouble was and what was done about it" (Llewellyn and Hoebel 1983 [1941], p. 21; see also Nader and Todd 1978, pp. 5–8; cf. Cain and Kulcsar 1982). This strategy yielded information on thirty-nine trouble cases at Playco. All trouble cases surfaced in interviews with participants, third parties, uninvolved witnesses, or through direct observation.

Tape recording initially produced self-consciousness in informants. Ethnographic data was thus recorded by jotted notes during conversational interviewing and informal observations, and by extensive note-taking during semistructured interviews. These notes became the basis of narratives written on a personal computer as soon as possible after exiting the field.

Appendix B: Glossary of Playco conflict imagery and hostile takeover equivalents[a]

Image	Definition
Ambush	Covert action to inconvenience an adversary (synonyms: "bushwhack," and "cheap shot"; "ambush" refers to a swift and premeditated takeover attempt in takeover imagery)
Amnesia	Feigned ignorance of a colleague's grievances
Art of	Description of the aesthetics of executive comportment
Black hat	An executive who often engages in covert action to manage conflict with opponents; from the practice of dressing villains in black hats in early Old West and pirate movies (synonym: "pirate"; cf. "black knight")
Black knight	An executive who often engages in covert action against opponents, does not support his intradepartmental colleagues in disputes (cf. "black hat"; "black knight" refers to an unfriendly acquirer from the perspective of an acquired firm in takeover imagery)
Blindsiding	An intentional and surprising public embarrassment by one executive at another's expense

Appendix B (*cont.*)

Image	Definition
Bozo	An executive who ineptly attempts to follow the code of honor to press his grievances against opponents (cf. "dick")
Bullets	Criticisms of an executive's plan by an opponent delivered in the midst of a meeting "duel" or "shoot-out"
Burning fighter	A particularly aggressive executive dispute
Bushwhack	Covert action to inconvenience an adversary (synonyms: "ambush" and "cheap shot")
Call out	Public challenge to a colleague for a "shoot-out" or "duel"
Cavalry	Departmental executives who come to a colleague's aid in an interdepartmental dispute
Cheap shot	Covert action to inconvenience an adversary (synonyms: "ambush" and "bushwhack")
Crying	Secretly complaining to a colleague about another's behavior without the offender knowing
Declaring war	Undertaking collective action to pursue grievances against a collective opponent aggressively and overtly (also expressed as "to go to war")
Dick	A belligerent executive who ineptly attempts to follow the code of honor to press his grievances against opponents (literal reference to the penis; cf. "bozo")
Dogs on a leash	Mental health (not having one's "dogs on a leash" indicates mental instability)
Duel	Ritualized contest of elaborate formal presentations used to settle an interdepartmental executive dispute (synonym: "shoot-out")
Executive in distress	Executive who ineptly follows the code of honor, but who colleagues feel can be saved; also an honorable executive caught in a "burning fighter" (see also "white knight"; similar to the notion in takeover imagery of

Appendix B (*cont.*)

Image	Definition
	"white knights" rescuing corporations in distress from unfriendly acquiring firms)
Failed gambit	Losing an executive "duel" or "shoot-out"
Flak vest	Suit vest worn by honorable executives during a "shoot-out" or "duel" to ward off "bullets" from the opposition ("flak" refers to impediments to a takeover raised by a target in takeover imagery)
Flight deck	The executive suites in the multistorey "main tower" at headquarters from which most "big ideas" are launched
Flying low	Not confronting an offender with long-standing grievances against his or her behavior
Gas attack	Nonverbal expression of scorn for an offending colleague
Hand grenades	Particularly aggressive insults expressed face-to-face by disputants
Hiding	Avoiding an opponent
Hunting big game	Looking for honorable executives with whom to dispute in order to establish a reputation ("hunting big game" refers to looking for large corporate takeover candidates in takeover imagery)
Iron Man	The senior vice-president of operations known for his "stiffness" in interpersonal affairs, his background in the steel industry, and his reputation as one of the most honorable executives at Playco
Italian lira money order	Reference to the worthlessness of an executive's promise (related to the takeover imagery of "Russian rubles" used to describe early, noncash takeover offers)
Jumping ship	Resigning from the corporation
Killing an idea	A principal's idea or proposal in a meeting duel is refuted by another principal and then wholly rejected as viable by a wider audience (cf. "withdrawal")

Appendix B (*cont.*)

Image	Definition
Life vest	Suit vest worn by less honorable executives when engaged in a "shoot-out" or "duel" to keep their heads above water
Meltdown	Physical fight between executives
Outlaw	An executive who handles conflict in unpredictable ways but who is regarded as especially task-competent
Patched up	An agreement to cease hostilities between disputants
Peace talks	Collective negotiations to cease interdepartmental hostilities
Pigeon	An executive who avoids all conflict and has a reputation as particularly "weak" (a "pigeon" refers to a highly vulnerable takeover target in takeover imagery)
Pirate	An executive who often engages in covert action to manage conflict with opponents but who is regarded as especially task-competent (synonym: "outlaw"; cf. "black knight" and "black hat")
Playing the game	Engaging in honorable vengeance
Princess of Power	The senior vice-president of marketing known to have the ear of the chairman of the board, thought to sometimes "succumb" to emotional outbursts, and believed to be the next president of domestic affairs
Raid	Covert action taken to inconvenience an opposition department (cf. "ambush," "bush-whack," and "cheap shot"; a "raid" refers to a hostile takeover in takeover imagery)
Rape	When an executive allows himself or herself to be publicly criticized by another colleague without "calling out" the challenger
Red line	An argument that unpredictably escalates to physical violence (derived jointly from the danger area on gauges for a nuclear reactor and the tachometer on a car)

Appendix B (*cont.*)

Image	Definition
Road blocks	Impediments raised by an executive to block another's decisions (similar to the hostile takeover imagery of "barricade" meaning impediments to a takeover attempt)
Second	An aide to a principal in a meeting "duel"
Serious player	An executive who adeptly engages in honorable conflict management (same as a "strong executive" or a "white hat")
Shoot-out	Ritualized contest of elaborate formal presentations used to settle an interdepartmental executive dispute (same as "duel")
Sit down	Negotiations between two principals to suspend a dispute
Skirmish	Intradepartmental argument between colleagues
Sleeping beauties	Executives enamored with their own abilities but ignorant of their negative perception by other top managers ("sleeping beauties" refer to vulnerable takeover targets in takeover imagery)
Small bursts of fire	Short public criticisms of a colleague delivered in rapid succession
Strong	An executive who adheres to the code of honor in handling trouble with colleagues
Sucked in	To become an ally in an interdepartmental feud through no purposive action of one's own
Target	An opponent in a conflict; typically used by less honorable executives to refer to adversaries
Temporary amnesia	Temporary feigned ignorance of a colleague's grievances
Terminator	Sales executive who adopted the nickname from Arnold Schwarzenegger's movie of the same name because he closes big deals for Playco and "hunts big game any way he can"
Texas boys	Texas takeover men (refers to "big-hat boys" who are Texas moneymen interested in hostile takeovers in takeover imagery)

Appendix B (*cont.*)

Image	Definition
Waltz around	Polite argument between less honorable executives (related to "dancing," which refers to preliminary negotiations during a takeover in takeover imagery)
War	Aggressive and overt collective pursuit of grievances against a collective opponent ("war" refers to an extremely hostile takeover attempt in takeover imagery; e.g., the American Express attempt to take over McGraw-Hill in 1979)
Weak	An executive who does not adhere to the code of honor in managing trouble with colleagues
White hat	An honorable executive (cf. "black hat," "outlaw," "pirate," "white knight")
White knight	An honorable executive who supports his colleagues in interdepartmental disputes and rescues executives in distress (cf. "white hat" and "black knight"; "white knight" refers to an acceptable acquirer sought after by a potential acquiree to forestall a hostile takeover in takeover imagery)
Wild Bunch	A successful product team known for its "outlaw" behavior; named after the Sam Peckinpah movie of the same name about a notorious band of outlaws in the Old West
Withdrawal	Unilateral concession of defeat in a "duel" or "shoot-out"
Wizard	Senior vice-president of R&D who has numerous inventions and patents, long hair, and wears loose, hopsack clothing
Wounded list	Executives who have lost individual conflicts in a larger "war" with another department ("wounded list" refers to executives of an acquired firm who develop health or career problems from the deal in takeover imagery)

Note: [a] Definitions of hostile takeover imagery in this table derive from Hirsch and Andrews (1983) and Hirsch (1986).

References

Berger, Peter L., and Thomas Luckman. 1966. *The Social Construction of Reality*. New York: Doubleday.

Berger, Peter L., Brigitte Berger, and Hansfried Kellner. 1973. *The Homeless Mind: Modernization and Consciousness*. New York: Vintage.

Black, Donald. 1984. "Social Control as a Dependent Variable." In Donald Black (ed.), *Toward a General Theory of Social Control*, vol. I, *Fundamentals*. Orlando, FL: Academic Press, pp. 1–36.

    1990. "The Elementary Forms of Conflict Management." In School of Justice Studies, Arizona State University, *New Directions in the Study of Justice, Law and Social Control*. New York: Plenum, pp. 43–69.

Bourdieu, Pierre. 1965. "The Sentiment of Honour in Kabyle Society." In J. G. Peristiany (ed.), *Honour and Shame: The Values of Mediterranean Society*. Chicago: University of Chicago Press, pp. 191–244.

Butler, Arthur. 1973. "Project Management: A Study in Organizational Conflict." *Academy of Management Review* 16: 84–101.

Cain, Maureen, and Kalman Kulcsar. 1982. "Thinking Disputes: An Essay on the Origins of the Dispute Industry." *Law and Society Review* 16: 375–402.

Dalton, Melville. 1959. *Men Who Manage: Fusions of Feeling and Theory in Administration*. New York: Wiley.

Davis, Stanley, and Paul R. Lawrence. 1977. *Matrix*. Reading, MA: Addison-Wesley.

Hirsch, Paul M. 1986. "From Ambushes to Golden Parachutes: Corporate Takeovers as an Instance of Cultural Framing and Institutional Integration." *American Journal of Sociology* 91: 800–837.

    1987. *Pack Your Own Parachute: How to Survive Mergers, Takeovers, and Other Corporate Disasters*. Reading, MA: Addison-Wesley.

Hirsch, Paul M., and John A. Y. Andrews. 1983. "Ambushes, Shootouts, and Knights of the Roundtable: The Language of Corporate Takeovers." In Louis R. Pondy, Peter J. Frost, Gareth Morgan, and Thomas C. Dandridge (eds.), *Organizational Symbolism*. Greenwich, CT: JAI, pp. 148–155.

Hoebel, E. Adamson. 1967 (1940). "Law-ways of the Comanche Indians." In Paul Bohannan (ed.), *Law and Warfare: Studies in the Anthropology of Conflict*. Austin: University of Texas Press, pp. 183–203.

Kanter, Rosabeth Moss. 1977. *Men and Women of the Corporation*. New York: Basic.

Koch, Klaus-Friedrich. 1974. *War and Peace in Jalemo: The Management of Conflict in Highland New Guinea*. Cambridge, MA: Harvard University Press.

Llewellyn, Karl, and E. Adamson Hoebel. 1983 (1941). *The Cheyenne Way: Conflict and Case Law in Primitive Jurisprudence*. Norman: Oklahoma University Press.

Macaulay, Stewart. 1963. "Non-contractual Relations in Business: A Preliminary Study." *American Sociological Review* 28: 55–67.

Moore, Wilbert. 1962. *The Conduct of the Corporation*. New York: Random House.

Nader, Laura, and Harry F. Todd. 1978. *The Disputing Process: Law in Ten Societies*. New York: Columbia University Press.

Pitt-Rivers, Julian. 1965. "Honour and Social Status." In J. G. Peristiany (ed.), *Honour and Shame: The Values of Mediterranean Society*. Chicago: University of Chicago Press, pp. 19–77.

Rieder, Jonathan. 1984. "The Social Organization of Vengeance." In Donald Black (ed.), *Toward a General Theory of Social Control*, vol. I, *Fundamentals*. Orlando, FL: Academic Press, pp. 131–162.

Stinchcombe, Arthur L. 1985. "Authority and the Management of Engineering on Large Projects." In Arthur L. Stinchcombe and Carol A. Heimer (eds.), *Organizational Theory and Project Management: Administering Uncertainty in Norwegian Offshore Oil*. Bergen: Norwegian University Press, pp. 225–256.

Thompson, James D. 1967. *Organizations in Action: Social Science Bases of Administrative Theory*. New York: McGraw-Hill.

Weick, Karl E. 1984. "Small Wins: Redefining the Scale of Social Problems." *American Psychologist* 39: 40–49.

White, Ralph K. 1965. "Images in the Context of International Conflict: Soviet Perceptions of the U.S. and the U.S.S.R." In Herbert C. Kelman (ed.), *International Behavior: A Social-Psychological Analysis*. New York: Holt, Rinehart & Winston, pp. 236–276.

Wyatt-Brown, Bertram. 1984. *Southern Honor: Ethics and Behavior in the Old South*. New York: Oxford University Press.

16

The role of cultural capital in school success[*]

Paul DiMaggio

It takes more than measured ability to do well in school. From Warner *et al.* (1944) and Hollingshead (1949) to Coleman (1961) and Cicourel and Kitsuse (1963), ethnographers have chronicled the impact of class on almost every aspect of the experience of American high-school students. More recently, ethnomethodologists and constituent ethnographers have documented the impact of cultural styles on students' relationships with counselors (Erickson 1975), test scores (Mehan 1974), and classroom instruction (McDermott 1977). Similarly, recent work in the status attainment tradition finds that measured intelligence explains no more than 15 to 30 percent of the variation in students' high-school grades (Crouse *et al.* 1979; Sewell and Hauser 1975).

At the same time, however, measures of family socio-economic status have been found to have a negligible impact on grades when measured ability is controlled (Crouse *et al.* 1979; Portes and Wilson 1976; Sewell and Hauser 1975). If measured ability is not the sole predictor of high-school grades and if measured differences in family background are not either, then to what do we attribute variation in student grades? And how may we square our survey research findings with the observations of ethnographers that schools are places in which status and culture matter and "particularistic leakages" (Erickson 1975) abound?

The answer may be that aspects of cultural style only loosely associated with such measures of family background as father's education or head of household's occupation make an important difference. Max Weber's notion of *status culture* (1968) may be useful in this regard. Weber noted that elite status groups – collectivities bound together by personal ties and a common

* First published in 1982 as "Cultural capital and school success: the impact of status culture participation on the grades of U.S. high school students," *American Sociological Review* 47(1): 189–201.

sense of honor based upon and reinforced by shared conventions – generate or appropriate as their own, specific distinctive cultural traits, tastes, and styles. This shared status culture aids group efforts to monopolize for the group as a whole scarce social, economic, and cultural resources by providing coherence to existing social networks and facilitating the development of comembership, respect, and affection out of which new networks are constructed. The content of a status culture is arbitrary; status honor "may be connected with any quality shared by a plurality" (Weber 1968, part 2, ch. 9).

The impact of a student's cultural resources on his or her success in school has been treated explicitly by Bourdieu (1977; Bourdieu and Passeron 1977), Collins (1975, 1979), and others. According to Bourdieu, schools reward students on the basis of their *cultural capital*, defined as "instruments for the appropriation of symbolic wealth socially designated as worthy of being sought and possessed" (Bourdieu 1977). Teachers, it is argued, communicate more easily with students who participate in elite status cultures, give them more attention and special assistance, and perceive them as more intelligent or gifted than students who lack cultural capital.

If, indeed, participation in prestigious status cultures represents a kind of cultural capital, we would expect to find the following:

> *Hypothesis 1: Measures of cultural capital are related to one another in a manner that suggests the existence of a coherent status culture of which they are elements.*

> *Hypothesis 2: Cultural capital is positively related to school success, in particular, to high-school grades.*

In much of both the ethnographic and the Weberian tradition, status cultures are seen as resources used to promote intergenerational status persistence; cultural capital is passed down from upper- and upper-middle parents to their children. If this is the case, then

> *Hypothesis 3a: Cultural capital mediates the relationship between family background and school outcomes.*

What is more, if, as Bourdieu has argued, cultural capital is inculcated in early childhood and the response of others to cultural capital is predicated in part on the social position of its possessor, then

> *Hypothesis 4a: Returns to cultural capital are highest for students from high status families and least to students from low status families.*

Let us call this, following Bourdieu, the *cultural reproduction* model.

By contrast, consider the possibility that, as Weber predicted, the rise of the market has severely corroded the status order. While ideal-typical status groups are well defined and strictly demarcated, in modern societies status cultures are more diffuse and more loosely bounded. As the potential membership of a status group becomes less known to any single member, the importance of the shared status culture – those cultural cues that define a person as a member to other members – becomes greater. Individuals may have a repertoire of status cultures that they draw on selectively (see, for example, Gumperz and Hymes 1972, on code switching). In such societies, status culture participation may be deployed unconsciously at the level of daily interaction.

For this reason, it may be more accurate to speak of *status culture participation* than of *status group membership*, and to think of status as a cultural process rather than as an attribute of individuals. A person who is "at home" in a prestigious status culture can display tastes, styles, or understandings that serve as *cultural resources*, making communication easier and indicating status group membership (see Collins 1975; Goffman 1951). In such a fluid world, childhood experience and family background may only partially and modestly determine a person's stock of cultural capital. Active participation in prestigious status cultures may be a practical and useful strategy for low status students who aspire towards upward mobility. By contrast, both high status students (who, presumably, receive cultural resources in the home) and nonmobile low status students may prefer to participate in adversarial youth sub-cultures while in high school (Coleman 1961).

If this is the case, we would expect the following:

> *Hypothesis 3b: Cultural capital's impact on school success is largely net that of family background.*

> *Hypothesis 4b: Returns to cultural capital are highest for students who are least advantaged.*

I will refer to this as the *cultural mobility* model.

Data and measures

The analyses reported below were undertaken with data from a random sample of white respondents to Project Talent. The sample includes 1,427 men and 1,479 women who were in the eleventh grade in public, parochial, and private high schools in 1960, when they were surveyed. The sample is weighted to reflect a cross-section of white American high-school students.

Following Bourdieu, I measure high-school students' cultural capital using self-reports of involvement in art, music, and literature. While it would be preferable to ground these measures in observed cultures of dominant status groups, in the absence of such a rigorous data base, high cultural measures represent the best alternative for several reasons. First, art, classical music, and literature represent the most popular of the prestigious art forms. Patterns of art museum visitation, concert attendance, and literature reading in the United States are similar to those found in France and other Western countries, with attendance and reading concentrated in the upper-middle and upper classes (DiMaggio and Useem 1978).

Second, to the extent that there is a common cultural currency among American elites, it involves at least a modest familiarity with the arts and literature. Such preoccupations as racquetball, wine, or ancient history are likely to characterize smaller, more localized status groups. Minimal familiarity with high culture, by contrast, transcends cleavages of age or region. Third, art and music have received relatively superficial attention in the curricula of American high schools (Rindskopf 1979). If, as Bourdieu contends, cultural capital consists of familiarity with precisely those subjects that schools do not teach but that elites value, then including art and music permits us to tap dimensions of cultural capital that are inculcated outside of the school. Finally, high culture is an element of elite culture that school-teachers appear to regard as legitimate. While American teachers are recruited largely from the lower middle class (Lortie 1975), they are overrepresented in arts audiences (in proportion to their share of the labor force) more strongly than any other group (DiMaggio and Useem 1978).

The first step in the analysis was to build a scale of measures of cultural capital. Three kinds of measures from Project Talent were employed. (1) *Attitude* measures asked students to rate their interest in specified artistic activities and occupations on a scale from one to five. Unlike aspirations questions, the occupational-interest questions simply asked the student to rate the attractiveness of a wide range of careers. In addition, four inventories or composites generated by Talent are included among the attitude measures. Three inventories combine questions tapping, respectively, artistic, musical, and literary interests. A fourth composite, the cultivated self-image scale, is based on ten self-evaluation questions, such as "I enjoy beautiful things," or "I am a cultured person." (2) *Activities* measures are based on questions about the extent to which students have created visual arts, performed publicly, attended arts events, or read literature. Except for the arts-attendance questions, which could include school trips, these questions explicitly exclude activities undertaken for school coursework. (3) *Information* measures are based on Talent-administered tests of information about literature, music, and art. All these tests tapped familiarity, appreciation, and historical knowledge, rather than technical skills of the sort developed in practice. In the music information test, for example, students were asked about famous composers rather than about the structure of tonic or dominant chords.

Analysis

Both the cultural reproduction model and the cultural mobility model yield the prediction that separate measures of high cultural involvements should be positively correlated with one another. This prediction inheres in the definition of cultural capital as the mastery of elements of a prestigious status culture. There is no *a priori* reason that students who care about any one art form – art, music, or literature – should be concerned about any other. Indeed, psychological research indicates that the practice of different art forms draws on substantially different cognitive skills (Wolf and Gardiner 1979). If we do find that measures of involvement in different artistic disciplines are related, we must look beyond psychological explanations for the answer.

The notion of status culture leads to just such an explanation. To the extent that art, music, and literature are part of a coherent status culture, we would expect students interested in music to be interested in literature and art, and vice versa. Milieus that inculcate an interest in any single artistic discipline will also be likely to inculcate an interest in any other high culture form. This expectation is particularly strong for the attitude and information measures. Participation takes time, so students who value the arts may tend to specialize in practicing one form, while maintaining interest in and knowledge about others. Of particular interest are correlations between measures of involvement in *different* forms. If high cultural involvements constitute elements in a coherent status culture, these between-discipline correlations should be consistently and significantly positive.

As expected, relationships among high culture attitude measures are strongly positive. Cultural information test scores in different cultural disciplines are also strongly associated, even when one controls for ability test scores in other areas. Finally, students who engage in one kind of cultural activity are more likely than others to be interested in any other high cultural activity.

It may be objected, however, that the positive correlations simply indicate that all of these measures tap some underlying personality attribute like creativity. Fortunately, Talent also reports activity measures for several middlebrow cultural pastimes – photography, crafts, woodworking, and needlework. If high cultural involvements really constitute part of a coherent status culture, we would expect to find these measures less strongly correlated with the high culture measures than the latter are with one another. Again, this is the case. Two-thirds and one-half of all correlations between cultural attitudes and cultural activities, for boys and girls respectively, are greater than or equal to 0.2. None of the correlations between cultural attributes and middlebrow activities reaches this level. Similar findings emerge when we compare correlations between pairs of cultural activities with correlations between cultural and middlebrow activities.

These findings are consistent, then, with the first proposition of each model, that different dimensions of involvement with different high culture disciplines are part of a relatively coherent status culture. Note, however, the weak relationships between attitudes or activities in any single discipline and scores on tests of information about any other. This finding suggests the importance of distinguishing among the three dimensions of cultural involvement in assessing and explaining their effects. It also suggests that, at least among teenagers in 1960, artistic attitudes and activities were more important elements of status culture participation than was cultural information.

In order to exploit further the recognition that different cultural dimensions may have different relationships to one another and to school success, and to simplify the subsequent analyses, the cultural measures were factor analyzed. Separate analyses for male and female respondents each yielded four similar factors with eigenvalues over 1.0. Factor 1, *cultural interests*, consists of all the attitude measures except interest in attending symphony concerts and cultivated self-image, which loaded onto factor 3. Factor 2, *cultural information*, consists of the three cultural information test scores. Factor 3 is the factor of greatest interest because it combines both attitude and activity measures that are particularly high cultural in nature. For this reason, it is interpreted as representing *cultural capital* in its purest form. Factor 4, *middlebrow activities*, consists of nonhigh culture creative pursuits, excluding, for each gender, those in which the fewest students reported participation. It also includes drawing, which, for both genders, clustered with the crafts rather than with the arts activities.

Each of these four factors represents a kind of cultural resource, and each represents a coherent set of interrelated traits. Factor 4 should have little, if any, positive impact on students' grades, unless, perhaps, it represents a measure of creativity. Factor 1 should have less of an impact on grades than factors 2 or 3, because it measures attitudes rather than actual behavior or information. If status culture participation influences grades because students display their knowledge in a manner that impresses teachers or boosts their performance on texts, we would expect factor 2 to have a major impact. If we believe that cultural capital consists of a set of interests, dispositions, behaviors, and styles that are learned and enacted socially, then we would predict that factor 3, cultural capital, would have the greatest impact. This is the case not just because factor 3 includes measures of high cultural activities, but because the factor is the only one that crosscuts question types as well. While all of these factors are, of course, only indirect measures of cultural resources that students bring to interactions with significant others, it is predicted that factor 3, cultural capital, will have the greatest impact on grades.

To test the hypothesis that cultural capital significantly influences grades, separate regressions were executed for male and female eleventh-graders. Independent variables include cultural factors 1, 3, and 4, the student's report of his or her father's educational attainment, and the student's composite score in the Talent vocabulary tests. Factor 2, cultural information, was excluded from the analysis because of its high collinearity (over 0.8) with the composite ability measure. The strength of this correlation suggests that students' cultural information test scores were largely determined by some underlying set of aptitudes, skills, and motivations that lead students to do well or poorly on tests. (Partial correlations, not reported here, indicated that the relationship between grades and cultural information test scores largely evaporated when measured ability was controlled.)

Dependent variables in the analysis were students' self-reported grades in English, in History and Social Studies, and in Mathematics, and a Talent composite of self-reported grades in all subjects. The use of self-reported grades, with restricted distributions, can be expected to depress R^2s in these analyses; but it does not affect the utility of the data for comparisons of the relative effects of independent variables (Picou and Carter 1976). English, History, and Social Studies are subjects in which cultural capital can be expected to make a difference; standards are diffuse and evaluation is likely to be relatively subjective. By contrast, Mathematics requires the acquisition of specific skills in the classroom setting, and students are evaluated primarily on the basis of their success in generating correct answers to sets of problems. Thus Welch *et al.* (1980) report that Mathematics achievement test scores are much more strongly influenced by years of school subject matter instruction than are achievement test scores in English and Civics.

The regression results are displayed in Table 1. They provide striking confirmation of the hypothesis that cultural capital is positively related to high-school grades. Standardized regression coefficients for cultural capital (factor 3) are significant at $p \leq 0.001$ for both males and females for grades in all subjects but Mathematics, where effects are smaller, but still significant. For English, History/Social Studies, and All Grades, the impact of cultural capital is of the same order of magnitude as the effect of measured ability. Cultural interests (factor 1) and middlebrow activity (factor 4) have no significant impact on grades. As expected, the impact of father's education is minimal.

These results support the expectation of both the cultural reproduction and the cultural mobility models that participation in prestigious status cultures has a significantly positive impact on grades. (Factors such as self-reported grades that depress the R^2s should not affect the relative weights of ability and cultural capital. The latter, rather than the total variance explained, is the focus of this analysis.) Indeed, the magnitude of the effects relative to those of ability was unexpectedly great. The findings also tend to disconfirm two possible alternative explanations of the association between grades and cultural measures. If these measures tapped some general dimension of academic achievement motivation, we would expect the impact on grades in Mathematics to equal those on other subjects. In fact, it does not. If the scores reflected some underlying dimension of creativity, factor 4 would have a significant impact on grades; again, it does not.

The findings provide limited support for the expectations of either model about the extent to which cultural capital mediates the relationship between family background and school success. While the inclusion of the cultural capital measures does reduce the betas for father's education by 20 to 80 percent, the original betas are so low that these figures are somewhat trivial. The extent to which these measures affect grades independent of the impact of father's education squares with the predictions of the cultural mobility model.

The third proposition of the cultural reproduction model holds that returns to cultural capital will be greater for students from high status homes than from low status backgrounds. By contrast, the cultural mobility model posits that the impact of cultural capital will be greater on the grades of less advantaged youth, for whom the acquisition and display of prestigious cultural resources may be a vital part of upward mobility.

The male and female samples were each divided into three groups on the basis of father's education: sons and daughters (respectively) of college graduates, sons and daughters of high-school graduates who did not graduate from college, and sons and daughters of men who did not hold high-school diplomas. Separate regressions were run on each of these six sub-samples.

Tables 2 and 3 indicate divergent results for men and women. Among women, the impact of cultural capital on all four grade measures rises

Table 1. *Results of regression of grades on ability (1), father's education (2), cultural capital (3), middlebrow activity (4), and cultural interests (5) for male and female eleventh-graders*

Dependent variable		1	2	3	4	5	R^2	Increase in R^2 with vars. 3–5	Reduction in beta of father's education with vars. 3–5
Males, n=809									
Grades in all subjects	b	0.5078	0.1158	2.2330	0.1488	-0.1256	0.1228	0.0286	0.0202
	s.e.	0.0623	0.0971	0.4330	0.4830	0.3830			
	beta	0.2791***	0.0409	0.1706***	0.0106	-0.0113			
Grades in English	b	0.0493	0.0223	0.2730	-0.0025	0.0412	0.1034	0.0310	0.0211
	s.e.	0.0077	0.0120	0.0540	0.0603	0.0476			
	beta	0.2255***	0.0660	0.1716***	-0.0015	0.0309			
Grades in History	b	0.0715	0.0012	0.2646	-0.0059	0.0259	0.1279	0.0254	0.0193
	s.e.	0.0080	0.0125	0.0561	0.0627	0.0495			
	beta	0.3096***	0.0033	0.1577***	-0.0033	0.0184			
Grades in Mathematics	b	0.0510	0.0189	0.1685	0.0133	-0.0387	0.0723	0.0102	0.0124
	s.e.	0.0082	0.0128	0.0575	0.0625	0.0507			
	beta	0.2223***	0.0531	0.1011**	0.0075	-0.0277			
Females, n=917									
Grades in all subjects	b	0.5988	0.0939	2.4314	0.4223	-0.1250	0.1897	0.0338	0.0297
	s.e.	0.0575	0.0857	0.3887	0.3925	0.3361			
	beta	0.3374***	0.0345	0.1901***	0.0346	-0.0124			

Grades in English	b	0.0602	0.0150	0.3412	-0.0062	0.0127	0.1683	0.0463	0.0300
	s.e.	0.0072	0.0106	0.0482	0.0485	0.0412	0.0106		
	beta	0.2797***	0.0457	0.2211***	-0.0042	0.0106			
Grades in History	b	0.0710	0.0111	0.3354	0.0352	0.0443	0.1713	0.0382	0.0294
	s.e.	0.0079	0.0116	0.0531	0.0534	0.0453			
	beta	0.2991***	0.0305	0.1790***	0.0218	0.0333			
Grades in Mathematics	b	0.0653	-0.0066	0.1302	0.0750	-0.0671	0.0857	0.0079	0.0091
	s.e.	0.0082	0.0121	0.0551	0.0555	0.0471			
	beta	0.2781***	-0.0185	0.0774*	0.0469	-0.0511			

Notes:
*$p \leq 0.05$, two-tailed.
**$p \leq 0.01$, two-tailed.
***$p \leq 0.001$, two-tailed.

Table 2. Results of regressions of grades on ability (1), cultural attitudes (2), cultural capital (3), and middlebrow activity (4) for male eleventh-graders with non-high-school graduate, high-school graduate, and college graduate fathers

Dependent variable		1	2	3	4	R^2	Increase in R^2 with vars. 2–4
Males with non-high-school graduate fathers, n=494							
Grades in all subjects	b	0.4384	−0.6358	2.0638	0.7770	0.0865	0.0297
	s.e.	0.0724	0.4530	0.5302	0.5828		
	beta	0.2515***	−0.0614	0.1616***	0.0583		
Grades in English	b	0.0559	−0.0743	0.3026	0.1267	0.0998	0.0404
	s.e.	0.0093	0.0586	0.0693	0.0764		
	beta	0.2604***	−0.0577	0.1885***	0.0752		
Grades in History	b	0.0632	−0.0195	0.2549	0.0061	0.0957	0.0223
	s.e.	0.0098	0.0618	0.0732	0.0806		
	beta	0.2796***	−0.0144	0.1508***	0.0034		
Grades in Mathematics	b	0.0345	−0.0560	0.0490	0.0492	0.0257	0.0025
	s.e.	0.0098	0.0622	0.0736	0.0811		
	beta	0.1572***	−0.0426	0.0299	0.0286		
Males with high-school graduate fathers, n=298							
Grades in all subjects	b	0.5397	0.6665	2.0630	−0.3403	0.1216	0.0289
	s.e.	0.0986	0.6205	0.7008	0.7307		
	beta	0.2903***	0.0596	0.1568**	−0.0258		
Grades in English	b	0.0504	0.0172	0.2396	−0.0888	0.0951	0.0387
	s.e.	0.0129	0.0804	0.0910	0.0954		
	beta	0.2184***	0.1264*	0.1482**	−0.0549		

Grades in History	b	0.0857	−0.0374	0.3433	−0.0570	0.1760	0.0422
	s.e.	0.0128	0.0799	0.0904	0.0948		
	beta	0.3568***	−0.0264	0.2039***	−0.0338		
Grades in Mathematics	b	0.0608	0.0230	0.2385	−0.0731	0.0809	0.0189
	s.e.	0.0142	0.0881	0.0997	0.1046		
	beta	0.2424***	0.0156	0.1357*	−0.0415		
Males with college graduate fathers, n=130							
Grades in all subjects	b	0.4274	0.2767	1.5914	0.1906	0.0702	0.0178
	s.e.	0.1735	1.0292	1.0230	1.2428		
	beta	0.2088*	0.0237	0.1315	0.0135		
Grades in English	b	0.0242	0.1253	0.1774	−0.0555	0.0337	0.0175
	s.e.	0.0214	0.0493	0.1243	0.1553		
	beta	0.1010	0.0371	0.1276	−0.0337		
Grades in History	b	0.0651	0.2500	0.0723	−0.0339	0.0959	0.0285
	s.e.	0.0233	0.1361	0.1350	0.1687		
	beta	0.2421**	0.1676	0.0463	−0.0183		
Grades in Mathematics	b	0.0625	−0.1276	0.0963	0.1436	0.0670	0.0123
	s.e.	0.0233	0.1362	0.1351	0.1688		
	beta	0.2362**	−0.0867	0.0625	0.0787		

Notes:

*$p \leq 0.05$, two-tailed.
**$p \leq 0.01$, two-tailed.
***$p \leq 0.001$, two-tailed.

Table 3. *Results of regressions of grades on ability (1), cultural attitudes (2), cultural capital (3), and middlebrow activity (4) for female eleventh-graders with non-high-school graduate, high-school graduate, and college graduate fathers*

Dependent variable		1	2	3	4	R^2	Increase in R^2 with vars. 2–4
Females with non-high-school graduate fathers, n=582							
Grades in all subjects	b	0.5006	0.3136	2.2030	0.7400	0.1453	0.0310
	s.e.	0.0660	0.3966	0.5010	0.4966		
	beta	0.2930***	0.0331	0.1636***	0.0614		
Grades in English	b	0.0440	0.0906	0.3312	−0.0195	0.1148	0.0452
	s.e.	0.0086	0.0504	0.0651	0.0633		
	beta	0.2093***	0.0788	0.2036***	−0.0133		
Grades in History	b	0.0654	0.0958	0.2638	0.0213	0.1358	0.0272
	s.e.	0.0093	0.0546	0.0705	0.0685		
	beta	0.2840***	0.0761	0.1479***	0.0145		
Grades in Mathematics	b	0.0450	−0.0693	−0.0005	0.1535	0.0442	0.0075
	s.e.	0.0098	0.0577	0.0745	0.0724		
	beta	0.1943***	−0.0548	−0.0003	0.0951*		
Females with high-school graduate fathers, n=342							
Grades in all subjects	b	0.6216	−0.8526	2.7058	0.3466	0.1776	0.0494
	s.e.	0.0980	0.5542	0.6034	0.6064		
	beta	0.3266***	−0.0844	0.2238***	0.0301		
Grades in English	b	0.0629	−0.0831	0.3641	−0.0114	0.1755	0.0659
	s.e.	0.0115	0.0657	0.0715	0.0722		
	beta	0.2906***	−0.0720	0.2608***	0.0086		

Grades in History	b	0.0634	−0.0008	0.4029	0.0278	0.1640	0.0611
	s.e.	0.0132	0.0749	0.0816	0.0824		
	beta	0.2585***	−0.0006	0.2546***	0.0185		
Grades in Mathematics	b	0.0870	−0.1431	0.2245	0.0647	0.1384	0.0230
	s.e.	0.0141	0.0804	0.0875	0.0884		
	beta	0.3356***	−0.1034	0.1343*	0.0406		
Females with college graduate fathers, n=113							
Grades in all subjects	b	0.7317	−0.6325	4.1952	−0.2707	0.2034	0.0910
	s.e.	0.1738	1.0617	1.1567	1.2902		
	beta	0.3714***	−0.0530	0.2968***	−0.0174		
Grades in English	b	0.0913	−0.0148	0.4244	−0.0566	0.2093	0.0729
	s.e.	0.0214	0.1264	0.1386	0.1561		
	beta	0.3894***	−0.0108	0.2649**	−0.0317		
Grades in History	b	0.0673	−0.0764	0.6174	0.0944	0.1644	0.1160
	s.e.	0.0247	0.1459	0.1600	0.1801		
	beta	0.2557**	−0.0496	0.3431***	0.0470		
Grades in Mathematics	b	0.0702	−0.0924	0.3971	0.0661	0.1216	0.0578
	s.e.	0.0235	0.1387	0.1521	0.1713		
	beta	0.2877**	−0.0647	0.2380*	0.0355		

Notes:
  *$p \leq 0.05$, two-tailed.
  **$p \leq 0.01$, two-tailed.
  ***$p \leq 0.001$, two-tailed.

monotonically with father's education. As the cultural reproduction model predicts, returns to cultural capital are greatest to women from high status families and least to women from low status families. Among the former group, the impact of cultural capital exceeds that of ability on grades in History and approaches it even for grades in Mathematics.

By contrast, among males the positive impact of cultural capital on grades is restricted to students from lower and middle status households. Sons of college graduates were no more likely to receive good grades if they scored high on factor 3 than if they did not. These results for males are consistent with the expectations of the cultural mobility model.

Gender differences

The male and female samples differed markedly in the relationships between family background and returns to cultural capital. As the cultural reproduction model would predict, cultural capital had its largest impact on those daughters whose fathers were college graduates. Effects on grades of daughters of high-school graduates without college degrees were smaller, and effects on grades of daughters of men without high-school diplomas were smaller still. By contrast the impact of cultural capital on grades was substantial, relative to that of ability, for sons of men in the two less educated groups, but negligible for sons of college graduates. This finding is consistent with the cultural mobility model.

The divergent findings for male and female samples were part of an overall pattern of gender differences that together suggest that cultural capital plays a different role in the mobility strategies of men and women. First, the girls in the sample expressed substantially more interest and reported greater participation in high culture activities than did the boys. Second, the individual cultural measures were more strongly related to ability scores for males. Third, the specific attitude, activity, and information measures were, in every case, more strongly correlated with family background (both father's and mother's education) for girls than for boys. And the intercorrelations among the cultural measures were stronger for high status girls than for lower status girls, suggesting that a more coherent status culture participation pattern existed within the high status group. No such differences appeared for boys. (Three-way cross-tabulations, controlling for father's education, were executed for each pair of the cultural interest and cultural activity questions. The bivariate relationships were strongest among college-educated men's daughters, but not among their sons.)

These findings suggest that cultural interests and activities were culturally prescribed for teenage girls, while for adolescent boys they were less strongly prescribed, perhaps even negatively sanctioned by peers. High cultural involvements may have been part of an identity kit that academically successful, high status girls, but not similar boys, possessed.

Conclusions

While firmer conclusions await analysis of the impact of an array of background measures on students' cultural capital, these findings lend tentative support to Jencks and Riesman's assertion (1968) that the level of cultural mobility in the United States has been relatively high. The findings also suggest that cultural capital is less strongly tied to parental background traits than Bourdieu's theory or similar discussions of class and culture in the United States would predict. The data show that cultural capital has an impact on high-school grades that is highly significant and that in non-technical subjects, approaches the contribution of measured ability. This finding confirms rather dramatically the utility of the perspective advanced here. It remains, however, to assess the impact of cultural capital on such outcomes as educational attainment, college quality, marital selection, and occupational attainment; to develop better measures of cultural capital; to assess the differing role cultural capital may play in the mobility strategies of different class segments; and to compare the influence of cultural capital in different kinds of educational and occupational settings. In all these arenas, conceiving of status as a cultural process which influences success by affecting the outcomes of interactions may yield important gains in our ability to understand the status attainment process as a whole.

References

Bourdieu, Pierre. 1977. "Cultural Reproduction and Social Reproduction." In Jerome Karabel and A. H. Halsey (eds.), *Power and Ideology in Education*. New York: Oxford, pp. 487–511.

Bourdieu, Pierre, and Jean-Claude Passeron. 1977. *Reproduction in Education, Society, Culture*. Beverly Hills, CA: Sage.

Cicourel, Aaron, and John Kitsuse. 1963. *The Education Decision-Makers*. Indianapolis: Bobbs-Merrill.

Coleman, James C. 1961. *The Adolescent Society*. New York: Free Press.

Collins, Randall. 1975. *Conflict Sociology*. New York: Academic.

  1979. *The Credential Society*. New York: Academic.

Crouse, James, Peter Mueser, and Christopher Jencks. 1979. "Latent Variable Models of Status Attainment." *Social Science Research* 8: 348–368.

DiMaggio, Paul, and Michael Useem. 1978. "Cultural Democracy in a Period of

Cultural Expansion: The Social Composition of Arts Audiences in the United States." *Social Problems* 26: 180–197.

Elder, Glen. 1974. *Children of the Great Depression*. Chicago: University of Chicago Press.

Erickson, Fred. 1975. "Gatekeeping and the Melting Pot." *Harvard Educational Review* 45: 44–70.

Goffman, Erving. 1951. "Symbols of Class Status." *British Journal of Sociology* 2: 298–312.

Gumperz, John J., and Dell Hymes. 1972. *Directions in Sociolinguistics*. New York: Holt, Rinehart, and Winston.

Hollingshead, August B. 1949. *Elmtown's Youth*. New York: Wiley.

Jencks, Christopher, and David Riesman. 1968. *The Academic Revolution*. New York: Doubleday.

Lortie, Dan. 1975. *Schoolteacher*. Chicago: University of Chicago Press.

McDermott, R. P. 1977. "Social Relations as Contexts for Learning in School." *Harvard Educational Review* 47: 198–213.

Mehan, Hugh. 1974. "Accomplishing Classroom Lessons." In Aaron Cicourel *et al.* (eds.), *Language Use and School Performance*. New York: Academic.

Picou, J. Steven, and Michael Carter. 1976. "Significant-other Influences and Aspirations." *Sociology of Education* 49: 12–22.

Portes, Alejandro, and Kenneth L. Wilson. 1976. "Black–White Differences in Educational Attainment." *American Sociological Review* 41: 414–431.

Rindskopf, David. 1979. *Arts Education in Public Secondary Schools: Offerings, Enrollments, and their Determinants*. Technical Memorandum #AH–46. St. Louis: CEMREL, Inc.

Sewell, William, and Robert M. Hauser. 1975. *Education, Occupation, and Earnings: Achievement in the Early Career*. New York: Academic.

Warner, W. Lloyd, Robert J. Havighurst, and Martin B. Loeb. 1944. *Who Shall Be Educated?* New York: Harper and Brothers.

Weber, Max. 1968. *Economy and Society*. New York: Bedminster Press.

Welch, Wayne, W., Ronald E. Anderson and Linda J. Harris. 1980. *The Effects of Schooling on Math Achievement*. Mimeo. University of Minnesota.

Wolf, Dennis, and Howard Gardiner. 1979. "Style and Sequence." In Margery Franklin and Nancy R. Smith (eds.), *Symbolic Functioning in Childhood*. Englewood Cliffs, NJ: Lawrence Erlbaum Associates, pp. 117–138.

Index